Nation and Religion in the Middle East

Fred Halliday

# Nation and Religion in the Middle East

Saqi Books

British Library Cataloguing-in-Publication Data
A catalogue record for this book is available from the
British Library

ISBN 0 86356 044 X (pb)
ISBN 0 86356 078 4 (hb)

Saqi Books
26 Westbourne Grove
London W2 5RH

# Contents

# Introduction

The texts included in this volume cover a range of topics and genres: some are analyses of the workings of ideology and power within the contemporary Middle East, some are engagements with particular debates that concern both the Middle East and the Western world, some address the ways in which identity has been defined and changed. I have tried in previous books to address these issues, both in regard to particular countries on which I have written, most notably Iran and Yemen, and in more general discussions of the contemporary Middle East.[1] These essays pick up and, I hope, take further the discussion in these earlier volumes.

There are three themes in particular which I hope that these essays, in their diversity, can address. The first is that of the formation of culture – be it national, or religious. Against those within the Middle East and outside who analyse the region in terms of constant cultural or religious identities, I seek to show here how what is defined as the national or religious is itself subject to change: what is presented as 'true', 'traditional', 'genuine' is liable to differing interpretations that draw both on themes from outside the region and from variant interpretations of the past. In the analysis of religion, as much as in that of nationalism, I hold to a modernist position: the pretense of both nationalism and religion is that they represent a true reading of a given, the past or the doctrine; the reality is that different groups, in power or out of it, in the region or in exile, constantly redefine and reselect to serve contemporary purposes. What is today presented as the 'true' representation of a past tradition is in fact a contemporary, modern creation, designed to meet contemporary needs, not least the interests of those defining the tradition. Ideology is in this sense instrumental, for those in power – states, elites, classes, religious authorities, men – and for those challenging power.

My second theme is the impact on the Middle East of the external context – be this economic, military, political or cultural. Contemporary focus on globalization may run the risk of confining discussion of such international factors to the recent past: but the Middle East as a whole, and the variant states and peoples within it, have been influenced by the external, just as they have influenced the external world for millennia. The defining moment in the original definition of classical Greece, and hence of Europe, was the battle of Thermopylae in 480 BC, between Greek defenders and Persian invaders. Later one need only think of the impact on Europe of Christianity and Islam, both of which originated in the Middle East, or of the impact on Mediterranean countries of the Arab and Turkish Islamic empires. From the eighteenth century onwards European imperial expansion, above all that of Russia, Britain and France, was to dominate the history of the Middle East. The Middle East of today has been formed, above all, by the workings of modern capitalism.

This relation is not the expression of some timeless antagonism. In much of the twentieth century it took a specific form, conflict between colonial and anti-colonial forces. The form that states, economies, but also religious and nationalist ideologies, have taken in the modern Middle East reflects that interaction. The role that anti-imperialism took was itself two-sided – serving to emancipate peoples from foreign oppression, but also in its turn serving to legitimate new forms of indigenous oppression.

Today there is much discussion of the relation between cultures: but I do not see such a relation as necessarily antagonistic or, conversely, as conducive to benign monotheistic accommodation. While the interaction between cultures is changing, variant, a reflection of political and social needs, the fact of interaction cannot be avoided: cultural autarky is, and always was, an impossibility. In the contemporary Middle East no society is immune to the international context, as the contrasted but convergent fates of Wahhabi Saudi Arabia and revolutionary Iran demonstrate: the question is how these societies react to changes in the external world, and whether they can respond creatively to them.

The third and for me most important theme that this book addresses is that of the possibility of discussion, on analytic and moral issues, between peoples and cultures. No understanding of the contemporary world, and not least that between the Middle East and the West, can fail to recognize the profound inequalities, and persistent hierarchy of power, that define these relations. That is why it is essential to recognize the continuing impact on the Middle East of the period of imperialist domination. A recognition of that past is a precondition for an understanding of the present, let alone for a resolution of the issues that divide the Middle East from the West. Contemporary, capitalist globalization accentuates the inequality, but recognition of this should not lead us to explain all developments in the Middle East in terms of imperialism. The end result of that can all too easily be conspiracy theory. Nor should a recognition of imperial domination and cultural difference, or the hierarchy inherent in globalization, lead to the denial of discussion of issues that are common to the Middle East and the West. It is possible to address issues of analysis and ethical position that are shared.

This possibility of discussion across national and cultural boundaries is true of, for example, the role in politics of nationalism and religion. This is an issue that arises in many parts of the world, including that country from which I originate, namely Ireland. I do not believe that being reared in the context of Irish nationalisms, for there are more than one, necessarily allows one to understand the rest of the world. I am wary of how many in the Middle East, both Arab and Zionist, have drawn lessons to suit their purpose from the Irish case. I do, however, think the Irish story instills both a recognition of the enduring force of nationalism, of its cultural and political importance, and an element of scepticism about the claims of nationalists, not least those who so confidently mix nationalism with religion.

I am, for these reasons, strongly against the trend, pervasive in much contemporary Western and Islamic political thinking, that seeks to deny the possibility of a common, universalist intellectual endeavour. Whether it be in regard to issues of democracy and human rights, or in regard to the claims of nationalists and fundamentalists, or in arguments about secularism, I believe there is a possibility of a shared political space: that shared space is a product of a common humanity, and common membership of a single world economic and political system produced by modernity. Indeed it is only on the basis of such an aspiration to shared, indeed universal, values that the recognition and overcoming of the international system of hierarchy, so central to globalization as it was to imperialism, can be addressed. The disputes that do divide peoples and nations are not primarily about values or civilizations. They are about interests, territory, power, and about the impact of competition for power within particular states on the international system. The earlier, contestatory universalisms of liberalism and socialism recognized this commonality of value in a world of material inequality.

No-one familiar with academic and political discussion of the contemporary Middle East can think that it will be easy to win the argument on these issues. There is too much of an accumulation of myth and half-truth, and too many people with a vested interest in propagating such myths, for them easily to be overcome. Yet it is important for the debate to be held, for those whose simplifications affect discussion in the Middle East and outside to be challenged. Here I would cite three people who, in my view, have made an exceptional contribution to this endeavour: Maxime Rodinson, the French orientalist, whose substantive work and critique of myths on the Middle East has set a model for us all; Sadeq al-Azm, the Syrian writer, who has over many years written with courage and clarity, against the tide of nationalist and religious obscurantism; and Muhammad Khatami, current president of Iran, whose writings have argued for a dialogue, not a clash, between civilizations and whose own philosophical work is an outstanding attempt to explore the implications of liberty, seen by him as a universal aspiration, with religious and cultural identity. In a world of simplification, dogmatism – secular and religious – and demagogy it is voices such as these which mark the possibility of a distinctive, reasoned and universalist approach.

In conclusion I would like to acknowledge the generous help of the Trust, which funded research used in this collection, in particular chapter 1. I would also like to take this opportunity to thank those who have contributed to the production of this book: Jennifer Chapar, at LSE; Emma Sinclair-Webb, an editor at once sympathetic and exigent; and the many friends from the region whose hours of conversation have informed these pages.

*Acknowledgements*

Chapter 1 was written as part of a research project funded by the Leverhulme Trust, whose support is gratefully acknowledged. Other chapters in this book are versions of texts published or preserved in earlier form. Chapter 2 was first published in *Middle East Lectures*, no. 3, The Moshe Dayan Center for Middle Eastern and African Studies, Tel Aviv University, 1999. Chapter 3 first appeared in James Jankowsi and Israel Gershoni (eds.), *Rethinking Nationalism in the Arab Middle East* (New York, Columbia University Press, 1997). Chapter 4 was published in *Arab Studies Quarterly*, Association of Arab-American University Graduates and the Institute of Arab Studies, vol. 9, no. 2, Spring 1987. Chapter 5 appeared in Joseph Kostiner (ed.), *Middle East Monarchies: The Challenge of Modernity*, (Boulder, Lynne Rienner, 2000). Chapter 6 was published in *Cahiers d'études sur la Méditerrannée orientale et le monde turco-iranien*, no. 22, 1996. Chapter 7 appeared in Akbar Ahmad and

Hastings Donnan (eds.), *Islam, Globalization and Postmodernity* (London, Routledge, 1994). Chapter 8 was published in two parts in the *New Statesman*, 17 and 24 August 1979. The postscript appeared in the *New Statesman*, 27 January 1984. Chapter 9 was first published in *London Review of Books*, vol. 19, no. 14, 17 July 1997. Chapter 10 was published in *Soundings*, October 1999. Chapter 11 first appeared in *British Journal of Middle Eastern Studies*, vol. 19, no. 2, 1992. The conclusion was published in *Middle East Reports*, no. 213, Winter 1999. I am grateful for permission to republish these articles here.

PART I

# Political Theory and Nationalist Ideology

### CHAPTER 1

# Liberal Theory and the Middle East

*The Rise of 'Hegemonic Abstentionism'*

Why should I worry about Saddam Hussein? He's no worse than the Los Angeles Police Department. (Gore Vidal, interview with BBC TV, 1990)

In the West above all, the past two decades or so have seen a remarkable split, or divergence, between two forms of public discourse supposedly concerned with the same question. On the one hand within international law and on the agenda of non-governmental organizations and some states, concern with universal human rights codes has grown: there are now over ninety such codes enshrined in the body of UN resolutions.[1] On the other hand, a significant trend within political theory has come to question the possibility, or desirability, of any universal conception of rights. Against this background, the following discussion has two aims. It is intended to explore the implications of this theoretical trend for those involved in discussing the Middle East. It also seeks to examine the presuppositions underpinning this theoretical trend itself, by reference to a specific part of the real world. It is about something that I find troubling and do not claim to have resolved in either its theoretical or Middle Eastern dimensions.

I have used the term 'hegemonic abstentionism' to refer to those political theorists who, from a variety of philosophical starting points, seek to limit the application of universal concepts of human rights. Numerous terms for such an approach exist – communitarian, relativist, tradition-based, anti-foundationalist, post-modernist, realist. There are philosophical differences between them, but their practical conclusion, their implication in the real world, is broadly similar. Following this approach, the concepts of a desirable society, and specifically of rights, as they are espoused in Western political discourse, are limited in large measure or entirely to the West. Consequently the attempt to develop and implement universal codes is fundamentally mistaken. Such an approach is distinct from relativism of the kind articulated in or on behalf of (or supposedly on behalf of) non-Western societies: in the name of Asian or Islamic values, or as part of a critique of ethnocentrism or imperialism. The latter I would term relativism from below, since it seeks to resist the imposition of something from outside.

The current I want to examine in this paper is rather a claim, from within the West, that there are limits to what can be prescribed for other societies, and that it may even be in everyone's best interests to so abstain. This is what I term 'hegemonic abstentionism'. It is hegemonic in that it comes from a standpoint within the dominant liberal-democratic states and reflects a choice about how to use existing forms of power. A theory that advocates doing less or doing nothing when more could be done, it raises many interesting questions.

The idea that values are specific to particular regions or communities is far from new. As historians of political thought point out, it runs through Western political thinking, from Plato to Spinoza, Rousseau, Hegel, Marx, and is implicit in much anthropological and sociological thinking.[2] It would nonetheless be accurate to say that over the past two decades or so we have witnessed a coherent and widespread reassertion of this approach. This can be seen in the writings of, among others, philosophers such as Alasdair MacIntyre, Stuart Hampshire, and Charles Taylor, and in the work of political theorists such as Michael Walzer, Amitai Etzioni and John Rawls in the USA, in Britain David Miller, Raymond Plant and John Gray. While most of these writers would regard themselves as in some sense within a liberal category, there is, of course, nothing especially or necessarily liberal about this view. The concept of community has authoritarian as well as democratic potential. The idea that rights or political ideals were only applicable to the Western elite states was very much a stock-in-trade of nineteenth-century colonial thinking, mixed as it was with ideas of social Darwinism. Huntington's espousal of this position, replete be it with misused quotes from Walzer, is of an equally illiberal, conservative kind.

Here let us summarize the views of some other thinkers in this vein. Thus MacIntyre, in a series of writings, has questioned the possibility of a rational and hence universalist approach to rights. He has insisted on locating all discussions of morality within the context of tradition and tradition-related communities.[3] MacIntyre would appear to take pleasure, in the vein of Jeremy Bentham and Margaret Thatcher, in mocking the very idea of rights.

Hampshire is equally sceptical of universalist or rationalist approaches. He believes instead in the possibility of some minimum, 'a non-divisive and generally acceptable conception of justice, however thin a conception this may be, amounting at its minimum only to fair procedures of negotiation'.[4]

Walzer also denies the possibility of a universalist, rational approach to moral issues and rights, but allows of some dialogue between different groups: he distinguishes between a 'thick' and a 'thin' morality, the former being principles inherent within communities, the latter being only those values that we can observe as recurring, reiterated, between communities. As universal values are few, and weak, he advocates a moral minimalism in the international arena. For Walzer we have an entitlement to criticize other societies but within limits: were he to be invited to China to lecture on democracy, he writes, he would explain his own views about democracy but would defer to what he terms 'local prerogative'. It is up to the Chinese to define what they mean by rights and democracy.[5] Samuel Huntington echoes these themes from the very different perspective of defending Western civilization. He argues that belief in the universality of Western culture is 'false, immoral and dangerous'. This leads him to enunciate what he terms 'the abstention rule', one of three maxims for regulating conflict between civilizational blocs in the next century.[6] Huntington has little to say about rights or justice, but the implication of what he is saying would seem to be clear enough. Later in this essay I want to take as an example of this approach the lecture given by John Rawls in Oxford in 1993 on what he terms 'the law of peoples' and relate it to the Middle East. First, however, it is necessary to spell out what some implications of this turn in political theory might be for the debate on rights in the Middle Eastern context.

*Implications for the Middle East*

I would argue that this development in political theory marks a new stage in the Western discussion of human rights in the Middle East, and a new challenge to those concerned with the issue. Very broadly one might identify three earlier stages in the discussion of rights in this region. The first, what one might term the 'Bulgarian Atrocities' approach, is associated with the colonial era and particularly with the clash over the treatment of Christians in the Ottoman Empire. Explicitly selective and non-universalist, the concern of this approach was with the fate of Christians and citizens of Christian states, in the Muslim world. The second stage associated with the rise of nationalism and inter-ethnic conflict, saw the discussion of rights and condemnations of violations of rights used instrumentally in rival claims of different sides in conflicts. Thus while one's own side were innocent, provoked, occasionally made mistakes or committed regrettable excesses, the other side were murderers, to the point that their whole claim was illegitimate. We can see such a partisan use of human rights, combining denial with denunciation, in the Palestinian-Israeli context, in Cyprus, and in Ireland. More recently it has been reproduced in post-communist ethnic conflicts, such as Bosnia and Nagorno-Qarabagh: indeed one of the most depressing features of debate on the post-communist world has been the recurrence of just the same half-baked and partial arguments about rights that one finds in the Middle East. This trend invokes universal codes and international opinion but is not universalist at all, based as it is on selection and competitive comparison.[7]

The third debate has been around the issue of relativism – what I have termed above 'relativism from below'. This takes the form of a critique of Western domination and ethnocentric concepts. As I have written elsewhere, for all its supposedly anti-imperialist and authentic character, this approach is questionable.[8] Be it in the Far or Middle East, a relativist argument is often made not by those whose rights are denied but by those who, in the regional context, are denying them, or by their Western friends who derive financial and strategic benefit from so doing.[9]

All three of these discourses are still with us: they are not mutually incompatible, nor are they specific to the Middle East. The emergence of the current of 'hegemonic abstentionism' could then be said to mark another phase in the discussion of human rights. It does so in at least four ways. First, if generally accepted, it would provide a rationale for Western states, as well as for Western media, universities, non-governmental groups and the like, to drop or downplay the issue of human rights and more broadly the issues of democracy and justice in the Middle Eastern context. Secondly, it would (and indeed visibly does) provide a rationale for those in the Middle East who, for their own reasons, wish to limit external criticism of their human rights practices. This goes for those in power, but also for those who, in the name of regional authenticity, be they nationalists or religious fundamentalists, deny the application of universal codes. Thus if the rulers of Saudi Arabia, Iran or Iraq want an argument to fend off criticism of their policies on individual human rights, of if Turkey, Sudan or Israel want to fend off criticism of their denial of collective rights, they will find succour in the arguments of the hegemonic abstentionists. Equally, those opposition groups whose own practices and programmes are themselves in conflict with universal human rights principles will be reassured by these arguments. Little wonder that Islamists like Huntington: he is telling them what they want to hear.

Turning the question around, we can see how in several respects the Middle East could act as a test case for such theories of moral minimalism or abstention. Most obviously we can ask two practical questions. First, what would be the implications for the region if such theories were applied as policy? This is a simple, if rather dramatic, thing to do. Secondly, one can enquire whether in relation to the Middle East the minimalist principle being advocated – be it Hampshire's rules of procedure, or Walzer's thin morality – would in fact be applicable. The theorists themselves claim to be formulating ideas that have some, mediate, relation to the real world. Rawls, for example, regards himself as engaged in what he terms 'non-ideal theory', that is, speculation that is supposed to have a relation to real-world situations and to guide real-world choices. He invokes principles of 'political realism' and plausibility.[10] We are entitled, therefore, to assess how 'real' the 'non-ideal' is.

Another way in which the Middle East could be used to probe these theories of hegemonic abstentionism would entail inquiry into the underlying assumptions about the nature of politics and communities embedded in such theories. Without derogation to the separate and necessarily theoretical world of political thinkers, we are entitled to examine some of the assumptions that underlie their thinking. Here I would mention five: the idea of communities or nations as historically discrete entities; the idea of tradition as something given and unequivocal; the idea of communities as self-regulating and their rulers as representative; the notion that tradition is immune to criticism; and the common characterization of what the preconditions for liberalism are.[11]

### 'The law of peoples'

One formulation of hegemonic abstentionism is to be found in John Rawls' *A Theory of Justice*, published in 1971, a rich and complex attempt to derive from first principles a liberal theory of justice. In this account justice, rather than freedom or equality, is shown to provide the basis for a liberal political order. In particular the thesis rests upon the notion that values can be universalized through a set of procedural mechanisms. Rawls was concerned, quite properly, with the ordering of a particular liberal community, but appeared to leave open the possibility of applying his theory internationally. It was this hint which others, including Brian Barry and Charles Beitz, took up when they argued that the procedures for attaining justice *within* particular societies could be applied internationally, to encompass economic redistribution, rules of war, the protection of treaties, and human rights.[12] They argued, in other words, that Rawls' theory could be developed to encompass both the issue of international relations in the strict sense, that of relations between states and communities, and universality, the application in each society of principles evolved on a liberal basis. In applying Rawls' theory writers such as Barry and Beitz were not, therefore, hegemonic abstentionists but were, rather, liberal universalists.

Twenty years after the publication of *A Theory of Justice* Rawls himself entered the fray to draw different and more limited conclusions. It is these conclusions which put him in my hegemonic abstentionist camp. This contribution to the debate took the form of a lecture, given in Oxford in 1993, entitled 'The law of peoples'. This term was meant to imply not international law as we now have it but those laws which all peoples have in common, that is, a set of principles shared across frontiers and cultures. These pertain, *inter alia*, to the issue of how liberal societies, constituted internally on Rawlsian principles, should relate to illiberal ones. Rawls' argument, in summary, is that the law of peoples does not entail that all societies should be liberal, but only that they respect certain minimal principles. Non-liberal but in a minimal sense law-abiding states are termed by Rawls 'well-ordered hierarchical' societies. He writes:

> . . . a liberal society must respect other societies organized by comprehensive doctrines, provided their political and social institutions meet certain conditions that lead the society to adhere to a reasonable law of peoples.[13]

When he comes to specifying what such a society would look like he lays down three requirements. First, 'it must be peaceful and gain its legitimate aims through diplomacy and trade, and other ways of peace.' It cannot be expansionist and must fully respect the civic order and integrity of other societies. Secondly, the legal system must be 'sincerely and not unreasonably believed to be guided by a common-good conception of justice'. It must take into account people's essential interests and impose moral duties and obligations on all members of society. This second condition also involves what Rawls terms 'a reasonable consultation hierarchy'. Thirdly, such a regime should respect basic human rights. Religion may be a source of authority, but the religious and philosophical doctrines of such a society should not be 'unreasonable': they should allow some freedom of thought, no other religions should be persecuted, and there should be a right of emigration. For Rawls this set of conditions would form an adequate basis for the application to the international arena of the principle of justice as fairness evoked in *A Theory of Justice*.

Rawls appears to regard the category of the hierarchical well-ordered society as a realistic one, that is to say he sees it as more than a mere exercise in the rearrangement of principles. He clearly hopes that the category and the three requirements that underpin it will provide a means both of recognizing the limits of liberalism in an international context and of answering some of the concerns of other societies. Thus a notion of universalism is shown not to be the underlying criterion for a principle of justice and at the same time Rawls demonstrates that liberalism respects non-liberal societies. As such, Rawls' theory allows, even invites, the test not only of philosophic clarity but also of plausibility and realism.

In making this argument, Rawls accepts that there may be societies that do not meet these criteria and he goes on to identify two types of states. There are those which are aggressive and which he terms 'outlaws', and there are those that exhibit what he terms 'unfavourable conditions'. In his words, they lack the political and cultural traditions, the human capital and resources necessary for a well-ordered society. Towards such states he adopts a markedly more interventionist stand. The outlaws, he argues, should face sanctions and be refused admission as members in good standing into the 'mutually beneficial practices' of well-ordered states. As for those societies that do not have the conditions for being well-ordered, he argues that it is the obligation of wealthier societies to assist in trying to rectify matters, including through the promotion of human rights. Rawls lays particular emphasis on the role of political culture and on the religious and philosophical traditions that underlie a state's institutions. Among the evils of such societies he mentions oppressive government and corrupt elites, and the subjection of women.

*Applications to the Middle East*

Earlier on, I mentioned two questions which one might ask of any theory of rights when applied to a particular region. The first would ask how the states of the region look when viewed in light of this theory. To provide a straightforward answer, let us take the three obvious sources of documentation on this issue: the reports of Amnesty International, Human Rights Watch and the US State Department. If we apply Rawls' two main categories of the well-ordered liberal state and the well-ordered hierarchical state to the Middle East, not one state in the region qualifies for inclusion in either category. To make it clear, no state in the contemporary Middle East can, on Rawls' criteria, be categorized either as a liberal state or as a well-ordered hierarchical state, of a kind that would permit them to be, in his terms, in 'good standing' in the international community.

There are, of course, gradations. There will be protests from readers. Some states do respect part of the criteria for being well-ordered: certain Arab states allow certain political freedoms, Israel permits a judiciary to function with considerable independence. But there are two major problems, one with regard to human rights of a group or collective kind, one with regard to individual rights. Those countries with a strong showing on such issues as democracy, and which could be argued to meet Rawls' second and third criteria, have a poor showing on his first criterion, and in particular on respect for the collective rights of others. Thus Turkey not only denies reasonable group rights to the Kurds, but continues, through a regime that everyone knows to be a subaltern entity, to occupy part of Cyprus; Israel has a strong showing on democracy, the rule of law, and freedom of expression for Israeli citizens, but long continued in defiance of international law and opinion to deny proper independence and statehood and a fair measure of territorial integrity to the Palestinians, and refused to allow refugees to return to Palestinian territory. When it comes to individual human rights, no state in the region respects the Rawlsian minimum let alone the liberal maximum: whether it be in the denial of freedom of expression, or in controlling emigration (a remarkably common practice) or in the distortions of the judiciary in all Arab states and in Iran, or in the use of torture, practised by Turkey, Israel and Arab states, these violations are clear and documented. In the Arab world and Iran we have widespread violations of gender rights, including those which pertain to equality between men and women. We also see in an increasing number of Muslim countries, the infliction of what international humanitarian law considers as cruel and inhuman forms of punishment.

Equally, the concept of the well-ordered but hierarchical does not apply to the kind of society being envisaged by the opposition forces currently on the scene in the region. All of the Islamist groups, from the more peaceful Turkish Virtue Party and more moderate Egyptian Muslim Brotherhood, to the most extreme military groups, espouse illiberal programmes in relation to women, non-Muslims, homosexuals, and where freedom of expression and assembly are concerned. In Israel we see the rise of a religious right whose programme includes serious infringements of individual rights on issues such as the Sabbath or Jewish identity, and whose spokesmen often espouse racist views towards Arabs. The secular groups fare no better: the political records of the PKK, or in the Iranian context the PMOI\NCR, are authoritarian, demagogic, profoundly illiberal. Since 1991 we have seen what the two main Kurdish forces, the KDP and the PUK, have done with their national and democratic mandate in northern Iraq. We should not be surprised by, nor should we indulge, the illiberal, 1950s-style corrupt, nationalist dictatorship being created in the Palestinian Authority area which nearly matched in three years the record for Palestinian deaths in custody which the Israelis reached in over twenty. Stripping aside all the apologetic claptrap and official, and unofficial, denial in which commentators frequently engage, and the nationalist misuse of critiques involving of ethnocentrism, imperialism and the like, we have a region that is, on these criteria at least, seriously in default. Following the Rawlsian framework, we are left with states that are to be classified either as outlaws or as lacking the preconditions for being well-ordered societies. Rawls does not spell out what this might entail, beyond hints of what look like very familiar, muscular assertions of hegemonic universalism. The limits of the 'non-ideal' approach would, therefore, seem to arise here as well.

The other question which the application of the Rawlsian framework to the Middle East raises is that of plausibility, in the sense of whether it makes sense, even with the necessary distance of political theory, to talk in terms of these two categories of well-ordered society. Rawls does not give examples, contemporary or historical, of what he means by a hierarchical well-ordered society, but he would seem to have the Middle East at least partly in mind since he talks of states in which 'religion may be on some questions the ultimate authority within society and control government policy on certain important matters.'[14] At the same time, as we have already seen, he stipulates that such a society should meet certain conditions: it should not seek to extend its authority politically to other societies, these religious and philosophical doctrines should admit of liberty of conscience and freedom of thought, no other religions should be persecuted, and there should be a right of emigration. But in the Middle Eastern context what does this mean? What we see is a situation in which the very way in which religion is formulated, by those in power, precludes respect for these minimal criteria. No Muslim state allows complete freedom of thought for those who seek to change their religious belief. None permit full equality of men and women. Many limit the rights of other religions: Iran suppresses the Baha'i, and inhibits its Sunnis; Saudi Arabia denies all beliefs other than those derived from the Wahhabi interpretation of Hanbali tradition. Elsewhere – in Egypt, the Emirates, and now in the Palestinian Authority – the rights of Christians are constrained by pressure from society and/or state.

We need also to look at how Rawls characterizes such a society. We may note that the distinction he implies between religious and political authority contains the questionable assumption, present in Rawls' formulation, that religion is a given, separate from political power. The point is, however, that the denial of human rights in these societies may be legitimated in terms of religion, but we have to ask whether this is but another idiom for authoritarian political and social practices described as religion. To accept religion as being the legitimation, just because those in power say so, is to beg many questions. There is, moreover, the central problem of what Rawls quite rightly calls 'representation': where religion is the legitimation for a hierarchical illiberal society, the rulers or state officials cannot with any validity be termed 'representative'. They do not recognize a form of consultation, as stipulated by Rawls, nor do they recognize a duty to reflect the wishes of their people. Once again, the well-ordered hierarchical society turns out to be an empty and arguably misleading category.

Is the concept of a well-ordered hierarchical society therefore invalid? Not necessarily. It may be that, for example, nineteenth-century European states which were not colonialist, and were peaceful and law-abiding, but which did not allow universal suffrage and other rights, were candidates. Some third-world states, like Singapore, that do not torture or kill and do not threaten others, might be candidates. In the Middle East one can think of some states, arguably Oman, Tunisia or Jordan, which do not threaten others and which display some evidence of being well-ordered. But one has to say that, in the contemporary Middle East at least, the concept of a well-ordered hierarchical society, where religion is presented as defining the system, not only does not apply but is inapplicable. Insofar as it is intended to allow of a resolution or application of the issue of how liberal societies relate to non-liberal ones the concept does not appear to help. It leaves the option of illiberal intervention, yet this would not seem to be a course of action most, or any, of these writers would favour.

*Tradition, community, religion: historical and moral problems*

This brings me to the question of whether Rawls' theory is in fact an adequate basis for thinking through the problem of how to relate to non-liberal societies. Here I would draw attention to a number of issues which, while not extensively explicated in his text, do nevertheless underpin it and which to a considerable extent surface in the work of other thinkers of this school.

*(i) historical distinctiveness*
First there is the problem of discreteness, of cultures or religions or communities being assumed to be separate entities into which the world is divided. This has philosophical import because beneath the talk of tradition and religion we discover a historical premiss shared by Rawls, MacIntyre and Walzer. This premiss is that of historical separateness which continues in some sense to characterize the contemporary community or individual. But this model of distinct traditions and of discrete communities which only subsequently proceed to interact and in some way overlap is simply false (just as it is for the history implicit in the international relations theory of 'international society' which envisages such a society as a set of states who gradually build contact with each other). The communities/nations we have today in fact grew out of the breakup of earlier, much larger entities, entailing the severing of transnational links. They are also constituted by the appropriation of international ideas, currents, populations and technologies for national ends. The state, nation, community of today presents as particular and indigenous what is in fact drawn from a variety of sources. Whether in liberal or illiberal contexts, the language they present as specifically theirs is in most cases the appropriation of an international concept now presented in national, pseudo-specific form. One example is universal suffrage. Another is national independence and territorial integrity.

States give national form and allege national histories for their political institutions when these are neither traditional nor indigenous institutions. The same goes for much else in what appears in Walzer's formulation as the 'thick', that is, all that is apparently specific to a particular, separate group.

One can counterpose to the minimal or, in Walzer's term, reiterative universalism a 'diffused' universalism. In other words, shared values are there not because of chance coincidence but because of a history of political and cultural transnationalism and universalization, spuriously denied by current state and ethnic divisions. This is true for politics, as it is for language, cuisine, custom, but it is most of all so for religion. Once you invoke religion as a legitimation or description of difference, then you have forfeited the right to talk in terms of divisions in the contemporary world, sovereign states or 'national' cultures. This is evident throughout history, but very much so today in the Middle East: no state has a religious life limited by the frontiers of that state. For Muslim countries this interaction is widespread, and takes the form of both influence and aspiration. But it is equally evident for the apparent exception: the debates within Israel on Judaism, and on the identity of Jews, are linked theologically and politically to the two thirds of the world's Jews who do not live in Israel, just as the supposedly national Christianities, in Greece or Armenia, are interlocked with diaspora debates. There is a core, a much larger, thicker core than appearance suggests.

### (ii) essentialism

Closely related to this historical premiss is that of the essentialism of tradition or religion. Throughout the communitarian, or hegemonic abstentionist literature, there is an assumption that our moral philosophical problem is that of relating to a given 'other'. Rawls implies this with his model of the hierarchical well-ordered society where religion plays a constitutive role. A comparable premiss underlies Huntington's idea of 'civilizations' as unitary givens. One could make a similar argument with regard to the nation. And of course this is exactly what many people, including people in the Middle East, do: by essentialising culture or religion you claim that your interpretation is the true one. In the Islamic context the invocation of 'Islamic government' or 'Shari'a' is similar. The moral philosophers say they have to accept this and then worry about how as liberals they can relate to it.

However, no national culture or language or religion is unequivocal in this way. All allow of different interpretations and implementations. There is no one true 'Islam' or Shari'a or anything else. This is what the whole debate within Islam and Judaism, and in the West within Christianity and liberalism, is about. The obverse of this is that the most difficult and divisive disputes are not between communities at all but within them. All the debates of modern times on political form, nationhood, gender relations and so on can be fought out with recourse to the language of specific communities. Yet the appeal to community allows for no means of adjudicating these, except either by the assertion of authority (and the denial of other interpretations) or by introducing other, international, supposedly 'thin' but actually transnational and, therefore, transcendent values.

### (iii) authority and interpretation

The premiss of communities being determined internally, and of the issue being of relations between liberal and illiberal societies, also begs a set of questions about who defines the values of the community and indeed the criteria for deciding on the accuracy of claims to authoritative definition.[15] When Walzer goes to China, we are not sure on what basis he assesses what 'local prerogative' really is. Yet being a committed liberal in practice, he chose those more consonant with his views. It is here, above all, that the apparently liberal tolerance of illiberalism may edge imperceptibly into an abandonment of common sense, let alone elementary sociological critical spirit. For the presupposition of Rawls is that when confronted with an illiberal other, a community based on different principles but potentially well-ordered, we should accept this as a given. But when a society is illiberal we cannot know whether those who claim to speak for it actually do so. As already noted, Rawls uses the term 'represent'. But faced with a claim by a group of people – males in power – caution is in order. The self-appointed abound in these cases, not least on gender issues. Moreover, even when one can plausibly argue that a particular practice – for example female genital mutilation – has the support of the majority of the society at any one time, one has to pose the sociological question of how such 'assent' gets reproduced, manufactured, through social and ideological pressure.

### (iv) the right to dissent

The espousal of the authority of tradition, community and culture raises moral as well as historical questions. Most directly we face the issue of whether the individual located within such a community loses the right to reject, criticize or escape the codes of the community. There is no need to labour this point: the challenge of dissenters, apostates, the gender 'deviant', the human rights activist and the rest is not to the veracity of 'the tradition' – he or she may accept, as culturally or historically accurate, the claim that something is part of the country's tradition. No doubt genital mutilation, public execution, family violence and the rest can be proven, on statistical grounds most of us would accept, to be part of a tradition. This does not preclude, or should not on liberal grounds, preclude the right of an individual, or a minority of dissidents, possibly even inspired by universal codes or transnational discourses, from challenging it. The ultimate paradox of this story is that liberalism, which is if nothing else associated with individualism, ends up by denying the individual's right to reject what is presented as tradition. Rawls recognizes a right to emigrate, but this implicitly denies the right to stay and dissent.

## (v) the preconditions for liberalism

There is a final area where the historical and political premises of Rawls' argument are open to question. This pertains to the preconditions for liberalism itself. The argument he presents, albeit in summary form, is again based on the model of discrete societies. We have, on the one hand, 'a closed and self-contained democratic society', on the other societies that 'lack' the conditions, the know-how, the resources to make being well-ordered possible. The point about this model is that it is not only unreal, but profoundly misleading. No democratic society is closed or self-contained, or ever has been. The same goes for the non-liberal societies of today. Trade, empire, invasion, cultural interaction have characterized them throughout history. The liberal societies of today got there in part by five centuries of domination of the rest of the world. The non-liberal societies are not just non-liberal because they 'lack' something, any more than they are poorer because they have not been incorporated into the global economic system. In political as in economic terms one can avoid a globalist, dependency-type reductionism, but still note that the dictatorships, the nationalist and religious demagogues, and corrupt administrations of the contemporary non-liberal world were created as part of the modern state system and owe much to it.

No discussion of the relation between liberal and non-liberal societies can avoid this issue of a shared modern history. This history has constituted both the liberal and the non-liberal: it entails a common moral space. The universal espousal of the principle of national self-determination, a good old Western European concept, is one example. There is also a problem of consistency here: one cannot invoke the critique of Western domination at the atemporal moral level against universal moral codes, only to deny it as the historical level, that of explaining how these regimes came to be there in the first place, and to stay in power. Rawls to some extent recognizes a transnational moral commitment when he argues for raising, or assisting, societies with unfavourable conditions to reach the level of being well-ordered. But he is unable to spell out the philosophical implications of this, namely that liberal states are, historically as well as morally, interrelated with non-liberal societies. The latter's very social and economic conditions, or whatever other conditions are deemed relevant to their illiberal state, are a product of a historical process of interaction. Causation *and* responsibility are shared.

### Conclusions

One cannot but be struck by the similarities, of implication and then denial, in the work of Rawls and of the other communitarians and hegemonic abstentionists. It is almost as if some professional rootedness as political theorists within states inhibits them from developing an internationally relevant moral theory. What appears as a legitimate procedural caution about the implications of their work becomes a form of international abstention, based not just on philosophical care, which may be justifiable, but on a refusal, expressed as a rather lofty distance from the realities and real moral choices in these societies, to recognize what other kinds of society are like. The mere fact that internal intolerance and external aggressiveness persist renders their solutions untenable.

This would suggest that this trend in political theory, initially plausible as it may appear, does not offer a way of resolving the broader debate on human rights and their application to areas such as the Middle East. One can, one should, recognize the force of the critiques of rationalist universalism and of the association of this universalism with the imperial past and the hegemonic present. But if plausibility, or realism, is one legitimate test of a political theory, and if the constitutive role of certain historical and moral premises in theory are laid bare, then there are major difficulties with the alternative approach. The challenge faced by all concerned with human rights in the Middle East is not to produce theories of community or tradition, but to address the very real problems, ethical and practical, in applying the universal codes that exist and which most regional states have signed up to uphold. So far, it would seem, the best we have is enlightenment universalism, grown wiser and more cautious with time, but potentially the more effective for that. And, by any criteria, Saddam Hussein is worse than the L.A.P.D.

### CHAPTER 2

# The Middle East and the Nationalism Debate

It is foolhardy in the extreme to discuss the subject of nationalism and the Middle East. Nationalism itself is a subject of lively, often acrimonious discussion amongst social scientists. In the world at large it is associated with some of the most bitter and unresolved conflicts of modern times. Recent history has given us some reminders of these problems: we have seen an unexpected and bitter case of inter-nationalist war in the Balkans, just as we see around us political movements, generically termed 'fundamentalist', that combine a return to holy texts with a militant assertion of nationalist themes. The modern history of the Middle East has been and will continue to be bound up with a range of nationalisms – Iranian, Arab, Turkish, Israeli, Kurdish. Not simply a clash between a group of unitary, consistently defined forces, this history exhibits within each nationalism subdivisions according to religion, district, left-right orientation and much else. At the same time, and as elsewhere in the world, hitherto silenced or marginal currents are seeking to redefine the nation, or assert their own distinctive place within it – on the basis of social class, gender, region, cultural current. The main constitutive goal of nationalism is, of course, independence, but nationalism does not stop with the attainment of that goal: there are always arguments about how the formal status accords with reality, whether juridical independence does not conceal a continued 'neo-colonial' status. Equally, the official or predominant definition of national identity continues to change, and is contested by others within the national community.

The best defence for tackling this subject can only be that one puts one's view as reasonably and carefully as one can, and that if offence is caused it is caused equally to both or all parties involved. This essay takes up that challenge of relating discussion of the Middle East to broader discussions of nationalism: it is an opportunity, in the light of contemporary debates on nationalism, and in the light of the still on-going history of nationalism in the Middle East to explore how far the general debate on nationalism can be applied to the region. More particularly, it explores how far what has been termed the 'modernist' approach to nationalism can be applied to the ideologies and movements associated with nationalism in these countries. It is, therefore, an attempt both to throw light on Middle Eastern nationalism from a comparative perspective and to take the examples of Middle Eastern nationalisms as challenges to this broader theoretical debate.

*The nationalism debate: cosmopolitanism and internationalism*

When we talk of nationalism we talk of two things, interrelated but distinct, each of which has prompted dispute in academic and political contexts. The first is nationalism as an ideology, a set of ideas about how the world is run and, equally, about how it should be run. Nationalism has no great founding thinker, but from the history of the democratic and popular movements of Europe in the late eighteenth and early nineteenth centuries a certain set of basic tenets associated with nationalism arose. This ideology asserts that the world is divided up into peoples, that they have distinct characteristics and history, usually a distinct language, that they have entitlement to a particular piece of land, and that those who are born into the nation have an obligation to respect it.[1] In the famous definition of Ernest Gellner nationalism is 'a political principle which holds that the political and the national unit should be congruent', in other words that nations exist and that they ought to have, are entitled to be represented in, independent states with their own territory and customs.[2]

At the same time, nationalism is used to refer to a set of movements – political movements arising at particular times with specific leaderships. In addition to claiming self-determination and usually independence for their peoples such movements also set out to define what the nation is, what its characteristics are, its history, the proper way of speaking its language, who is and, very importantly, who is not part of the nation. A nationalist movement is one that, broadly speaking, espouses the doctrine and which sets out, as any proponent of a normative theory should, to make it happen. This is what Arab nationalism has done since the early part of the twentieth century, what Iranian nationalism has advocated since the 1890s; it has been the programme of Jewish nationalism, or Zionism, since the movement's founding congress at Basle in 1897. Nationalism in this sense is necessary and modular: every state in the world now has to espouse it and whatever its origins or particular content, every nationalist ideology has to meet the modular requirements of this ideology, just as every state has to have a flag, a capital, a national airline, a football team, folklore, a national cuisine, and so on. Like marriages, nationalisms may start for the most unexpected and bizarre of reasons; accident and even illusion may play a role, but once contracted nationalisms conform to certain basic tenets. The bigamist or the polygamist still recognizes what marriage is.

The title of this essay is 'the nationalism debate' but it would be more accurate to talk not of one debate but of several, revolving around the two meanings of the word nationalism. The first debate, which preoccupied thinkers and politicians in the nineteenth and much of the twentieth centuries, was whether nationalism was a transitory or permanent phenomenon, a relic of an atavistic pre-modern age, or an accompaniment of modernization, indeed a necessary accompaniment of modernity itself. One sceptical response reflected the outlook of the pre-modern or cosmopolitan world, a world in which cultural and other differences indeed existed but did not take a nationalist form. We can discover such a response in those who favoured some continuation of the Ottoman empire, or who, in the European context, believed that forms of cosmopolitanism could resist or prevail over the rise of nationalism.

We may think we know better now, especially in light of the tragedies of the twentieth century. However, for much of the nineteenth and early twentieth centuries most liberals, socialists and Marxists expected that nationalism, a doctrine that divides peoples up and at the same time asserts a unitary view of the community termed nation, would sooner or later disappear. This was the approach associated with ideas of internationalism, some Marxist or 'proletarian', some liberal and cosmopolitan. Just as in the Middle East cosmopolitanism drew on poets like Rumi, and even on verses in the Koran. Some of the greatest European internationalists, among them many Jews, were people who drew on elements in religious tradition: one need only think of Marx himself, of Spinoza, Freud, or later Marxists, notably Leon Trotsky and Rosa Luxemburg.[3]

In the Middle Eastern concern both forms of resistance to nationalism were evident. In the nineteenth century and beyond there were those within the Ottoman empire who sought to preserve a pre-nationalist diversity. In a different vein the work of my late colleague Elie Kedourie, who saw nationalism as a set of aberrant ideas mistakenly spread by intellectuals, reflected a similar perspective.[4] Yet for all the calculations and manipulations involved, the rise of specific linguistic nationalisms within the Ottoman empire and its successor states swept such cosmopolitanism aside and produced a Middle East in which nationalist movements with their aspirations to nation-hood prevailed. From the other perspective, that of a post-nationalist internationalism, there were many who sought to build links across ethnic frontiers, not least in the Arab-Israeli context or, under different circumstances, in the French communist movement and within the nationalisms of North Africa. Yet here too it was nationalist movements, nationalist sentiment, and nationalist animosities, that prevailed.

In the Arab-Israeli context this was not an all or nothing matter, as the work of Joel Beinin has shown, but there was little chance in such circumstances of an effective cross-national movement developing, let alone prevailing.[5] Some left-wing groups, notably Israeli and Palestinian communities, did seek to maintain such an internationalist approach, but the mainstream of Zionism, including that of Mapai, most certainty did not. Zionism embraced chauvinism and denial. From the 1950s the Arab left almost universally espoused militant nationalism, seeking to outbid its more rightwing rivals in hostility not just to the policies of the Israeli state but to the very existence of Israel and to the right of its people to their own state. In the 1960s and 1970s no groups were more opposed to mutual recognition than the 'Marxist-Leninist' factions of the Palestinian movement. When in 1977 an Arab leader, Anwar al-Sadat, did courageously make the break, the Arab left universally joined the chorus denouncing capitulation. The espousal by the Arab left of such nationalism is not specific to the Arab-Israeli conflict: such attitudes have been repeated in other cases, in the support by much of the Arab left for Iraqi aggression against Iran, or by most Moroccan communists and socialists for Hassan II's assault on Western Sahara.

Where this failure of internationalism has been less obviously so has been in regard to the largest inter-ethnic frontier of all in the Middle East, that of the Kurds with their neighbours. Here the record is a more mixed one. In Turkey, partly as a result of an intransigent Kemalist ideology imposed by the state, there has until very recently been little room for political recognition between Kurd and Turk. Tragically, the Kurds were pushed further and further into the arms of an extreme far left party, the PKK. Yet opinion in Turkey can change, as the late President Özal indicated. In Iraq the picture has been less absolute, with enduring cooperation between Arabs and Kurds in opposition to governments in Baghdad. Certainly, this has been a limited case, made the more complex by divisions within Kurdish ranks themselves. Surprising as it may seem, the most successful multi-ethnic country in the Middle East is probably Iran: despite the chauvinisms of Shah and Imam alike, the majority of Iranians, Persian and non-Persian, appear to be integrated into the Iranian economic and political system and to see their future within it. 'Democracy for Iran, Autonomy for Kurdistan' was the slogan of the Kurdish Democratic Party in the relatively free elections of 1979. As for the largest non-Persian ethnic group in Iran, the Azeris, representing perhaps a third of the population, they on the whole continue, despite nationalist expression in the first half of this century and now the existence of an independent Azerbaijan to the north, to see their future within a single Iran. One of the factors locking the Azeris into this position is dislike of the Kurds.

It would, however, be too simple to dismiss as irrelevant the entire Marxist tradition on the national question. In the first place, some of the ideas of this tradition mattered: despite Marx's own view of imperialism as progressive, the discourse associated with twentieth-century Marxism in both its Soviet and Chinese forms, in particular the discourse around an economic theory of imperialism, came to carry almost universal appeal throughout the third world. Even amongst movements that were in other respects anti-Marxist, the argument against imperialism was central, and with it came a certain form of internationalist solidarity. Moreover, Marxism draws attention to something that merits study in its own right, the relation of ideology to social groups. The Marxist argument on nationalism and social class in the form stated by most Marxists was simplistic and linked to a false view of history. However, it is undeniable that nationalist movements do have particular links to social class, and that different social forces have distinct nationalist programmes. Freed of progressivist historical myth or reductionism, a Marxist perspective enjoins us to examine how this was the case in the Middle East as elsewhere and allows us to get beyond the nationalist self-image of the single undifferentiated nation.

Especially now in an era of globalization, the Marxist view of the transience, or growing irrelevance, of nationalism in the modern world has in one respect been proved valid. Globalization in some ways promotes nationalism and national sensitivity, not least in the field of cultural nationalism. We can see this today in the Iranian obsession with *tahajum-i farhangi*, cultural assault. But in the field of economics the story is different. As Eric Hobsbawm has pointed out, we see the increasing abandonment by nationalist states and movements of the belief in a distinct 'national', autarchic approach to economic development. From the 1970s in the former communist countries and in the third world there has been a shift towards the opening up of markets and a belief that it is integration into the world market, not separation from it, that carries the best promise of economic advancement. This move signifies a very significant reduction in the nationalist claim: those who seceded from communist states did so not because they believed in autarchy, in closed economies, but because they believed that they could thereby ensure a more advantageous place in the global economy. In the Middle East the record has been mixed, but nonetheless represents a move in the same general direction: the abandonment of a separate 'socialist' economic programme has been perhaps most evident in Israel, but is also evident in Egypt with its *infitah*, and elsewhere.

Finally, amidst all the nationalist clamour of the region over the past decades, and with many accommodations by supposedly Marxist or left-wing forces to nationalism, it has to be acknowledged that the communist parties and those close to them have, more than any other current, sought to preserve a belief in cooperation between peoples of different nations. This has been true of Arab-Kurdish relations in Iraq, and in the Arab-Israeli context. For years it was the communists, and independent Marxists such as Isaac Deutscher and Maxime Rodinson – two people who greatly influenced my own generation – who almost alone insisted on the need for a two-state solution, resisting the exclusivist claims of mainstream Zionism and Palestinian nationalism alike.[6] I think of Emile Habibi and my friend, the late Emile Touma. Above all I recall Sa'id Hammami, representative of the PLO in Britain and courageous advocate of Arab-Israeli dialogue, who was assassinated by agents of a rejectionist Arab state in his office in central London in 1978. For a long period the views of such principled opponents of nationalist intransigence were sidelined: but now at a time when some broad schema of coexistence is accepted by many, including by the USA which for so long refused to recognize the rights of the Palestinians, we should remember those who in more difficult times held to the principle.

*Perennialism and modernism*

The second great area of debate on nationalism is that concerning the origins of nations. The critical cosmopolitan and liberal attitude to nationalism was not just of political import but also had significant academic consequences, accounting to a large extent for the strange silence of social scientists on the subject until well into the latter part of the twentieth century. Historians such as Hans Kohn and Hugh Seton-Watson wrote the histories of particular nationalist movements; others, within a nationalist framework, wrote of nations as ancient and continuous entities; but sociologists had apparently nothing to say. Nationalism was assumed to be a passing phase of no concern to the student of modernity. One sociologist who did recognize the importance of nationalism was Max Weber: but since he thought it was a good thing he treated it as intellectually unproblematic.

It is only in the last twenty years or so that a fully developed social science debate on nationalism has emerged, constituting what one may term the second debate about this topic. The essence of this debate concerns the issue of nations themselves, and the degree to which they are, or are not, products of modernity. In the view of nationalists, who it should be remembered make up the overwhelming majority of human kind, nations are far from being products of modernity, and are indeed historic entities which have developed over the centuries but have their origins in the mists of time. Tradition, roots and long historical narratives show this, as do supplementary activities like archaeology, the study of folklore and oral tradition. This is the approach dictated by nationalism, often referred to as 'primordial' and aptly termed by my colleague Anthony Smith as the 'perennialist'.

The alternative approach is what Smith calls 'modernist', and is associated with such writers as Ernest Gellner, Tom Nairn and Benedict Anderson.[7] There are important differences between these thinkers, but for the sake of argument I shall treat them as convergent. For Gellner and Anderson nationalism is a product of the transformations of industrial society, providing a means of bringing a newly literate and displaced peasantry into a wider society, and giving legitimacy and meaning to the new state and society produced by industrialization. The invocation of history is a means by which aspirant elites can mobilize support; but beneath a supposed continuity it involves not the reproduction of a given identity or tradition so much as the selection, reformulation and, if necessary, invention of symbols and narratives to suit present purposes. There is no one given past or identity on which the nationalist can draw, but rather a set of available meanings and symbols which are selected for contemporary purposes by political movements. Such discursive processes are not, however, haphazard, or in themselves formative, as post-modernists might have us imagine; it is these political movements, and the state interests they may embody, which shape nationalist ideology.[8] This may involve selection or reformulation, or it may involve outright falsification: as Ernest Renan said, getting your history wrong is part of being a nation. For the modernists history does not explain what peoples or movements do in the present. What they do in the present is dictated by present concerns, and the past is the source from which legitimation, justification and inspiring example can all be drawn.

One example of such selection, discussed further in chapter 6, is that the conflict in modern times between the Arabs and the Persians. It is easy to cast this in perennialist terms, going back through Qaddisiya to the Medes and the Persians. This is what Saddam chose to do when he denounced Khomeini as a *magus* or Zoroastrian priest, provoking Khomeini to characterize Saddam as an anti-Shi'a tyrant, a Yazid. But this picture of an enduring Arab-Persian conflict is misleading. It is so first because for much of history the two peoples have interacted and intermingled via trade and religion. And secondly, the animosities we have seen in the past two decades or so are the product of policies and images propagated by revolutionary elites, of very recent vintage, the Iraqi one that issued from the revolution of 1958 and the Iranian one from 1979. In the history of Iran up to the time of the revolution conflict with the Arab world, or nationalist mobilization against it, were insignificant.[9] It was the Arab nationalism of the Iraqi Ba'th, strongly influenced by Sati' al-Husri, that cast the Persians as the historic enemy of the Arabs. We have to look at how contemporary states, drawing on and reformulating the past, have used tradition to pursue current ends, in this case nationalist mobilization within and inter-state competition without.[10]

These two approaches, the perennialist and the modernist, are two poles in what is a very diverse argument. Anthony Smith himself, uneasy with both positions, has proposed a third position, somewhere in between, one that recognizes the modernity of the construction of nations but also identifies the continuity of such nationalisms with earlier ethnic communities and traditions.[11] He lays stress in particular on the survival over the centuries of areas of shared culture and symbols that go a long way towards shaping the modern map of nations that we have: hence his term for his approach, 'ethno-symbolism'. Those in the Marxist tradition, on the other hand, shared with the modernists the view that nationalism is a product of the transformations of the past two centuries, but less the acceptance of nationalism remaining a permanent feature of modern society. For most of the Marxist tradition, nationalism remains an unwelcome development, at once transitory and an aberration, something that will dissolve in the broader process of historical development.[12] For the modernists history shapes nationalism, but does not abolish it.

My own view is broadly sympathetic to the modernist perspective. Cultures, peoples, languages have existed throughout history and we can trace some of those that exist today back a long time, just as we can trace back our own families and ancestors: but this does not mean that they were nations in the modern sense, or that the past distribution of cultures, peoples and languages explains the present set of nations. Too many candidate nations have disappeared on the way, too much selection as to what constitutes identity has occurred and is occurring for the past to explain the present. There are no seats in the UN for the peoples of Amnon, Amalek, Lydia, Nabatea, Himyar, Saba, Phoenicia. We hear much about Samaria, but there is no embassy of the Samaritan Republic.

Nations are not perennial or teleological products, but reflect the interaction of a set of factors associated with the modern world, which shape the usages of that past. This modernity allows us, in particular, to identify two aspects of nationalism. One is its inevitability. It is universal and unavoidable: in this sense nationalism is necessary the world over, no region being exempt from it. We can include amongst such formative trends the universalization of the European state system, through colonialism and diffusion, the workings of the world economy, the spread of a particular vocabulary reflected in the very discourse of nationalism itself and the entry into politics of the people. At the same time nationalism is contingent and constantly changing. What is contingent is the particular division of the world into the nations that we see today, and equally the content which is attributed to these nationalisms: while the perennialists insist that the division into nations and content of their nationalisms is given, what we instead see is that chance historical factors and the outcome of conflict has produced the map we see before us. The map shows 193 sovereign states and some other, clearly identifiable, peoples claiming such representation. But the map itself could have been very different. The existence of contemporary nations is not a product of history but of contingent factors, which are themselves shaped by universal factors whose modular forms allow of comparison. Hence I opt for the term 'comparative contingency'.

At the same time, while the map has more or less been stabilized by world history of this century, the content of these nationalisms has not. Marx's observation about the constantly changing character of capitalist modernity ('all that is solid melts into air . . .') has never been truer than it is today, be this in regard to the realm of technology, or to that of ideas, culture and symbolism. Here nationalism has a problem: necessarily framed in terms of the essential, true, one and only interpretation of the nation, what we see the world over are unceasing debates about nationalism and its core essence, of definition and redefinition. Nationalists cannot understand this because for them there is one true, fixed definition of the nation and all else is treason or distortion; but what we are seeing is the working out, in the realm of nationalist ideas, and uses of the past, of this constantly changing modernity.

To assert the modernist case in the context of the Middle East is, of course, to invite the wrath or suspicion of nationalists of all kinds. Yet if we step back from the claims of ideology, what we see is how a set of political movements in different contexts sought to attain power through promulgating nationalisms and, once in power, to retain it in this way. At the centre of the story lie not nations or identities but something much more concrete, namely states. For it is through states that nationalism is formulated and then inculcated into successive generations, through text books, socialization, rituals, saluting the flag, and later forms of induction such as military service. Where do Middle Eastern states come from? They reflect the division of the Middle East in the post-1918 settlement: over a large part the British and French determined borders, in Arabia the Saudis and Yemenis fought to a standstill, in the case of Turkey and Iran non-colonial regimes managed to reassert control of territory. In all of these cases it would seem that the nations did not capture the state. Instead, the state captured or rather created the context for the formation of the nation.

Was history different in the case of Israel? Only to some degree. The two elements, state and nation, have come together as they did everywhere else. The national was produced by Zionism: this movement turned a set of religious and cultural traditions into a modern political identity, with the programme of creating a state. A liturgical language was modernized and a cultural and religious tradition interpreted to meet the needs of creating a modern nation. Equally a set of sacred texts were used to elicit a political justification for this state, based on claims derived from a particular, legitimating historical period. Zionism has distinct, and uniquely tragic, origins, but it has conformed to the requirements of the nationalist ideological model. As for the state, in the sense of a defined territory with a functioning administration it was a product of British colonial and war demarcation. In 1948, to apply the formulation of Ernest Gellner, the political and national became congruent.

In the Middle East as elsewhere this process of definition and redefinition has involved a relationship, itself ever-shifting, with the pre-nationalist past. The process well illustrates the selectivity, the contingency and the choice involved in the construction of tradition. Such selection and choice is, to repeat a point made earlier, continuous: nationalism as an ideology allows of no fixed state. It is not a matter, as nationalists present it, of a 'true' versus a 'false' definition of identity, but of shifts in identity and arguments about it, corresponding to shifting social and political relations. In an earlier epoch it was common for nationalists, inspired by ideas of the modern, to reject or disparage parts of the pre-nationalist past. Thus Pahlavism in Iran, and the anti-Arab nationalism of someone like Ahmad Kasravi, sought to reject the Islamic Arab period as one of decadence and to revive the symbols of the pre-Islamic period. In Turkey, while the corruption of the Ottoman period was rejected, much was made of the Hittites. In Israel, Zionism sought with its secular and socialist orientation to cast off the trammels of the *shtetl* and what it considered to be obscurantist clerical associations. In *Der Judenstaat* Herzl insists that there will be no theocracy, no room for clerical influence in the Zionist state: in words that sound ironic today, he insisted that the clergy should keep to the temples, as the army should keep to its barracks.[13] In the Arab world the greatness of the early Arab empires and of warriors such as Saladin was used to legitimate the enterprises of the modern state. In Saudi Arabia today there has been a subtle shift away from the reliance on a legitimacy based on religion and the place of Wahhabism, towards a stress on the Al Saud family, the warrior component of the regime, as the sole legitimating instance.

These modernizing, mainly secular nationalisms sought to provide a modern definition of the new nation in the contemporary context and in so doing took available history, language, culture and moulded it as they needed. Of course, the claim was always that what was being presented was the one true version: this is what nationalist doctrine dictates that you do. Equally the claim was made that the historical record justifying present claims was unequivocal. But it rarely was. The Turks played fast and loose with their origins, claiming continuity with ancient Anatolia when in fact they had come from Central Asia. Pahlavism involved a denial of the fact that when the Arab Muslim armies invaded after Qadissiya they had been widely welcomed by a population sick of Zoroastrian corruption, and it even downplayed the important Persian contribution to Islamic civilization: Pahlavism after all was an all too modular application of European, specifically German, nationalism to Iran, replete with the claim of a common Aryan origin. Zionism too had to mould history to its needs, taking the Kingdom of David which lasted for an eighty-year period, as its contemporary legitimation. At the same time, in its eastern European context it had first to break with the other claims – socialist internationalism and Bundism – that were being made on the Jewish population, and was initially seen by the communists as but another diversion from the unity of the class struggle.

Arab nationalists, depending on choice, made much of pre-Islamic poetry, of the *jahiliya*, of the crusades, or of the Arab empires. Arabs also saw fit to call up for suitable deployments the pre-Islamic past, one with which there was little real continuity: thus Nasser invoked Ramses, Saddam invoked Hamurrabi, and Ali Abdullah Salih in Yemen, especially when in conflict with Saudi Arabia, has appealed to the sons of Saba and Himyar, an identification with the ancient settled civilizations that points up the contrast with the parvenu Bedouin regime across the frontier. In Tunisia the revival of interest in the Carthaginians, in Amilcar and Hannibal serve both to promote tourism and to assert a distinctive Tunisian identity.

Equally language was deployed and shaped to meet modern political needs: words for nation, state, republic, revolution were formed, and older terms resuscitated for current needs. We can see this with Arabic words *watan, qaum, umma* and so forth.[14] In Hebrew we can chart the peregrination of Hebrew words deployed for the purposes of modern political vocabulary *am, leum, Zion, eretz, ge-ula* to name but five.[15] Some had religious resonance but others – *leum, am* – did not. The symbol of state, the candelabra, is a sacred object given national and political form. The symbol on the Israeli flag, the six-pointed star or *magen David*, not Herzl's choice for a national emblem,[16] uses a mediaeval symbol not originally specific to Judaism for contemporary purposes. A feature of such linguistic deployment found in many nationalisms is that of coming up with an ancient, supposedly nationally specific, word for the legislature: thus we have in the Middle East *knesset, majlis, shura*, and, elsewhere, *duma, sejm, dail* and *parliament*. But there is a sleight of hand here: these words do not acquire their meaning, let alone practical definition, from the pre-modern contexts from which they are drawn, and what they do mean is part of a modern universal politics – involving universal suffrage, the equality of citizens, the rule of law and so on.

These definitions of nationalism were never the only ones, nor did they settle the debate once and for all. As a reflection of the very changes within modernity we have seen the emergence, in opposition to the first generation of nationalisms and nationalist regimes, of a new definition of politics that takes a different attitude to the past and makes quite different usage of it. Within the Arab world the pace varies from country to country. In Egypt, the concern with *turath* or heritage, and a gradual return to Islamic values, may be dated from the trauma of 1967 and the realization of the failure of Nasser's socialist experiment. In Algeria, it came two decades later with the rise of the FIS in opposition to the FLN. In Iran it was associated with the revolutionary upsurge of 1978-9 and its consequences. In Israel, the seeds of restatement were laid after 1967, but it took another decade for this more conservative, religiously inclined movement to gain significant political force. The search for roots is itself modular – stressing the primordial, yet conforming to modern type. This is evident in the words for 'heritage': thus Arabic *turath*, Hebrew *mesoet* and *shoreshim*, Turkish *töre*, Persian *miras* and *asar*. In each case we see a rejection of earlier, more secular definitions of nationalism and of the modernist aspirations associated with them. In each we see a growing concern with cultural identity, as defined by those making the definitions: thus great effort goes into defining the true nature of being an Arab, or Egyptian, or Muslim, or Jew. The sense of external cultural threat is often there. In Turkey Erbakan's party (now closed-down) Welfare Party made much of the threat posed to Turkish *ahlak*, or morals, by foreign culture and tourists. Khomeini's favourite slogan was the need to be *bidar*, to be alert or vigilant; there may be some overlap of meaning in the Hebrew term *harid*, a term expressing an analogous cultural sensitivity and anxiety, and with a religious dimension. The social scientists need neither accept as 'natural' nor reject as 'invented' such formulations: the point is that for all its apparently retrospective character, nationalism's search for such roots is a contemporary and necessary endeavour.

*Middle Eastern exceptionalism*

So far I have discussed two aspects of the 'debate' on nationalism, the issue of its permanence and that of its origins. I would now like to turn to the question of universality as it pertains to nationalism in general and to nationalism in the Middle East in particular. To put it another way, to what extent can we apply the concept of nationalism, as ideology and movement, across all states and societies. All that glitters is not gold, all the movements that talk or talked of democracy were not democratic: perhaps not all that talks of the nation is really nationalism.

This denial of universality is itself universal, another modern reflex. It takes three forms. One is that of denying the claims of peoples without independent states to such states, on the grounds that they are not really nations, just tribes or groups of immigrants or one section of our existing nation who have been bribed to come up with some factitious identity. In former Yugoslavia, the Serbs accuse the Bosnian Muslims of being Slavs who converted to Islam because the Ottomans paid them to do so. In Ireland, it was common in the nineteenth century for Catholic nationalists to accuse the Protestant third of the population of being 'soupers', implying by that former Catholics who had converted to Protestantism because they would thereby receive food, in the form at least of soup, from the English occupiers. In the case of the Middle East we hear many claims, with often unstated political agendas, that seek to deny the legitimacy of other nations. Amongst the Arabs it is common for those with the best claims to a long millennial history to scorn the others. Thus it is no accident that the description of Arab states as 'tribes with flags' was made by an Egyptian diplomat, my good friend Tahsin Bashir. Equally when the Yemeni foreign minister visited London in 1996 he began his speech at Chatham House by pointing out that Yemen had a long history of settled civilization, unlike some of its neighbours whom he did not need to mention. One of the greatest sources of prejudice in the Middle East is the Persian attitude to the Arabs. Equally it applies within countries: for the Turkish state, the Kurds are not considered to have a distinct identity and were until recently described as *dağ Türkler*, 'mountain Turks'.

Such an argument for delegitimation has been used, repeatedly and with clear purpose, in Arab arguments about Israel, as in Israeli arguments about Palestinians. For decades the reason given for denying the legitimacy of the state of Israel was the denial that it represented a people with a legitimate claim to its own state. On top of arguments about its colonial origin came the charge that Israelis were 'just immigrants'. Another ploy was of course to claim that Zionism was just a form of racism, and thus not a nationalism: that there were in Israeli nationalism, in common with every nationalism on this earth, some elements, some myths, some terms pejorative towards non-Israelis could hardly be denied. But such a suggestion was not the point of the claim of racism: the point was rather to deny the right of an Israeli state to exist. It was part of the denial of universality on spurious, historical or ideological, grounds. It was not, of course, matched by any comparable identification of racist themes towards Persians and Jews, above all, to be found in many currents of Arab nationalism.

A second issue in the debate on universality concerns the wider claims of religion, and in particular the argument that Middle Eastern nationalisms are in some sense not 'real' nationalisms because of religious transnationalism. Religions are not in the main associated with national entities, not least because religions predate nationalism and make claims that cut across or defy the prime claim of the state which lies within nationalism. All religions – even Judaism, which is perhaps the one most linked to a specific people – make claims that are distinct from those of states and allow for claims that cut across national frontiers and are supposedly superior to them. 'In Islam there are no frontiers,' Khomeini used to proclaim, or as the Muslim saying proclaims, la hudud wa la sudud, 'no borders and no barriers'. Many is the non-Muslim academic who has endorsed the view that nations, nation states and nationalism are somehow incompatible with Islam.

All three Middle Eastern monotheistic religions allow for arguments that deny the legitimacy of particular states, often on the grounds that the establishment of such a state does not meet the ethical or scriptural expectations which the religion lays down. Thus a considerable body of Iranian *mulla* deny the legitimacy of the Islamic republic and the institution of *velayat-i faqih;* likewise, when Pakistan was established the Deobandi movement of fundamentalist Jama'at-i Ulema opposed its creation. On the Jewish side, there remain in Jerusalem and New York minorities of orthodox Jews who refuse to accept the legitimacy of the state of Israel and continue to use Yiddish as their language of communication.

This questioning of the applicability of nationalism can, therefore, take a religious form. Delegitimation can, however, also be found in a third, secular form, in arguments that highlight imprecision, the conflicting aspirations and mixed identities of nationalist movements. Here the conclusion is that the existence of such conflicts within nationalism undermines its legitimacy. A nationalist movement and ideology is expected to denote a nation, a particular people, whose rights must be realized and living (it is generally hoped) in one state. One can therefore come up with a syllogism of delegitimation: nations are communities with one unitary identity, but since people 'X' do not have a unitary identity, people 'X' are not a nation. Such clarity and such identification of a unitary people is rare in the Middle East, but equally in the world as a whole. This is most obviously so for the Arabs: nationalism in the Arab world takes two secular forms, the nationalism of the Arabs as a whole, and that of the particular state within which the movement is located, an Egypt, a Jordan, an Iraq, an Algeria. There is the *qaumi* 'national' and the *qutri* 'local'. The term *watani* is also used, but a study of Arabic nationalist discourse would show that this term is used to apply to both *qaum* and *qutr* depending on the circumstances. There is also for Arab Muslims the third dimension of Islam. Its vocabulary pervades Arab nationalism, from *mujahidin* to *fedayin*, and part of the claim of Arab nationalism has been the special place of the Arabs within Islam: hence the very secular Michel Aflaq stressed the *risala khalida* of the Arabs and allegedly converted to Islam in his last years. Equally the term *umma* is used both in the Islamic sense, and to refer to *al-umma al-'arabiyya*, the Arab nation.

Such ambivalences are not confined to the Arabs. For a Turk there have, over the past century, been at least four different identities: Ottoman; Turkish, in the sense defined by Gökalp and later Atatürk; pan-Turkist, involving the Turkish peoples of the *dünya*, from the Adriatic to the Pamirs; pan-Turanist, based on the mythical ancient land that stretches to Afghanistan; and finally, and not least, whether for Jamal al-Din al-Afghani or for the *Refah Party* and its successors, Islam. For Iranians, we have seen comparable shifts: between an authoritarian Pahlavism from above, and the secular, very anti-Arab nationalism of Kasravi from below, in between the liberal nationalism of Mosadeq, and later the militant Islam of Khomeini. The Ayatollah began his time in power by denying that Iran was a legitimate entity at all, and shocked many Iranians by introducing many Arab world, Quranic terms redeployed for populist purposes into the political language of the Islamic Republic.

Distinct but in some ways comparable issues of multiple and conflicting identity references arise in the case of Israel. Zionism began with the claim that the Jews were a nation and entitled to their own state. This is what in a straightforward modernist way was envisaged by the founders of Zionism, from Moses Hess to Theodor Herzl: there is no claim to conceptual originality in Herzl's book, rather the insistence on the application of the modular ideology to the Jewish people. It involved a particular project, tenaciously and successfully carried out, of ingathering in the hope that all Jews would be brought into one state, gathered as one people *ahad ha'am*. The state creation has succeeded, but the other part has not and, barring a major and world-wide rise of anti-Semitism, is unlikely to. *Shelilat ha-golah*, the negation of exile, has only partly taken place. Two thirds of the Jews of the world live outside Israel. Some are coming, but others are leaving, as is normal in any country: there are *aliyim*, those who make the ascent, but also *yordim*, those who go down, that is, leave Israel.

The question this now poses is, of course, whose state is Israel: is it the state of Jews, or the state of Israelis? The answer, without normative implications, is of course both, but with the passage of time Israeli identity, formed over the past century of settlement and reproduction, is getting stronger. One can note similar patterns elsewhere – in the former dominions of the British empire, where perhaps two generations ago Australians or Canadians would have regarded themselves as British, new national identities and interests have emerged. This is not a sudden or officially proclaimed process, but it is a historical trend. In the context of Israeli-Diaspora relations, there may be a Zionist version of Oscar Wilde's comment on the English and the Americans – that they need to learn that they do not speak the same language. For their part, Israelis made the same bogus argument in denying Palestinian rights to a state.

Such challenges to the concept of nation are not, of course, specific to the Middle East. The suggestion that Israel was an immigrant or colonial creation may have sounded a convincing argument in the Middle East, but could hardly stand a moment's broader comparative reflection: within modern history this is true of all the nations of the Americas, Australasia and such countries as Singapore. In the long-term, probably every nation in the world has been created through immigration of one sort of another. The issue of uncertain identity, or of multiple identities, also used against the Arabs and the Turks is hardly peculiar to the region: every inhabitant of Britain, as much as of any Arab country, has two nationalities, a *qaumi* or British one and a *qutri* or regional one, be this English, Welsh or Scottish. In France and Italy centralizing ideologies of the classical kind long denied it, but here too there is ethnic diversity within the framework of the state. The two largest nations in Europe have, in this century, had enormous and still continuing difficulties about how to define their nation: the Germans were and still are in a muddle about German citizenship, *Volksdeutschen* and the rest, whilst in Russia there are three different terms for the people – *russki*, *rossiiski*, and *rossianin*, the last being an ancient term revived after 1991 by Yeltsin and his associates.

Here again we see the tension between the aspiration of nationalism and the reality. Nationalism seeks to assert one common, timeless, unitary identity: in fact there are always different levels, and the definition for any individual or group changes over time. Again, modernity condemns everyone to having a national identity, but it also constantly shifts the terms and context of such a definition. Nor have I yet introduced politics, everywhere the most important factor of all: political movements and states shift their definitions and the combination of elements as they see fit. Thus Egyptian leaders have switched, from the time of Saad Zaghlul and the Wafd Party onwards, between the Egyptian, the Arab and the Islamic, depending on the needs of the moment. Gershoni and Jankowski have written extensively on the history of this 'misrification'.[17] When Nasser wanted to impose his will on Syria and other Arabs, he stressed the *qaumi*. When Sadat wanted to make his peace with Israel and downplay his responsibility for the Palestinians he stressed the *qutri*. Within Zionism, there has been a parallel evolution – as the relation between secular and religious, and between socialist and free market, definitions illustrates.

As for religion, in varying degrees it does play a role in the national ideology of Middle Eastern states. Even the most secular, such as Atatürk's Turkey or post-independence Zionism, deploy terms that have religious origins. But etymological origins do not give contemporary meaning: I share with orientalist scholars, notably Bernard Lewis, an interest in and vigilance about the etymology of words, but would use etymology not to define present meanings but rather to begin charting how over time words acquire new meanings and often end up meaning something very different from what they meant before. Thus even the most secular of nationalisms has words of religious origin. This is separate from the fact of movements and ideologies that make explicit use of religion, and which formally proclaim it as part of their programme. But here too we are not looking at a uniquely Middle Eastern phenomenon, or one that would disqualify these from being considered nationalist. If one thinks of European nationalisms, whether those of Western Christianity in Ireland, Poland or France, let alone of Eastern Christianity, in Greece, Serbia, Russia or Bulgaria, then in each case the issue of religion is present. There is moreover the issue of instrumentality. In these instances it is as much a case of the political movement using, or framing, the religion as the other way around; in the longer run it is the need of the state that shape the requirements of religion.

Nowhere is the import of the political, and with it the instrumental use of religion, more evident than in the case of Iran. The Iranian revolution appears to reject nationalism as a secular, alien and limiting ideology. Yet if one looks at what Khomeini has said and done before coming to power and afterwards a familiar nationalist political programme emerges.[18] The main language he drew on was populist: he referred to the struggle between *mostazafin* (the oppressed) and *mostakbarin* (the oppressor); the main enemy was imperialism, described as *istikbar-i jahani*, or world arrogance; his Iranian foes were corrupt traitors and agents; the Shah was *sag-i karter*, the running dog of Jimmy Carter. One of Khomeini's most successful revivals was of the term *taghut*, the Quranic for a golden idol, in Hebrew *avoda zara*, which he then applied to the Shah, Carter and Saddam. The term in a way operated as a Persian equivalent of Mao's 'paper tiger'. All this is familiar third world nationalist rhetoric. After coming to power, and even more so when Iraq invaded Iran in September 1980, Khomeini began to talk of *in mellat-i aziz*, this dear nation and, later, to stress the primacy of the state and its *maslahat*, or interest, above that of religion. Khomeini's revolution was framed and worked out through the imperatives of the nation-state: now it is increasingly being recognized that Iran is adopting an ideology that can be termed 'national-Islamism', but this was ever so.[19] The same applies to the programme of other fundamentalist groups: the factions of Algeria, the FIS and the GIA, talk repeatedly of imperialist oppression and the need to change it; the charter of the Palestinian Hamas talks of Palestine as an oppressed nation. Those in the Arab world who sought to reconcile nationalism and religion quoted the *hadith* 'hubb al-watan min al-iman', 'love of the homeland comes from faith'.

Transnational claims and identities are also marked out instrumentally and never entirely disappear. America claims to stand for universal values. France and Britain still exert influence over their former colonial areas and linguistic domains. China has claims on its overseas communities. In the Middle East the Turkish interest in the broader Turkic world, long denied by Atatürk and Lenin, has revived with the collapse of communism: but very much as a function of Turkish state politics. There is no suggestion that this could entail the fusion of states, or mass immigration of former Soviet Turkic people to

Turkey: 'We are not Zionists,' one Turk said to me, 'we don't want our poor relatives coming here'. Iran too uses its Islamic claims, and claims over Shi'ites, for political purposes, but where inappropriate, it would oppose such solidarity. Thus it supports the Shi'ites of Lebanon, in their confrontation with Israel, but backs Orthodox Christian Armenia against Shi'ite Azerbaijan. Iran has common interests with Hindu India and has said little about Kashmir. Israel's relation to the Diaspora is an intensely political one, with both government and opposition seeking to mobilize support amongst Jews abroad, and to export their domestic arguments to these communities. However, at the end of the day, it would seem that the Diaspora carries little political authority when it comes to key decisions in Israel itself.

As for the Arab world, two further arguments about regional exceptionalism are often made. One suggests that nationalism has only a partial or superficial hold on Arabs, and that other claims, in particular the claim of religion, are more binding.[20] This may be true but, as I have already suggested, this may be to apply inapposite criteria. Recently it has become common to say that Arab nationalism is dead. Obviously the goal of creating one Arab state failed, with the *infisal* of Syria in 1961 and the downhill trajectory of Nasserism thereafter. The attempt by Saddam to create another kind of *wahda*, this time with tanks in Kuwait in 1990, also failed. I welcomed the unification of the two Yemens, also in 1990, but would suggest that it represented a particular, sub-regional development and not a harbinger of a broader unificatory drive of the kind that one Nasserist at the time referred to as a *masira indimajia* in the Arab world.[21] Nonetheless, the demise of Arab nationalism in the pan-Arab sense seems to me to be overstated, not least because it is in the interests of states to sustain it, even as they manipulate it. There remains a coexistence of pan-Arab and state-centred nationalism: it is not a question of it being resolved one way or the other, in the direction of a full political *wahda* or, conversely, by the end of the pan-Arab dream, but rather by shifts from one plane to the other.

Certainly, specific states are asserting themselves more and more: even Qatar claims its own perennial identity, Qaddafi rails against the delusions of Arab nationalism. But pan-Arab identity still matters: every Arab can tell you where they were on 2 August 1990, just as an older person can tell you where they were on 5 June 1967. Arab politics is becoming more fragmented and economic integration never worked: but money, culture, ideas and jokes travel perhaps more than ever before around the Arab world. The greatest figure in Arab unity of the twentieth century was perhaps a woman, Umm

Kalthoum. Those who have read the marvellous and very serious work of the Iraqi Khalid Kishtainy, *Arab Political Humour*, will know how pervasive this form of shared cultural expression is.[22] In Latin America the dream of Simon Bolivar, of creating a united state out of the four *delegaciones* of the Spanish American empire, failed. Like Nasser, Bolivar felt the bitterness of attempting such a union. Instead twenty or so new states emerged and have endured for nearly two centuries. But Latin Americans still feel themselves to have a common history, identity, language, and when new opportunities arise, as they do now with regional trading blocs, they draw closer together. One can and should expect the same thing in the Arab world: two hundred years from now Nasser will be remembered, as is Bolivar, when other more pragmatic and perhaps more successful politicians have been forgotten.

To conclude on this issue of universality. We are getting it wrong if we start with a model of a full, ideal type nationalism supposedly to be found in Western Europe and then measure other peoples against it. Even the Western Europeans measure up less well to this model than might at first appear. In all of these cases there is a state-promoted history of nationalism, a concern with official versions of the past and of current identity, a diversity of identities and ethnicities within countries and involving transnational links, and most importantly of all a process of constant change and redefinition. All the challenges we have seen to the hitherto prevailing, top-down history in Europe – from social historians, feminists, regional experts, ethnic minorities and, last but not least, individuals who do not feel they 'fit' the official model – can be reproduced elsewhere. The Middle East has a system of states, created by the post-1918 settlement, within which nationalisms of various kinds have developed. If they draw on different cultures and have very different points of origin, they are nonetheless forced to operate within the constraints of this state system and of the broader, structural and discursive constraints of modernity. These states are condemned by the logic of nationalist ideology to promote their differences, but are equally condemned by the logic of the contemporary world to perform similar functions.

*Future choices*

I would like to conclude by drawing out some of the implications of this discussion for the study of the contemporary Middle East, and in particular turn to the analytical and ethical implications of the argument about modernity. In writing the history of nations and nationalisms in the Middle East, as social scientists and historians we look at how the very framework of modernity, encompassing but not restricted to the Franco-German ideological creation of the early nineteenth century, came to shape the political and value systems of the region. Hence we look at state formation, at the building of administrative and military infrastructures, at the writing and formalization of history, at linguistic policies, at socialization, at the creation, invention and reproduction of tradition. In this sense, we write the histories of nationalisms from a perspective of comparative contingency and also, without reductionism, we would do well to examine with an open mind the intersection of movements and ideologies with social class. Endeavours of this kind will necessarily involve touching on raw nerves because they entail a certain 'revisionism': as the Irish historian Roy Foster has said revisionism is a necessary, indeed inevitable part of any historical or political analysis. Each person writing does so from a vantage-point somewhat different from that of those who preceded and, it is to be hoped, on the basis of new information. Revision is not an affectation of the disaffected but an intrinsic part of the scholarly endeavour.

Turning to ethics, we know that perennialism has a clear normative consequence – nations are those communities which have existed the longest, and which can muster the strongest arguments based on history and appropriate sacred texts. On this basis nationalisms seek to make the most of their own case and, at the same time, to deny the claims of others as having less historical and perennial validity. In extreme cases we see mutual claims of delegitimation, as in the Israeli-Palestinian conflict or, in the strongest example of genocide in the modern Middle East, in the policies of Ottoman Turkey towards the Armenians. The modernist approach recognizes in the force of these arguments their undoubted ability to mobilize, but at the same time denies their validity. Claims going back hundreds or thousands of years have diminished, and some would say no, moral or legal validity. Arguments as to the illegitimacy of other peoples on historical grounds similarly lack validity. Two hundred years ago Singapore was a sandbank on the edge of the Malay Peninsula. Now it is a flourishing state of 4 million people: whatever Malayan and Indonesian nationalists may think, Singapore has as much right to be a state as any other. The same would apply in the Arab-Israeli context. Everyone can play games with Canaan and Amalek. Perennialism traps us not only into bad history, masked as the discovery of tradition, but also into a mutually incompatible set of contemporary claims. Modernity, on the other hand, accepts that nations are recent creations, often forged in conflict with each other, and that if there is political will conflicting claims can be resolved on the basis of reason and justice.

This argument may, however, have other implications for the study of the Middle East, in particular for the vexed and in the end unanswerable issue of how distinctive this region is in terms of its history and contemporary politics. It will be evident from what I have already said, and from what I have written elsewhere, that I incline towards a universalist view that regards the societies of the Middle East as in many ways similar to those of the rest of the world. I reject claims made on historical, religious or mental differences. During the Kuwait crisis of 1990 much effort went into trying to explain Saddam's actions in terms of the workings of the Arab or Muslim or Iraqi 'mind': but this was a waste of time, a form of psychological reductionism. Saddam Hussein was a dictator who had run out of money and had little to show his people for their eight years of war with Iran. So he decided to try to rob his neighbours: there was nothing particularly specific or Arab or inscrutable about that. By the same token, the supposedly artificial origins, confused identities or shifting secular-religious interactions of the Middle East do not, in my view, qualify them as being radically different from what we find elsewhere. The same would go for the tendency to conspiracy theory – contrary to fond Middle Eastern belief, this is prevalent in Beijing, Belgrade and New York. Of course there are differences, as there are in any region or cultural field: but the very impact of modernity is universal and, as I have argued, imposes a common format on states and on the ideologies and movements associated with them.

This universalist assertion may also have a small normative consequence: if in other parts of the world some degree of regulation of nationalist conflict, be this within states or between them, has become possible, then it may also be possible in the Middle East. Such accommodations require concessions on both side, and they also require a realization by nationalist leaderships that the time has indeed come when the benefits of compromise outweigh those of confrontation. We saw this in South Africa, we have not yet seen but may still see it in Ireland, and we have certainly not come to this point in former Yugoslavia. Such compromises tend not to come through the disappearance of nationalist movements and leaders and the emergence of new saintly replacements: they come through calculation by nationalist leaderships. This applies equally to the broader issue of security competition, arms race and military confrontation: we saw in Europe that it is possible, through at first limited arms control and confidence building measures, to build some trust and set in motion a virtuous spiral of disarmament and security building. The time has not yet come when this is possible elsewhere in the world, and especially in the Far East and the Persian Gulf, two areas where the security spiral is currently at its most disturbing. In the Arab-Israeli context the record is mixed, but in some of Israel's relations with its Arab neighbours there is already evidence of substantial achievement. With political will, the model in place can prevent the recurrent conversion of nationalism and national distrust into all-out war.

This brings me to the final prospective argument which I would like to restate. Again it highlights the contrast of perennialism and modernity. Perennialism, for all its stress on history, is profoundly ahistorical: it posits a nation, and identity, that is fixed in time, and implies that the task is to discover or locate that fixed point, that definition of identity, or land, or correct speech, or food, and to get there once again. Modernism makes no such claims, but sees the ways in which over time definitions change, using parts of the past, but selecting according to present needs and combining with elements from other cultures. It has, therefore, two virtues. It allows us to avoid the intransigence of normative claims derived from history, and it permits a more creative, tolerant, flexible and historically accurate picture of nationalism itself. Not always can normative aspiration and analytic accuracy so combine, but in this case it can be argued that they do.

### CHAPTER 3

# History and Modernity in the Formation of Nationalism: the Case of Yemen

*Wa ju'tak min saba' binaba yaqin* And I have come to you from Saba with good tidings (*Quran*, Sura of the Ant, verse 22)

Yemen has been relatively marginal to the study of the modern history of the Arab Middle East, which has tended to focus on Egypt and the Mashreq. Within writing on Yemen itself, there is frequent mention of nationalist movements but remarkably little sustained treatment of the issue.[1] Yet the development of nationalism in a country of 14 million people, is a significant part of the overall story of nationalism in the Arab world, and may also provide the occasion for examining in regard to one particular case a number of comparative and theoretical questions.

In the previous chapter I have discussed a general approach to the study of nationalism which I term 'comparative contingency' and contrast with much of the other writing on the subject. Here the intention is to illustrate this approach by giving an account of one of the less well known nationalisms of the Arab world. In so doing this chapter aims to explore how far it is possible to go in writing such a history within the framework of 'comparative contingency' outlined above. If the Yemenis may feel offended that I am denying them their essentialisms and their perennialisms, they may take comfort from the fact that I deny it to all the other peoples of the region and indeed the world as well.[2]

As already discussed in chapter 2, since the 1960s a substantial and theoretically diverse literature on nationalism has been produced to yield some by now relatively clear lines of debate.[3] Yet if social science has, late in the day, come to acknowledge the importance of studying this phenomenon in a theoretical or comparative dimension, much of the writing on specific nationalisms, and hence on 'nations', has remained innocent of it. My own summary view of the debate is that it has in some ways reached an impasse: an array of general theories is offset against a mass of individual accounts with relatively little interaction between the two. What is needed now is a moratorium on general theories, of which we have plenty, and indeed a questioning, as Sami Zubaida has suggested, of whether a general theory is either desirable or necessary.[4] What we need instead are comparative individual histories that are both written in the light of these general theories and which, critically, test them against the historical record.

As chapter 2 suggests, far from there being 'historic' and 'new' nations they are all modern, products of contingency in the new international and normative climate created from the early nineteenth century onwards, and of the process of state formation which has accompanied it. The solution to the problem of history of 'nations' is neither to assert a perennialism, nor to waste time, political or academic, in boosting or denying the historicity of particular 'nations': we can examine how what bits of the past have been selected for current uses, but this is not to ascribe causality to this past. The question of the political behaviour of 'nations', and indeed of the legitimacy of claims to people or territory, can therefore be delinked from that of history. To write about the nationalisms of any contemporary 'nation' is to write within the framework of such a comparative contingency. To suggest a working guideline: nothing more than two centuries old should be of relevance to either history or legitimation.

The research agenda which such an approach entails would comprise four major points. First, it would identify the *general historicity* of this 'nation' in the sense of how recently it was formed, and the dependence of this formation on a broader, international, context – it being one of the paradoxes of nationalism that while each claims its uniqueness all are modular variants of a simple code, products of a universal trend of the past century or two.

Secondly, it would seek to identify the *specific causation*, those particular historical factors which contributed to the formation of this nation, with the territory, culture, historical self-image it possesses. Such an account of causation would be *anti-perennialist* in that it would deny any necessary development to this nation, even as it examined, free of deterministic assumptions, how the past was used for modern purposes.

Thirdly, it would be necessary to delineate the *specific ideological content* of this nationalism, not by demanding that it conform to a specific unitary model, based on ethnicity, language or anything else, but rather by recognizing, beyond its modular, common, form which stipulates what all nationalisms must say, the diversity and contradictions within it, as well as the changes which could occur in even relatively short periods of time. There would be no place in such an account of discussion of which version of the national ideology is 'genuine' or not, or, conversely, for demonic revelations about the 'true' if secret intentions of an enemy.

Finally, as part of the investigation of cause and of contingency, it would examine the *instrumentality* of nationalism, the relation of this nationalism to identifiable social and political groups, in other words the history not of the emergence of a given or an essence, but of the creation of both ideology and movement by political forces. If nothing else, this would relate the apparently abstract history of an idea to material and real-world forces, and further preclude any argument to the effect that one group in a society rather than another has a more accurate claim to represent the 'genuine' national message. Much of this would involve a study of state-building, and of the ways in which those aiming to take power, or retain it, have generated and managed ideas of nation. In Marxist accounts, the role of states would itself be a function of the role of classes: elsewhere, this relation itself can be treated as contingent, so that the question becomes not how classes have used states to create 'nations', but whether and how far this has been the case, and how far other social groups, including those in control of the state itself, may have done so in a way that is not definably influenced by class. If class has somewhat less of a direct role than orthodox Marxists would suggest, it may provide more of the explanation than idealist or abstracted sociological accounts would claim.

The history of nationalisms in general could, therefore, be written from such a standpoint. This perspective would, however, suggest another, parallel, line of enquiry, an accompanying set of histories of nationalisms that did not develop, indeed of 'nations' that could, on historical and other grounds, be expected to have become distinct political entities in modern times but did not: California, Bavaria, Crete among them. This is the reverse side of a history based on contingency. It would identify two options: the failure of otherwise plausible groups to espouse nationalism and the preference of nationalist movements for a status less than independence. The Middle East could also be approached from this perspective, one that would free us both from the confusions of political debate about legitimation and delegitimation, but also from tireless discussions of essentialisms and teleologies. In the Middle East as elsewhere, nationalisms have been modern, contingent,

## Scripts of Ancient Yemen

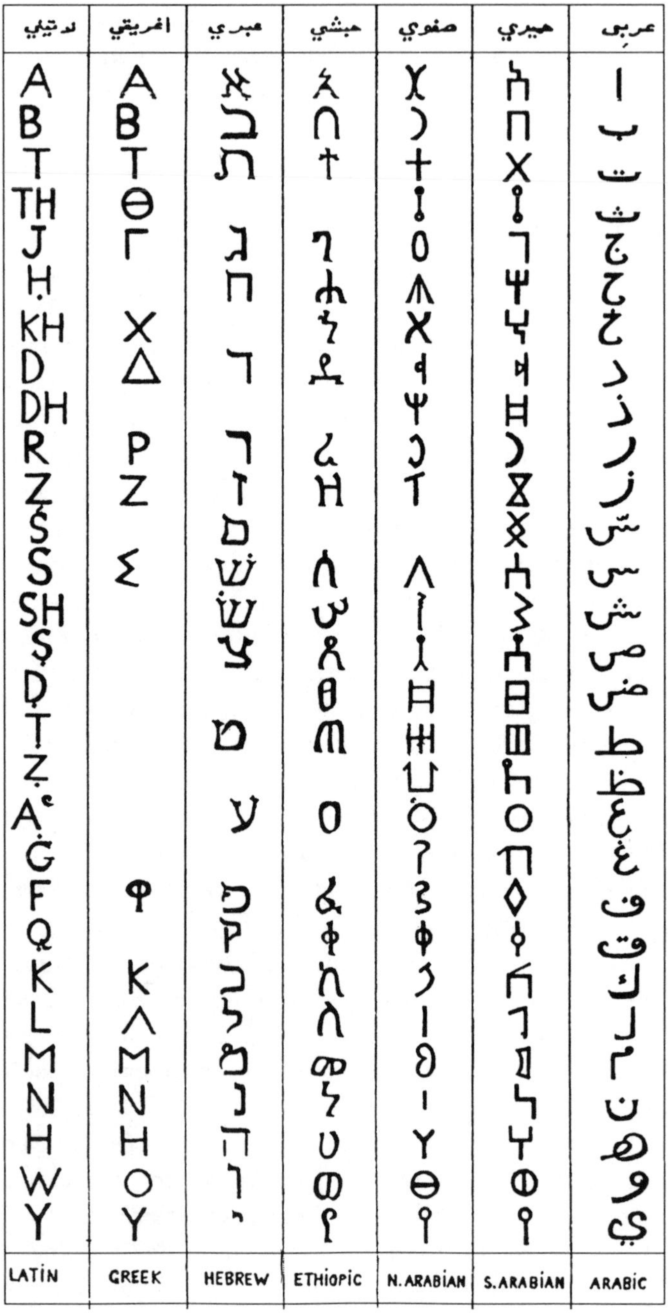

A table comparing scripts. Bottom row labels (left to right): LATIN | GREEK | HEBREW | ETHIOPIC | N. ARABIAN | S. ARABIAN | ARABIC

The Latin (leftmost) column reads, top to bottom:

A
B
T
TH
J
Ḥ
KH
D
DH
R
Z
S̱
S
SH
Ṣ
Ḍ
Ṭ
Ẓ
Ȧ
G
F
Q
K
L
M
N
H
W
Y

Source: Salah Museum, Ta'iz, 1984

confused and instrumental ideologies and the movements corresponding to them have reflected this. In what follows I shall take one particular nationalism, that of Yemen, and present, in outline form, an account of its formation.

### Yemeni nationalism

In the conventional nationalist account the Yemeni nation is an ancient one: for some millennia there has been a settled civilization in the fertile south-West part of Arabia.[5] The high point of this civilization was marked by the kingdoms of Ma'in, Saba and Himyar which have left extensive archaeological ruins. One illustration of the characteristically inclusive, 'perennialist' claims of Yemeni nationalism to the whole past is to be found in a poster of 'South Arabian Scripts' sold in the Salah Museum of Taiz, a former palace of the Hamid al-Din Imams.

The scripts designated as 'South Arabian' and hence part of the national inheritance are: Himyaritic, Sabaean, Arabic, Amharic, Hebrew, Greek, Latin. The south Arabian kingdoms were significant in the broader history of the Middle East in part because of the long-distance trade links to India and the states at the top of the Red Sea, in part because migration spread across the Red Sea to Ethiopia whose languages comprise several descendants of the ancient south Arabian tongues (Amharic, Tigrinya) and which use variants of the ancient scripts.[6] With the advent of Islam, Yemen became part of the Arab and Islamic worlds and contributed both militarily to the Islamic conquests and culturally to the mediaeval Islamic period.[7] From the tenth century onwards, Yemen ceased to be part of the broader Islamic empires and was ruled by a succession of dynasties until, in the early modern period, it fell under various degrees of external influence and control – in the sixteenth and seventeenth centuries the Dutch and the Portuguese yielding to the Ottomans, and in the nineteenth century the Ottomans and the British dividing the country between them.

In the twentieth century we can see, so the story goes, the gradual re-emergence of the Yemeni nation within the area of historic 'Yemen'.[8] Prior to World War I Ottoman rule was challenged by the forces of the Zeidi Imam, and it was he who took over the whole of North Yemen when the Turks departed in 1918. Although at first cautious about challenging the British to the South, the Imam gradually came to assert a claim to the whole of 'natural Yemen'. In the 1940s there began to develop political oppositions, to both the Imams in the North and the British in the South. The former, the 'Free Yemeni' movement, sought to free the North from the dictatorial rule of the Zeidi Imams and in 1948 staged an unsuccessful coup. Its critique of the Imam was initially phrased in religious terms, calling for an end to the Imam's oppression, *dhulm*, through various forms of taxation, and for an Islamic revival to be carried out through a corps of Islamic militants: these, the *shabab al-amr*, would travel through the country mobilizing support for the *nahda*, or renaissance, by overcoming the ignorance of the population.[9] The aim was as much to establish a truly Islamic Imamate as to replace it. Influenced by the Muslim Brotherhood in Egypt, these Free Yemenis only later turned to a more secular political vocabulary. In the South, political movements in the port of Aden began to articulate the demand for greater self-rule for Aden itself: the initial slogan, 'Aden for the Adenis' was directed both against the British and against the more conservative, 'backward' rural society of South and North.[10] By the 1950s, and with the rise of Arab nationalism elsewhere in the region, the predominant politics of the oppositions in both North and South was nationalistic and involved support not only for the general goal of 'Arab unity', but also for 'Yemeni' unity.

Nationalists in North and South differed on whether there could be unity under the Imams, but the assumption was that Yemen was one country, wrongly divided by colonial and dynastic oppressors whose removal would secure unity. Following the defeat of the 1948 revolution, the opposition in the North consisted of intellectuals on the one hand, and of subterranean officer groups on the other: it was to be the latter who, in September 1962, overthrew the Imam and proclaimed the 'Yemen Arab Republic'. From the early 1950s onwards there had been a gradual shift in the language of the opposition, so that when in 1956 the Free Yemenis had issued a new set of demands, *matalib al-sha'ab*, it represented the Yemeni people as part of the Arab nation and committed to Arab unity.[11] The earlier goal of an Islamic Imamate had gone.

The nationalist opposition in the South was originally based in the trades union movement in Aden and, as part of its support for Arab and Yemeni unity, opposed the British-backed plan for a separate south Arabian state in which the conservative rural rulers would play a predominant role. Following the outbreak of the revolution in the North, the opposition spread to the countryside of South Yemen and an active guerrilla movement developed. During the period 1963-67 the guerrilla movement became a major contender for power in both Aden and the countryside, in the process dividing into two groupings, the Nasserist FLOSY and the more radical 'Marxist-Leninist' National Liberation Front. It was the NLF which then came to power in the South and which, in various guises, was to rule there up to the unification agreement of 1990 and until its defeat in the war of 1994.

The period between 1967, when South Yemen became an independent state, and 1994, when the North conquered the South, was one in which both regimes espoused a nationalist position, asserting their place in the Arab world and calling for Yemeni unity.[12] However, contrary to the nationalist expectations, unity did not follow the departure of the British in 1967. Instead the two states set about supporting opposition movements within each other's territory: *both* claimed to be the bearers of nationalist legitimacy and to represent the whole country. As a result no diplomatic relations were exchanged, although political links between them subsisted intermittently. On two occasions, in 1972 and 1979, the two states fought short border wars, the first being an attempt by the North, with Saudi and Libyan backing, to conquer the South, the second being an attempt by the South, in alliance with the left-wing guerrillas of the National Democratic Front, to advance in the North. From the early 1980s relations improved and a set of 'unity' committees were set up. These made little progress, but in 1989-90 matters accelerated as the end of the Cold War and the internal weaknesses of both regimes led them to agree to a provisional unification. To much popular acclaim in both North and South, this occurred in May 1990, followed by general elections in April 1993: however, disagreements over the allocation of power within the post-electoral system, and rising distrust between the two leaderships, led to a de facto split in the country in early 1994, followed at the end of April by an outright Northern attack on the South. On 7 July 1994, Northern forces entered Aden, thus effectively unifying the country under one regime for the first time in several centuries.[13]

## Distinguishing features

In broad historical and ideological terms, the nationalism of the Yemen is part of the wider pattern of nationalism in the Arab world, and indeed the third world, delayed somewhat by the region's comparative isolation and later decolonization.[14] Thus it can be seen as having grown in the 1930s and

1940s under the influence of the changes taking place in Egypt and Iraq, and as having acquired a powerful impetus from the Egyptian revolution of 1952 and what followed. The emergence of a radical left, in North and South, came in part under the impact of the changes within the Movement of Arab Nationalists (MAN),[15] and to a lesser extent with the emergence of Ba'thi and Communist trends. The strength of the left-wing MAN was a result both of the radicalization of the Palestinian movement and of the Yemeni situation where the republican left, increasingly angered by Egyptian compromises with Saudi Arabia, developed well before June 1967 its own specifically Yemeni critique of the 'petty bourgeois regimes'.[16]

From the 1950s onwards the tone and vocabulary of Yemeni nationalism was therefore apparently that of other Arab nationalisms – against imperialism and Zionism and, in its later left variant, against the 'petty bourgeois' regimes and their allies. It also reflected changes in colonial policy and administration that were not specific to the Middle East: increased concern in the 1930s to assert control over previously autonomous areas, enhancement of particular colonies for reasons of imperial strategy, the rise of the oil industry,[17] the abandonment by colonial powers of a permanent commitment. The subsequent changes in nationalism also reflect shifts within the Arab context. However, the use of these apparently universal Arab nationalist terms may conceal more particular local meanings: thus the failure of 'petty bourgeois' Nasserism was primarily identified in Yemen as being about Egypt's inability to fight the Yemeni royalists and the Saudis. Hence what might seem to be an exogenous, mimetic adoption of general Arab nationalist terms concealed a modular, endogenous usage. There are, moreover, a number of other, more specific, features of this nationalism which merit attention.

In the first place, as a reflection of the division of Yemen into two states Yemeni nationalism had a *double genesis*, reflecting the different conditions in North and South. In the South nationalism was mainly the conventional third world variant, directed against British colonial rule and in favour of national independence. In the North it was more akin to that of the earlier anti-absolutist nationalism of Europe, being directed against the Hamid al-Din Imamate and initially aiming not to establish a republican regime but to install a more equitable Imam. But these nationalist strands were not completely separate since, while the North also espoused an anti-colonial element insofar as it called for the union of Yemen and the expulsion of British colonialism, the South had its own social radicalism reflecting the local division between the nationalist movement and the existing political hierarchy of sultans and tribal leaders within the South Arabian Federation. There was, therefore, both an anti-colonial and a politically egalitarian dimension to Yemeni nationalism, reflecting the two sources of the movement.

The second element of Yemeni nationalism that merits special attention then is its *social radicalism* and the espousal of an idea of 'revolution' directed not only against colonial rule but also against indigenous political and social elites. Forms of radicalism could be found in other variants of Arab nationalism, and the word 'revolution' (*thawra*) came to have a generic, promiscuous diffusion in modern political rhetoric. In the Yemeni case, however, the role of popular movements organized by radical political parties was perhaps greater than elsewhere, in part because of the more rigid social structure in the North and Southern hinterlands, in part because of the absence of that intermediary institution, the modernizing armed forces, that had played such an important role in many other Arab states. To adopt the terminology of the times, it was harder for 'petty bourgeois' regimes to establish themselves in Yemen than elsewhere, although in the end they did. Thus in much Yemeni political rhetoric the revolution was as much that of the oppressed poor (*al-kadehin*) as of the Yemeni nation as such.

If Yemeni nationalism presented itself as part of the Arab world and of the Arab nationalist movement, it also demarcated itself from these in a specific manner. This was not just a question of Yemen possessing a combination of ideological identities, as in the Egyptian or Iraqi cases: rather Yemeni identity was defined in opposition to that of the Arab world outside. At least three factors can be seen as playing a role here. First, while Yemeni nationalism embraced the country's Islamic identity, the past invoked to justify the 'nation' began with pre-Islamic civilizations. Thus for Yemenis the concept of *jahiliyya*, of the pre-Islamic period being one of 'ignorance', is unacceptable, not least because of the contrast which it highlights between what was happening in Yemen and what was taking place elsewhere in the Arabian peninsula. In their discourse, Yemeni nationalists often like to set the sons of Qahtan (the Yemenis) against those of Adnan (the Beduin, Saudis, etc.). Secondly, if Yemeni nationalism has been directed against external rule in the form of British and earlier Ottoman colonialism, it has also been directed against its Arab neighbour, Saudi Arabia. This is a factor relatively absent in other Arab states and is a reflection of the fact that in the period after World War I in which Arab nationalisms were formed, the Arabian peninsula was the only area where independent Arab states existed and could engage in inter-state, nationalism-provoking activities. The clashes in the 1920s and early 1930s with Saudi Arabia have been compounded by the treatment of Yemenis in Saudi Arabia during the oil boom and by the ongoing political, including border, disputes between the two states. It could be said, with only a little simplification, that the main 'national' enemy of Yemen is a neighbouring Arab state. This sense of contrast with other Arab states is further compounded by the experience of the Egyptian military presence during the 1960s: even among those republicans whom the Egyptians were supporting, there was a strong sense of antipathy to the supposed liberators, an antipathy well known to have been reciprocated by the Egyptians themselves.

This uneasy relation to Arab nationalism is well illustrated in the documents of the Southern nationalist movement. In the NLF's founding document of 1965 the Arabs are referred to as the people (sha'ab) to whom the Yemenis belong, but by the 1970s the Yemenis were to become the sha'ab and the Arabs the looser umma. Similarly, while in the 1970 South Yemeni constitution Yemen is a district (iklim) of the Arab world, by 1978 Yemen itself is the watan, the homeland.[18] Thus while Arab identity was in no sense rejected or overtly challenged, the Yemeni dimension came to be given greater centrality.

The role of 'unity' within Yemeni politics reflects both a general Arab aspiration and a particular Yemeni one. Thus the support for Arab unity, from the 1950s onwards, served both to express Yemen's membership of and participation in the Arab world, but was also used to secure military, political and financial support from other Arab states: in a sense, it reflected Yemen's relative isolation and poverty. However unity also meant the resolution of the specific, more local problem of the fragmentation of Yemen itself. Most obviously, this pertained to the division between North and South, ascribed as we have seen to the policies of colonial powers. Prior to the 1950s the area now known as South Yemen was known as 'Aden', or 'the Protectorates', later as 'South Arabia' (Junub al-Jazira al-Arabiyya) or the 'Arab South' (al-Junub al-Arabi) and it was only from the late 1950s that the names Yemeni South (al-Junub al-Yamani) or South Yemen (Junub al-Yaman) came into political usage, alongside South Arabia.[19] A proper charting of the shifting denomination of the 'Yemeni' area in the writing and political rhetoric of the period remains to be written: the most cursory review indicates, however, a fast, politically inspired shifting of nomenclature, with at any one time frequent uncertainties and alternative usages.[20] But there were further elements to this call for unity: the demand for the return of the three provinces occupied by Saudi Arabia in 1934; hostility to political movements in the South, be they Aden-based or more broadly 'South Arabian', that wanted to maintain the inherited divisions of the country;[21] and implicitly support for the idea of national integration and centralization in the face of a highly fragmented, regional and tribal society. This assertion of a Yemeni national identity was also designed to preclude the emergence of other potential 'nationalisms' at that period – Adeni, Hadhrami, Asiri.

*Contingency and instrumentality*

This historical overview, and the discussion of particular ideological elements that distinguish the case, together provide the raw material for an assessment of the contingent formation of Yemeni nationalism. In the first place, the *general historicity* of Yemeni nationalism, that is to say, the role of the international and universalizing context, can be analysed in terms of a number of processes: changes in international trade and strategy in the nineteenth and twentieth centuries; the impact of changes in colonial administration on the South;[22] the introduction of ideas of social and political organization from the Arab world and elsewhere (including the British trades union movement and Indonesian politics, the latter mediated via emigrés in South-east Asia); and the political evolution of the Arab world from the 1940s onwards. In short, the particular history and formation of Yemeni nation-alism took place within a broader, universalizing context.

Analysis of the specific causation of Yemeni nationalism would encompass both the pre-existing social and political structures in the country and the impact on Yemen of external events, among them the rise of Saudi Arabia in the 1920s, the explosion of the Palestine question in the 1940s (with the very specific impact on Yemen of the departure of the Jewish community, hitherto seen as part of the Yemeni people),[23] and the Egyptian revolution of 1952. It would, however, also address the contingency of this nationalism taking the form it did. In the first place, there is the contingency of space: there was nothing inevitable in 'national' Yemen either comprising or excluding the territory that it did. Given the divisions within Yemeni society prior to, and indeed accompanying, the rise of the nationalist movement, other outcomes are more than conceivable: Aden could have remained separate, becoming eventually a cosmopolitan nation-state, an Arab equivalent of Singapore to the rest of the Yemen's Malaysia, a Qatar or a Kuwait; the Hadramaut could also have broken away as could any of the other seventeen political entities in the South or the Zeidi parts of the North; political Yemen could have extended to include the southern Dhofar region of the Sultanate of Oman, an area historically claimed by Yemenis and with more geographic and social continuity with the Mahra province of Yemen than with the rest of Oman.[24] Had the Saudis pursued their conquests in 1934 then the whole of North Yemen might have been incorporated into Saudi Arabia, and Yemen would today have the status of Hijaz, an entity with some historical distinctiveness, but with, in Anthony Smith's terms, an unrealized substratum. Equally, had the British not been there, the Saudis might have annexed Hadramaut, a region where the sentiment of being 'Yemeni' was intermittent at best and which would have given the Saudis direct access to the Indian Ocean.[25]

This contingency extends to the realm of ideology. We see in Yemeni nationalism the combination of elements found in other Middle Eastern nationalisms – pre-Islamic, Islamic, Arab, third worldist, local, in this case, Yemeni: far from these being set by history, or necessarily contradictory, they are combined in a mutually supportive but changing manner. The history of school textbooks stresses a 'people' in continuous time and without tribal or other fragmentary characteristics who have acted to create the modern Yemen.[26] In declarations of state each of the four elements is deployed to endorse the existence of a historic, natural, Yemeni 'nation', with changing emphases reflecting changing circumstances: thus when Yemen faces conflict with Saudi Arabia, it is conventional to appeal to 'the sons of Saba and Himyar'; when Yemeni politicians respond to events in Palestine or the Gulf their 'Arabness' is highlighted; in times of rapprochement with Saudi Arabia, emphasis is given to Islamic fraternity and the contribution of Yemen to Islam. On the other hand, the varying emphases also reflect shifts in the political situation within the country: thus the 'Islamic' element has been prominent in two periods, in the 1940s with the rise of the Free Yemeni opposition, and again from the late 1980s with the emergence of an Islamist current, al-Islah. Again, there are no constraints on the combination or adjustment of these different ideological components.

Behind such accounts of ideology, and of definitions developed and changed, lies the question of instrumentality, of the use of these ideas by political leaderships in or out of power to serve their particular ends. Much of the discourse of nation and nationalism revolves around the state, not least through the efforts of states to promote a specific 'national' awareness against external and internal centrifugal forces. Nowhere is this more so than with regard to the question of 'unity' itself. While this corresponded to a widespread popular sentiment, one that combined easily with support for Arab unity, it was articulated by political leaderships for their own, instrumental reasons. Thus in the 1950s the Imam used 'Yemeni unity' as a means of advancing his dynastic claim to exercise influence over the South, the territory then occupied by the British. After the revolution of 1962, the Sana'a government used 'unity' as a means of enhancing their domestic legitimacy, countering British involvement in support of the royalists in the North and mobilizing support for their own regime from the population in the South. Once two Yemeni states came into existence in 1967, 'unity' became an instrument for conducting relations, mostly of rivalry, between the two regimes. While on the one hand 'unity' reflected some common interests between the two states on matters of economic development and tourism, little progress was made in this regard; more substantively, the two regimes used 'unity' to legitimate forms of pressure on the other.

For much of the late 1960s and 1970s this involved support for guerrilla opposition within the other state, but on two occasions it led to war. Both wars, those of 1972 and 1979, were attempts by one regime, using the slogan of 'unity' and in alliance with opposition forces within the other state, to advance their interests. For the South unity had long been, and remained, part not only of the reintegration of the Yemeni homeland but of the transformation of the North as well. Thus in the aftermath of independence South Yemeni officials insisted that 'Yemeni unity . . . is a unity of the toiling people, and must be made by them . . . This unity must be progressive and must not be racial or regional in character, and must be hostile to colonialism and reaction'.[27] The pre-1962 argument that there could not be unity until there had been a transformation in the North was now reformulated: unity would be achieved by actively promoting such a transformation.

This instrumentality remained central in the 1990-94 period of unification itself. Each regime hoped that it could use unification both to enhance its own position within its respective area of power and advance it in the area of the other. Unity, therefore, was not a policy aimed at fusion, but rather an instrument for inter-regime competition. If at first it appeared as if this was not a zero-sum game, and that both sides could benefit from and live with the unity agreement, the elections of 1993 showed that in reality each was bent on consolidating within its own territory: however, the political situation had so changed that the North now believed it could impose its will on the South, which it indeed proceeded to do after some months of preparation and misleading negotiation. Yemeni unity was thus achieved by the successful imposition of the Northern regime's power on the South, in alliance both with Islamists in the North and with dissident exiles from the South.[28]

As already noted, both between and within states 'unity' reflected the more general goal of state-building. North Yemeni society is more socially fragmented than that of any other country in the region with the exception of Afghanistan. This fragmentation is reflected in the lack of influence of the central government outside the major cities and the widespread distribution of arms in society. In most discussions of Yemen, by Yemenis and others, this armed rural population is referred to as 'tribal': few of these inhabitants of the rural areas are nomadic, and the term 'tribe' is used in a number of senses, but the fact of such diffusion of power, arms and identity is clear enough.[29] In the South, British rule made some impact on this 'tribal' system, and the Socialist Party went much further in the direction of centralization. Advocacy of 'unity' entailed both the creation of a single 'Yemeni' political culture, but also the strengthening of the powers of the state itself. At the ideological level this involved a denial, with mixed impact, of the 'tribal', regional and sectarian differences within Yemen, and hence an assertion of the legitimacy of the central state.[30] In practice, it meant that both states sought to reduce the power of the armed rural population, the South more success-fully than the North. In the North during the 1970s the regime of President Ibrahim al-Hamdi promoted closer ties with the South as part of an attempt to strengthen the central government.[31] Probably one of the main consider-ations of the Sana'a regime in entering the unity process in 1990 was its hope that it could use the Southern army and administrative apparatus to strengthen itself in the North. The irony was that, when it came to the war of 1994, Sana'a could only prevail by making significant concessions to the centrifugal forces.

To this discussion of the instrumental use by states of the notion of unity we can add a further chapter on class. It is not difficult to write a history of Yemeni nationalism in 'class' terms, seeing nationalism in general and the idea of unity, in particular, as the ideologies of particular classes, seeking to advance their interests against the prevailing, fragmented state structures. Thus in the North unity was espoused first by dissident *sada* and merchants, denied their proper status by the Imams, and then by the newly rising social groups – intellectuals, educated technocrats and army officers and, later, the incipient trades union and peasant movements. The radical left in the North, which clashed with the regime in the late 1960s and which waged guerrilla war between 1978 and 1982, saw itself as the vanguard of a mass movement of workers, peasants and intellectuals that would bring about unity through overthrowing the military and tribal forces dominating the country.[32] In the South it was the rising trades union movement in Aden, later backed by a radicalized rural population, that pioneered unity against those social interests – merchants in Aden, and sultans in the countryside – whose interest lay in preserving a separate and itself fragmented South.

Such 'class analysis' may often have taken a simplified and crude form, one that would have been inappropriate not just for any country in the Middle East but for any more developed society as well. To reject such reductionist use of class analysis is not, however, to rule out the fact of a wide-ranging and multiple interaction of classes with ideas of nation and nationalism: any history of nationalism in Yemen, as elsewhere, must take such interaction into account. Here again comparative contingency may be a suitable guideline: the question is not one of whether nationalism was determined by class, or unrelated to it, but how, within the general context of modernity and under the impact of exogenous political and social change, specific articulations of class and nationalist ideology occurred. While not every victory was the work of the undifferentiated 'proletariat', 'petty bourgeoisie' or, in the Yemeni case, *sayyadin* (fishermen), and not every act of resistance the doing of the *ikta'iin* (feudalists), these forces certainly played their part.

## Conclusion

This chapter has attempted to provide an analysis of nationalism in Yemen within the framework of 'comparative contingency'.[33] The aim has been to show neither that the Yemeni 'nation' existed for centuries or millennia, nor that such a pre-existing 'nation' 'arose' or 'woke up', but rather that a set of recent processes, some international and some within Yemen, have combined to produce a nationalist movement and discourse and to give it the particular content which it has. In accordance with the universal pressures operating on it and with the modular claims of other nationalisms, Yemen would inevitably have had to produce some form of 'nationalism' by the middle of the twentieth century. But that it took the particular form it did, at the time it did, reflects a set of contingent events and processes. Equally, while the population as a whole has been involved in this diffusion of a nationalist ideology, the actual content and emphasis of the ideology has varied over time and place, reflecting the instrumental usage of nationalism by aspirant political leaderships and established regimes alike. It follows that in the conditions of the modern world the Yemenis had to be part of some nationalist process; that they were incorporated into this particular nationalism was a result of the multiple contingencies discussed above. In neither case was the outcome the result of a historical determination derived from the existence of the 'nation' nor was the outcome pre-determined as to geographical context or ideological content. All of which is without prejudice to claims about contemporary belief or political legitimacy.

CHAPTER 4

# 'Terrorisms' in Historical Perspective

*Political Violence and the Mythology of 'Terrorism'*

*Article 4 – Fundamental guarantees*

1. *All persons who do not take a direct part or who have ceased to take part in hostilities, whether or not their liberty has been restricted, are entitled to respect for their person, honour and convictions and religious practices. They shall in all circumstances be treated humanely, without any adverse distinction. It is prohibited to order that there shall be no survivors.*

2. *Without prejudice to the generality of the foregoing, the following acts against the persons referred to in paragraph 1 are and shall remain prohibited at any time and in any place whatsoever:*

   *(a) violence to the life, health and physical and mental well-being of persons, in particular murder as well as cruel treatment such as torture, mutilation or any form of corporal punishment;*
   *(b) collective punishments;*
   *(c) taking of hostages;*
   *(d) acts of terrorism;*
   *(e) outrages upon personal dignity, in particular humiliating and degrading treatment, rape, enforced prostitution and any form of indecent assault;*
   *(f) slavery and the slave trade in all their forms;*
   *(g) pillage;*
   *(h) threats to commit any of the foregoing acts.*
      ('Humane treatment', Geneva additional Protocol II, 1977)[1]

Since the latter part of the 1960s the issue of 'terrorism' has played a significant role in political life and discussion in many countries, and in international relations. The Arabic term *irhabiyya* (terrorism) also came into common usage at that time. Persians had long used *terrorizm*. The lives of many people have been affected by actions classified as 'terrorist'; many more bear the psychological and physical marks of involvement in such actions. 'Terrorism' is not, therefore, a matter that can be avoided, a figment of the imagination of political opponents and repressive regimes. Yet it has become, above all in the Middle East, a subject of such distortion and myth that it is next to impossible to establish a balanced discussion of it. Some western writers on the subject have sought to abandon the term altogether on the grounds that the term is so overloaded with emotional and polemical associations that it cannot be used. They argue that there remain, however, two other phenomena that can be analysed: 'terror', a goal or instrument of political and military conflict, and political violence, of which 'terrorism' is a part.[2]

As far as is possible, this is a line of argument I would support. It is possible, and preferrable, to write about a range of political and military phenomena, everything indeed covered by the term 'terrorism', without using the term. Yet the term 'terrorism' has become so widespread and some of the actions it denotes so contentious that it may, nonetheless, be worth trying to assess some of the general issues involved. One of the casualties of the prevailing discourse on terrorism is the possibility of moral judgement. On the one hand, crimes by states are used to absolve the crimes of those opposed to them. Yet, as Geneva Protocol II stipulates, in all political conflicts those opposed to the state as well as the state itself are bound by moral and legal conventions. On the other hand, when states talk of 'terrorists' the crimes of opposition groups are used to deny the legitimacy of protest or of the right to resist and rebel: yet the latter is a central feature of Western and Islamic thought and has been given further meaning by modern concepts of democratic and national legitimacy.[3]

The challenge facing anyone who seeks to analyse 'terrorism' as a political phenomenon is, therefore, to take the phenomenon seriously, not to accept prevailing mythologizing, but to try to establish an independent terrain on which to discuss it. Attempting to find a middle ground is not possible: there is no middle ground where political violence is concerned any more than there is with racism. We need an independent position and the function of a comparative and historical perspective is precisely to help establish that independent ground. The aim of such an examination is two-fold: on the one hand, to use a critique of the prevailing discourse on terrorism to open up discussion of the varying uses of political violence in the contemporary Middle East and elsewhere; secondly, to bring into the open the moral judgements and possible moral principles that are relevant to the study of political violence, and above all to allow discrimination as to when it is legitimate for states and those opposed to them to use force.

Anybody who has been involved in the Irish or the Middle Eastern situations or any of the other comparable cases of ethnic and religious conflict realizes the complexity and danger of this question of 'terrorism'. It is a very difficult one, starting with the obvious fact that there is no agreed definition of the word 'terrorism'. One argument sometimes invoked states, that 'one person's terrorist is another person's freedom fighter'. This is a relativist fallacy: it means that if you believe that someone's cause is just, then whatever he or she does in pursuit of that cause is itself justified. There are, there must be, violent actions which everybody whatever their cultural background can agree are illegitimate. But because of the wide range of actions covered the act of definition is a complex one, as it is with any other social concept – religion, fundamentalism, or even war. Indeed one scholar has identified no less than 109 different meanings of terrorism.[4]

A second reason for the difficulty of discussion is the degree of mythologization and exaggeration we confront. To say that the issue of terrorism has been taken out of context and has been exaggerated and distorted is in no way to detract from the moral and human seriousness of the terrorist phenomenon. There does, however, seem to be a tendency to inflate and distort the question. The USA during the 1970s and 1980s made much of the issue, and presented it as a unitary, world-wide threat.[5] Governments in the Middle East have also made much of the issue to discredit their opponents, and conceal their own uses of political violence, domestically and internationally. Israel has long done this, in an attempt to discredit the Palestinian cause: Benjamin Netanyahu, in particular, made a career out of self-serving demagogy about 'terrorism'. Arab governments have also used the issue of terrorism to justify their own repressive policies, and to identify all political opponents with the cause of political violence. The Turkish government has used the term 'terrorist' to justify its refusal to develop a political solution to the Kurdish question. Yes there can be no legitimate criticism of the uses of political violence by opponents of a state if it does not permit a full and open examination of the right to rebel, and of the conditions under which such a right may apply. We can extract the issue of 'terrorism' from such political agenda through two paths, conceptual clarification and historical perspective. It may then be possible to address a third issue, that of the role which terrorism in its current, selective usage denotes in bringing about political change.

## Conceptual clarifications

Let me begin with the conceptual problem. The word 'terrorism' dates from the French Revolution, like many other now fashionable terms including nationalism, 'guerrilla' and 'counter-revolution'. It was originally used in 1794 to refer to the use of terror by governments against their own populations. That is where the concept originally comes from, an origin worth remembering. It was in this sense too that Leon Trotsky, whilst Commissar of War in the post-1917 Bolshevik government, used it to justify the use of political violence against the enemies of the state.[6] Trotsky argued that socialism could not be built in Russia under conditions of imperialist intervention without revolutionary violence and repression. Etymologies and meanings change, and the term certainly has developed many different meanings since. Yet it is important in any evaluation of the use of violence in politics, and in adjudication of crimes against humanity committed in the contemporary world, not to lose sight of what one can term 'terrorism from above'. The castigation by the governments of the USA, Israel, Egypt or Turkey of 'terrorist' opponents may not always be without justification: in their usage, however, it precludes assessment of actions in which they and their clients have also been involved. At the same time recognition of this use of illegitimate violence should not lead to denial of the crimes committed by those not in power, which we can call 'terrorism from below'. Today it is in this latter sense that the term is generally used: individual acts of violence separated from a war or civil war context but carried out for certain political ends. Today we are talking about political terrorism, not about lunatics or haphazard assassinations. We refer to kidnappings, hostage taking, hijackings, bombings, and so on. Terror is, therefore, capable of being used by those with state power and those without, as an act on its own or as part of a wider war or civil conflict.

If we look in more detail, there are four different aspects of the concept of terrorism, or four different meanings which we have to take into account. Once again it needs to be stressed that what we choose to call 'terrorism' is a matter of convention; it is not something that is automatically 'given' by facts or by history. The first, very important aspect is what is called enforcement terror, that is, the terror of governments. This is what I would term 'terrorism from above'. It has been said many times, but it loses none of its force to say it again, that the great majority of the acts of terror committed in the modern world and in history have been committed by those in power against those who are out of power. This is as true for what states have done within their own territories as internationally. This does not provide an answer to the question of moral assessment of hijacking, or bombs in supermarkets, but it does provide a moral corrective to some of the selective judgements that are made by academic experts and state officials. Even if one takes the case of the states which do carry out acts of terror outside their own frontiers, one had better start by looking at what they do to their own citizens, which is often much worse.

There are, secondly, acts of violence that are isolated, separate from the situation of a country at war and hence intended to cause terror itself rather than contribute to a broader conflict. By extension and in its narrow Western and Israeli 1980s sense, terrorism refers to acts of violence carried out internationally, in other words carried out in a third country, outside the context where its political causes can be located: an IRA action in a country other than Britain, a Palestinian action outside of the Middle East, an Islamist bomb in New York, a South Moluccan action in Holland. These would be regarded, in contemporary usage, as being acts of 'international terrorism' in the narrowest sense. This is the sense, for example, in which the US State Department's Counter-Terrorist Office was set up. Such actions have recurred. Yet the problem with this usage is that, in practice, it can be selective and self-serving. During the 1980s this usage was not used to identify acts of violence committed by states, the USA or its allies, in other countries – Israel in Lebanon, the USA and Pakistan in Afghanistan, the US-backed *contra* in Nicaragua. The term 'international terrorism' also contains the suggestion that somehow terrorism is itself organized internationally, that there is some world-wide network, aided or tolerated by certain states, which explains the incidence of terrorism, negatively defined, in a range of countries. That there are links – military, financial, political – between different groups using political violence, and that some states have aided them is indisputable. The idea of a unitary or co-ordinated 'international terrorism' is, however, a myth.[7]

The term 'terrorism' is also used much more broadly to describe the violent actions in a civil war or conflictual situation of any group of which you disapprove. The Geneva Protocol II of 1977 clearly identifies forms of violence that are impermissible in civil conflicts. The problem with this is that it too easily confuses the discussion of the uses of political violence by conflating the identification of violence with the legitimacy of the cause in which it is committed. First, political violence is a recurrent part of political change. People sometimes say that the British and the Americans had a 'peaceful' path of development. In reality, the history of both Europe and the USA is marked by the spilling of blood, civil wars, and the rest. That is how, in part, these states were established and how the boundaries between them were fixed. If other countries are now going through that experience, it may be alleviated or it may be condemned, but as a historical fact violence as part of political change is very widespread indeed. Moreover, in the context of many third world liberation movements and nationalist movements violence and acts of what in the narrow sense can be called terror have occurred. Therefore, the use of the term terrorist today is very often used to denote any liberation movement or nationalist movement of which states or people in the West disapprove. To avoid this slippage we need always to distinguish between a criticism of certain forms of violence, or of the resort to violence itself, and the validity of a cause itself.

There is a fourth aspect of terrorism which, looking from outside the Western framework, is important to bear in mind. This is 'terrorism' as a globalized anxiety and pretext, a *grande peur* of the late twentieth century. Here terrorism is a public concern, reflected and promoted as a state issue, as a subject of seminars in universities, as a subject of alarm and alarmism, rather like witchcraft, promiscuity, or spies. In this sense, the issue of terrorism has been inflated to cover many other phenomena and to justify and direct political action. There is distortion in the degree of emphasis laid on certain acts of violence internationally. So the degree of selection involved in focussing on one aspect of violence and ignoring others constitutes 'terrorism' as an ideology, as a set of political values, a set of political programmes which bear some relationship to the reality but which clearly serve other social functions as well.

This mythologization of terrorism is similar to other forms of orchestrated public anxiety, just as in other contexts the harassment of individuals accused of 'un-American' or 'un-Islamic' activities, or immorality, or spying, serves broader purposes. It can be used by states to justify general repression of political dissent. It can also occasion spontaneous hostility to forces that are not involved in the acts concerned. Such was the use of the Reichstag fire to foment anti-semitism in Germany in 1933. Such too was the widespread anti-Islamic response within the USA to actions – the Oklahoma bombings of 1995, the explosion of TWA 800 off the coast of New York in 1997 – which had no connection to Muslim groups or individuals. The issue is not to deny that acts of terrorism from below do occur, but rather to disentangle analysis of such acts from the broader context in which the issue of terrorism is discussed.

So, within the general category of 'terrorism' there are these four themes: the use of violence by states against their subjects; isolated acts of violence; the question of violence in liberation and nationalist movements; and, finally, the inflation for political ends of terrorism as an issue.

*Terrorism from below: three historical phases*

We can now attempt to place the issue of 'terrorism from below' in some historical perspective. There are certain things which a historical perspective will *not* do. It will not enable us to define what we mean by terrorism. We have to define that ourselves in order to look at the history. It will not give us a morality of terrorism; that is something we have to derive from our own principles. A historical view of terrorism will certainly not give us a theory of the 'terrorist personality', the very pursuit of which is an intellectually nonsensical activity, although one out of which a lot of people have made money and reputations and received research grants. Nor will it give us a general theory of the causes of terrorism: there is no such a thing.[8] However, it may help us to put today's phenomenon in perspective and to see what measures, what responses, we can come to.

The history of terrorism from below can be divided into roughly three phases.[9] There is what you could call the pre-history of terrorism, that is the history of terrorism up to the end of the eighteenth century, which is essentially the history of assassination, before bombs and, obviously, hijackings. This was found, for example, among the Zealots of Palestine, and among the *hashashin* – the assassins in the Middle East; it was found in ancient Rome and ancient Greece, occurred in subsequent societies as well, and of course has a continuing history. The point about the first or 'pre-historical' period is that the victim was often assumed or alleged to be guilty. Consequently, there was a theology or morality of assassination: it was said to be justified. Many is the state that erected statues to assassins: the

Athenians erected a statue to the tyrannicides Harmodias and Aristogeiton. While many of the assassinations that have taken place in the twentieth century lack any such justification, it is nonetheless worth remembering that the issue began with what allegedly was justified terrorist activity.

The second phase of terrorism is the nineteenth century, involving acts of violence, in Europe and North America, particularly by anarchists and later by nationalists. This is part of the radical politics of early modernity. One can argue that the high point of this second phase came between two assassinations: the assassination of Tsar Alexander II in 1881 and the assassination of Archduke Ferdinand of Austro-Hungary in 1914. Those were the two most politically spectacular assassinations, the ones with the greatest consequences. It was between those two that one saw the high point of 'propaganda of the deed', of men like Ravachol setting off explosions, of anarchists in Paris, of Johan Moste in New Jersey talking about bombs, though not doing much about it. This period also saw the rise of nationalistic assassination movements – in Ireland, Iran, Egypt, India and elsewhere. Among the nationalist movements were the two nationalities which have probably the oldest history of terrorist actions and which still maintain violent or 'physical force' elements in their tradition, the Irish and the Armenians. And it should not be forgotten that World War I was sparked by the assassination in Sarajevo.

The third period of terrorism is the period since World War II. We are dealing here again with different phenomena – in broad terms, actions by three kinds of group: the secular left, nationalist movements and religious fundamentalists. The first group, the secular left, comprises organizations active in the 1960s such as the Weathermen in the United States, the Rote Armee Fraktion in Germany, the Red Brigades in Italy, the Angry Brigade in Britain, and the various Japanese Red Army factions. These carried out bombings and similar activities in developed, democratic capitalist countries. They achieved nothing and they had, more or less, disappeared by the late 1970s. This wave of terrorism by groups of the far or anarchist left is no longer with us on the same scale. A related post-war phenomenon was that of the urban guerrillas in Latin America, particularly in Uruguay, Argentina and Brazil: they too were more or less defeated by the mid-seventies. As their critics on the Latin American left pointed out, the resort to armed resistance in the absence of a significant mass movement led to isolation for the guerrillas, and increased repression from above.[10] In the 1990s there was a revival of terrorist activity by ideologically more diffuse minority groups whose main aim appeared to be the disruption of life in urban communities: the Aum Shinrikyo (Supreme Truth) sect which unleashed nerve gas in a Tokyo underground in March 1995, killing 12 people and injuring several thousand, and the Oklahoma bombing by American right-wing militia elements in the same year. This 'new terrorism' has as yet not taken either a pervasive or effective form.[11]

Acts of terror by movements struggling for national independence comprise the single most important category and the one that was very much the subject of the widespread discussion of 'terrorism' in the 1980s. In the post-war period this began with the struggle of the Jews in Palestine for independence after World War II, and the attacks on British and Arab victims as part of that struggle. There have been many others which were equally successful and whose regimes were later generally accepted internationally: Kenya, Cyprus, South Yemen, and of course Algeria. Other nationalist forces have also used terrorism from below: the Palestinians, the Basques, the Moluccans, and those in Northern Ireland who pursued a struggle in the name of a united Ireland, 'physical force' as distinct from 'moral force' republicans, together with their 'loyalist' opponents.

A further development of terrorism since the 1970s has been that of actions by religious groups. Outside the Middle East this is easily presented as a function of Islam or, if not of the Islamic religion as such, then of political militants, Islamists, invoking Islam. Such anti-Islamic stereotyping is easily reinforced by the rhetoric of Islamist groups such as the GIA in Algeria, who call for an indiscriminate use of violence against all who collaborate with the 'apostate' (*mortadd, kafir, mulhid*) regime. In opposition to this rhetoric, three points need to be made. First, the incidence of political violence by groups invoking religion is by no means specific to Islam: Christianity, Judaism, Hinduism, Buddhism have all been invoked by those using violence from below and above. In Northern Ireland Christians of two sects – Catholics and Protestants – have invoked religion to justify their crimes. In Israel fanatical Jewish groups have advocated violence by the Israeli state when it has suited them, and independently when it has not. Baruch Goldstein, who killed 29 Palestinians in Hebron in 1994, claimed to be doing the work of God. In India, there has been an ominous rise in the use of violence by Hindu chauvinist groups, using again both state and unofficial means to terrorize their Muslim and Christian fellow citizens.

Secondly, it is nonsense to seek the causes, as distinct from legitimation, of violence in the texts or tradition of any religion. The doctrinal situation of each of these religions is clear: they allow of a pacific reading, as of a violent one. At the same time, each major religion and ethical tradition contains provision for discussion of just war, of the conditions under which it is legitimate to use force, and of what kind of force it is legitimate to use. The choice as to which reading is made depends on the political choice of the moment. In the Islamic case there is a concept of legitimate war *al-harb al-mashru'a* or *al-harb al-'adila*. The Quran (9.13 and 22.39-40) gives legitimation for war in self-defence but also enjoins the believer to respect limits in what they do (Quran 2.90).[12] Moreover, the Islamic tradition distinguishes between *jihad*, which is legitimate, and *ghazu*, invasion, or *'adwan*, aggression, which are not. In addition to this set of principles and vocabulary specific to the Muslim world, Muslim states are also committed, as are non-Muslim ones, by the international conventions regulating the conduct of war to which they have subscribed. Under Geneva Protocol II these apply also to non-state groups, rebel forces operating on the territory of these states.

There is, thirdly, in this identification of 'Islam' with 'terrorism' a misuse of the latter term for polemical political purposes: on the one hand, to delegitimate not just the actions but the very programme of political groups – in Palestine above all – who mobilize Muslim peoples, on the other, to confine discussion of terrorism only to Muslim states. The Middle East has seen terrorist actions from above – by states acting in the name of Islam, by Israel, and by secular regimes in Turkey. In his *A Clash of Civilizations* Samuel Huntington argues that 'Islam has bloody frontiers': he does not, however, provide an accurate account of where the responsibility for this bloodiness may lie – in some cases prime responsibility lies with Muslims, in others not. In Bosnia, Kosovo, Palestine, Kashmir, to take but four examples, it does not.

How do we assess this second wave, the wave since World War II, in particular those terrorist activities that have developed since the 1960s? First of all, it is important to be clear, for all the people who say terrorism is always with us, that the urban guerrillas in Latin America and the urban guerrillas of Manhattan, North London, Tokyo and so forth were defeated. Secondly, if we take the international aspect of terrorism in a national liberation context, that is, the hijackings and other acts of violence which will continue, we must recognize that while this is a serious problem, it is a subaltern problem. It is not *the* major problem for international peace and law and order. It is a problem which has to be dealt with in a serious way, both politically and technically; but the degree and the extent of contemporary terrorism are greatly exaggerated. One could speculate about what would happen if the television news, in the morning or evening, were to give the same prominence to every car crash, with gory photographs and interviews with all the victims and so on, that it gives to terrorist incidents. The issue of car crashes, which is not an insignificant one, would be very much more on our minds.

To put it in proportion, and without diminishing the horror involved, it is worth citing one statistic that in the two decades up to 1995 the numbers killed by 'international terrorism' in any one year were under a thousand.[13] Each death was a tragedy, an unnecessary loss, but the cost of terrorism has not reached the epidemic proportions that we are sometimes led to believe. Of course, all the people involved who survived will remember it for the rest of their lives, and the psychological scars will remain. But we are not dealing with a problem on the scale of private ownership of handguns in the USA (where there are close to 10,000 deaths a year as a result of shootings), the international drug traffic, the proliferation of nuclear weapons, poverty and war in Africa, and five or ten other major international issues which confront us today and for which we equally do not have solutions.

## Terror and communal conflict

It is not the terrorism of small groups but two other kinds – 'terrorism from above', or the violent actions of states, and political violence in the context of communal conflict – that in human costs and international consequence are the most serious. In any comparative perspective, the most worrying feature of all 'terrorism from below' in the international context today is not hijacking and bombing and the seizure of embassies: it is the growth of terrorism in communal situations in third world countries, and in confessionally divided countries such as, until recently at least, Ireland. This is where you have violence between Turks and Greeks living adjacently in Cyprus, Protestants and Catholics in Northern Ireland, Hindus and Sikhs in the Punjab, Arabs and Israelis in the Middle East, the different communities of Lebanon, Muslims and Christians in the Philippines, the Tamils and Sinhalese in Sri Lanka and, more recently, in former Yugoslavia. Here acts of violence by members of one community against another produce a counter-reaction: they produce hatred, they undermine any possibility of a lasting coexistence of the two communities. A spiral of hatred, fear and vengeance takes place. This worldwide phenomenon is killing and maiming thousands of people in the world each year. The focus on involvement of Western citizens as the victims of acts of 'international terrorism' obscures this much larger use of violence in situations of inter-ethnic conflict: long a matter of mainly non-European concern, and occurring only in isolated pockets such as northern Ireland or the Basque country, it was to become a major preoccupation in the 1990s with the onset of mass inter-ethnic violence in former Yugoslavia.

Such inter-communal terrorism is going on every day and in many places. Those people who do stand independently, such as the Palestinian spokesman Sa'id Hammami, the Social Democratic and Labour Party in Northern Ireland, the non-violent opposition of the Kosovo Democratic League or other comparably courageous people, are cut down by the hatred on both sides; they are spat upon or worse as traitors and moderates. The decomposition of communities where people of different ethnic or religious backgrounds did previously live together in some way with whatever prejudices and grievances is a widespread contemporary phenomenon. It is, arguably, the most worrying aspect in the contemporary world of the misuse of violence by those who are not in power. Here 'terrorism' means terror used against other citizens of the same country, not against international targets and not, to a large extent, against the state.

*Some historical conclusions*

Some conclusions can be drawn from this history. First of all, there is no general 'theory' of terrorism, a general psychology of terrorism or even a general causation of terrorism. What drives Palestinians or Armenians or drove the Zionists just before they became independent in Palestine is very different from what drove American Weathermen or the Rote Armee Fraktion to use violence. But there are some philosophic preconceptions which are very widespread among terrorists, three of which merit a mention. One is the simple idea that you can shortcut social and political change. In other words, that you do not have to get elected, you do not have to mobilize popular forces, you do not have to create a rebel army, you can just break through the oppression of the state or the social opposition you face by killing a few people or by carrying out a certain dramatic act. The classic example was *Narodnaya Volya*, the People's Will, in Russia during the 1870s, who believed that if you killed fifteen members of the government the whole regime would fall. The same assumption lies behind hijacking and other contemporary actions of terror; it lies equally behind the facile assumption of counter-terror as practised by Israel and the United States in the Middle East which deems that if you kill a few of the other side then the problem will be solved. This fundamental, simplistic assumption that social and political problems can be solved by killing a few people, by terrorizing them, by shortcutting the whole process is the one central and almost universal feature of 'terrorism from below', whether this comes from oppressed groups or from nations. There is a refusal to see that you have to mobilize support, that you have to gain consent. There is also a refusal to see how strong your opponents are. It is a politics born of desperation, not in the sense that people are necessarily destitute or desperate, although some of them certainly are, but in the sense that all other means of change are apparently exhausted.

The second aspect of terrorism, the second fallacy which goes with it, is the idea that 'propaganda of the deed', be it blowing up a Paris restaurant in the 1880s or hijacking a plane or kidnapping an ambassador in the 1980s, will mobilize your own side. This is the simplistic assumption that the scales will fall from people's eyes, that they will rise up and seize power and all will be solved. The fact that you get your picture on the front page of the *New York Times* for a day, or get worldwide diffusion of some communiqué, does not mean you are going to change the world, although too many people have imagined that it does. The fact that you get prime time news coverage will be forgotten tomorrow. Both forms of philosophical simplification remain prevalent: they reflect a refusal to understand what is required for serious political change.

Thirdly, in contexts of terrorism against other ethnic groups and in communal situations, there is a recurrent moral evasion: since terrorism is illegitimate against other human beings, the answer is not to foreswear terrorism, but to deny the humanity of the other side. This may range from rage and contempt, to the denial that the other side constitute a legitimate ethnic group with any collective right to self-determination, to a deeper denial of the very entitlement of the other side to basic considerations of dignity and survival. Such attitudes could be found in the rhetoric which characterizes the other community as 'animals', 'vermin', 'insects' and the like. It is reinforced by propaganda promoting hatred and attempting to degrade the other side. In its denial of the entitlement of the other side to humanitarian treatment, something going beyond rage or reprisal, it seeks to square the moral circle, purportedly upholding the principles of humanitarian treatment in the name of which oppression suffered by one's own side is contested whilst oppression of the other side is simply denied. It is a dramatic example of that very rejection of universality which is so central to the nationalism discussed in chapter 2.

The first step in countering terrorist arguments is, therefore, the assertion of the entitlement of all humans to humane treatment. The second concerns the distinction between combatant and non-combatant: for it is the denial of this difference which provides the other philosophical prop for terrorist actions. Less absolute than the argument about the sub-human character of the opponents, the argument that runs, 'They are all guilty' provides an equally suitable legitimation for indiscriminate violence. Yet this has as little validity as the first: in all societies, industrialized or not, or with whatever degree of political consensus, there is a distinction between combatants and non-combatants, between those who may be objects of legitimate violence and those who may not. Again, universality may provide the answer, for, in the final analysis, none of those who argue that all members of the enemy society are militarily active would for a minute accept the argument as applied to their own society.

This leads to the question of efficacy: does terrorism work? Terroristic actions and counter-terroristic actions may work if they have a very specific goal; for example, to get some prisoners released or to get a very specific government policy changed or a minister removed, to get a ransom paid, to get some dismissed workers taken back. In the history of the American labour movement in the late nineteenth century, certain terroristic actions produced such a positive result. But precisely because it is circumventing political and social change, terrorism cannot achieve major social change on its own. If we look at the history of anarchists and other bombers in the nineteenth century, they got nowhere. The same goes for the urban guerrillas in Latin America and for the Weathermen and the Rote Armee Fraktion.

If, however, we take cases where national liberation movements have used violence and terror, some of them have succeeded. It can be argued, though, that in each case their success is attributable to reasons other than the use of terror. The Zionist movement in Palestine did not achieve statehood primarily because of the use of terror. It was organized, it was funded, it fought, it had a political organization: it was for those reasons that it succeeded. The same goes for the Algerians, as it does for the Irish in the first phase of the independence movement up to 1921. The same would go for

Kenya, South Yemen, Cyprus and so forth. Terror was not the central factor in their victories. If we look at cases where nationalist movements have used terror and have not succeeded – the IRA, the Basques, the Québecois, the Armenians of *ASALA*, the South Moluccans – we can see that their failure to date is attributable to the fact that they lack the necessary social and political strength to enforce their cause. The case of the Palestinians is also instructive in this regard: years of 'terrorism from below', from the mid-1960s to the mid-1980s, produced little response from either Israel or its main supporter, the USA. On the other hand, the proclaimed willingness to have a political dialogue with Israel, announced at the Algiers conference of the PLO in November 1988, combined with the political pressure of the *intifada* which had begun in 1987, did produce a context where substantive negotiation was possible and culminated in the Oslo agreement of 1993.

This does not mean, of course, that terrorism does not have consequences. It does have consequences, and quite serious ones. The most obvious is that terrorism usually renders states more repressive. It leads to various forms of state crackdown including intensified 'terrorism from above'. We saw this in a comparatively minor way in West Germany in the 1970s with the *Berufsverbot*, the attempt to root out of state employment (and that includes primary schools) anybody who had radical left-wing connections. We saw it in a much less polite way with military regimes in Argentina and Uruguay in the 1970s; we saw it in Turkey in 1980 when the military junta came in on a law and order platform. Even the ancient Greek tyrannicides, Harmodias and Aristogeiton, failed in their attempt to overthrow the Athenian tyranny and went on to provoke greater dictatorship. The second consequence that follows from terrorism is retaliation. What the United States and Israel did in Lebanon in the 1980s and 1990s are examples of this retaliation: they did not achieve their results. With their use of state violence, they suffered from the same moral as well as political deficiencies as their opponents.

The third and by far the most important consequence of terrorism perpetrated with communal motivations is, of course, that it generates hatred. It breeds fear, it makes it much, much more difficult for people to cross the communal lines to try to build family or political or other ties. The result is that in Lebanon and in Northern Ireland you now have generations of young people who have been brought up to hate the other community and to see them only as killers. The piles of martyrs mounted and there are always justifications. I recall the IRA person who said to me, 'Oh, we're not against them because they're Protestants, we're against them because they're fascists.

Don't you know the difference?' Some such justifications can for a minute being to sound quite revolutionary and non-sectarian. But the reality is that communal hatred of this kind is highly sectarian, has no revolutionary character and always intensifies. It is the major consequence of terrorism.

The only adequate response to the challenge of terrorism, from above or below, is to develop a moral and legal position to deal with the conduct of war and to place terrorism in such a framework. As I have already argued, there is sufficient basis in both Islamic and other traditions for moral discussion of the legitimacy of violence by states and by those opposed to them. These elements of guidance are reinforced by the very precise provisions of the Geneva Conventions – the four Conventions of 1949 regulating the conduct of states in war, and the two Protocols of 1977, which regulate not only war between states and opposition groups but also the actions of opposition groups themselves.[14] These enshrine the limits on state power, but equally allow for the right of revolt by those suffering national or social oppression. The Geneva Conventions make possible moral dialogue between conflicting political groups and across supposedly fixed civilizational and religious boundaries.

Following the Geneva Conventions, then, when is it legitimate to use violence at all? This right is termed in contemporary writing as *jus ad bellum*.[15] It is illegitimate to use political violence in societies that are democratic. This would apply in the cases of the IRA, and ETA; their use of violence is not legitimate *tout court*. Beyond the question of the right to wage war there is also the question of right in war, *jus in bello*. Here we have to be clear that certain acts constitutive of what is conventionally called terrorism are in any situation unjustifiable: civilians and prisoners of war are to be treated properly; all use of violence is to be proportionate; certain weapons are in themselves illegitimate.

The essential guideline in discussing 'terrorism from below' is proportion. The phenomenon of international terror is a secondary phenomenon. It is not the major threat to international order. It is not a major phenomenon in international relations today. It is very unpleasant for anybody associated with it and for anybody who fears it, and that includes anyone who gets on an airplane. It must nevertheless be kept in proportion and not inflated for other political ends.

The crucial moral guideline is that when a group commits acts that could be regarded as terrorism, these must be separated from our judgement of the justice of its cause. People whose causes one dislikes can behave well, and people whose causes and whose grievances one considers to be justified can and do commit acts of terror. The act no more disqualifies the cause than the cause justifies the act. One must recognize that the frequently made attempts to discredit by reference to their tactics the Palestinians, or the Armenians or the Kurds in Southeast Turkey, all of whom are people with legitimate national grievances, are fallacious and to be rejected.

Finally, to return to the question of policy, we can say that beyond all other considerations the search for political solutions has to go on. From those places I know a bit about – namely Ireland, Palestine, Sri Lanka and the Punjab – I would argue that terror has made political solutions even more difficult. At the same time, it has made them all the more necessary. The protagonists in this war – the advocates of 'law and order' on one side, the defenders of 'progressive atrocities' on the other – have to yield to dialogue, and ultimately, to democracy.

PART II

---

# Modernity and the State

CHAPTER 5

# The Fates of Monarchy in the Middle East

There is a story told of the weeks following the Yemeni revolution of September 1962. Possibly reflecting a certain urban bias, the story tells that, as news of the overthrow of the Imam spread, tribesmen came flocking into the city. When asked why they had come, they answered that they had heard that a beautiful woman, *jumhuriyya* (republic), had appeared there and they wanted to see her. The tribesmen were in a way right for their time. In the early 1960s and for much time before and some after, it appeared that republicanism, in the minimal sense of the end of dynastic rule, was sweeping the region.[1] This is what the revolutionaries were saying. It was also what social scientists, amongst them Huntington and Lerner, were suggesting. My own first book was entitled *Arabia without Sultans* – the sultans of South Arabia had gone, as had the Imam of the North, and the book gave an account of the campaign by the revolutionaries of Dhofar to overthrow the Sultan of Muscat, as he was then called. The aspirations of the Dhofari guerrillas did not, of course, stop there. As evening came on and the fighters gathered round their camp fires I listened to them shout slogans reflecting their political hopes: '*Yasqut kul al-shuyukh, wa al-muluk, wa al-imam, wa al-salatin, wa al-umara, wa al-shah fi al jazira wa al-khalij al-arabi al-muhtall.*'[2] Imperialism, Zionism, 'Arab reaction' and a generic foe termed 'Revisionism' were also denounced. Not much was left out.

The Yemeni tribesmen were to a considerable sense right too for the Middle East as a whole in this century. Of the three major monarchical systems existing at the start of the twentieth century – the Ottoman Sultanate in Turkey, the Qajar Shah in Iran, the Alawi Sultan in Morocco – only the last survives, as does the Al Bu Said Sultanate in Oman.[3] Of the monarchies that emerged in one way or another under colonial rule in the Arab states, a considerable number have also been overthrown: in Egypt in 1952, in Iraq in

1958, in Libya in 1969. So too have long-established monarchies installed in important states that impinge on the Middle East and whose demise was to have significant consequences for them: the Romanovs went in Russia in 1917, the Indian *maharajahs* after 1948, the Greek monarchy in 1967, the Mohammadzai in Afghanistan in 1973, the Solomonic dynasty of Ethiopia in 1974.

Monarchy, like democracy or peasant revolution or a return to holy texts, is legitimated and delegitimated by demonstration effect: what is happening elsewhere or what is believed to be happening elsewhere matters. The Shah took fright in 1958 when the Hashemites fell in Iraq, as he did again after the 1973 coup in Afghanistan. The Saudis have been alarmed by what appear to be democratic developments elsewhere in the peninsula, be it the tentative parliamentary openings in Kuwait and Bahrain of the 1970s, both of which they encouraged their local allies to close down, or the Yemeni elections of 1993 and 1997. In 1981, when their Iraqi and Iranian foes were distracted by their war with each other, the six peninsular monarchies banded, one might even say huddled, together to form the Gulf Cooperation Council. Republicanism was, therefore, the dominant trend in the Middle East of the twentieth century, as it was in Europe. Yet of the twenty-five states that comprise the Middle East today, eight are still ruled by monarchs: if population ruled is taken into account, then we are looking at around 15 per cent of the region's population being under monarchical rule in the 1990s. If appropriation of oil revenues is the criterion, then the figure is much higher – probably two-thirds of the region's oil revenues go to the Gulf monarchs. The Sultan of Oman has remained with some help from his friends, as have his royal confreres in the smaller Gulf states and, above all, in Saudi Arabia. The monarchies of Jordan and Morocco have also survived, and have to a considerable extent even prospered. In the case of the oil-producing GCC states they too have enjoyed comparative stability and prosperity. Kings Hussein and Hassan, with much less money available, manoeuvred in such a way as to defy their critics: they were unseated neither by revolt from below nor by recurrent threats from the military. The Palestinian challenge of 1967-70 in Jordan is remembered if only because of the manner in which it ended. Yet we retain only a dim memory of the military challenges of Abdulla al-Tal in 1948 or the dissident officers to 1957 to the Jordanian monarchy. Likewise, in the case of Morocco, the mass socialist challenges of Ben Barka and the UNFP in the early 1960s[4] or that of Mohammad Oufkir in 1972 now seem remote.

When did the tide turn? In retrospect one can see that for Arab nationalism it began after the great defeat and delegitimation of 1967: monarchy, like Islamism, benefited from the failure of the secular nationalist project. Significantly, after this point there began to be a certain nostalgic talk of monarchy and discussion of the uses of the monarchical system. As reality shifted, so social scientists too have begun to look again at the monarchies, not as anachronisms living on borrowed time but as enduring aspects of Arab states and as objects of study. The literature on the enduring monarchies, although often hampered by opacity of object and state censorship, allows for a comparative discussion to take place.[5] History, and social scientists, have abandoned any assumptions about the inevitable fall of monarchy, of a republican telos in politics: though to say this need not imply an alternative belief in monarchical continuism. In the Middle East as elsewhere, the establishment and survival of monarchies bears no *necessary* relation to modern politics: it is a contingent matter, established, maintained and, when it happens, terminated by the balance of political forces. If it does survive it is not in spite of but because of the workings of modernity within the country and internationally. Monarchies endure not by remaining the same or because they are 'traditional', but rather by finding new forms of support within the societies they rule, within their economies and within the international system. The explanation of why and how they have survived rests on identifying this interlinking of monarchy with modernity.

*Political consolidation, international context*

There are some broad conclusions which appear to follow from this thirty-year ebb of a determinist republican orthodoxy. In the first place, most obviously but most importantly, monarchy is and may well remain a significant part of the politics of the Arab world. The eight monarchies have endured a range of challenges and have been able to use the financial and political resources provided to them, to consolidate their positions. The various reasons for this domestic success include plentiful wealth, the adoption of nationalist policies, and assiduous efforts at state-building. Monarchs also rule through building coalitions with armed forces, with the middle classes, with clerical institutions and, more generally, through forms of controlled mobilization. These alliances shift: the Saudis have lessened their dependence on the Al Shaykh, the descendants of Muhammad Abd al-

Wahhab, and on the clerical establishment, the al-Sabah in Kuwait have distanced themselves from the merchants. However, all monarchies involve coalitions. It is easy to see what happens when oil rent and monarchical conceit combine to make rulers believe they can dispense with coalitions, as the case of Muhammad Reza Pahlavi showed all too clearly.[6]

These monarchies have, also, benefited from external support: the GCC states, Jordan and Morocco have all been supported by the West, and have pursued astute diplomacies to balance the conflicting pressures upon them. External support is not everything, however, and even if they were set up by colonial powers, it is mistake to regard their survival as simply a matter of imperialism. But the monarchs of the region have also known what happens when they get it wrong. All of the existing monarchies of the Arab world, and some of those that survived as long as they did, owed their survival at some point to the intervention of external forces: Morocco was saved in 1912, and again in the early 1960s and 1970s; Jordan was saved in 1958 and again in 1970; Oman was saved in 1957 and again in the early 1970s; Kuwait in 1961 and 1991; Saudi Arabia called for help in 1963 and again in 1990. The same applied to the others, prior to their fall: had it not been for the British, the Egyptian monarchy might have ended much sooner than it did; the Iranian was helped into being in Reza Khan's coup of 1921, and saved in 1953; the Iraqi could have foundered in 1941. Conversely it was the inability of the British to act in Iraq in 1958, and in Libya in 1969, and of the Americans to do so in Iran in 1978, that spelt doom for those regimes. Thus, while it would be simplistic to attribute the emergence or survival of these regimes solely to external military or indirect security support, it would be misleading in the extreme to ignore the importance of such backing at key moments. There is no mystery about their survival, and no need to invoke religious tradition either.

A second broad conclusion about Middle Eastern monarchy is that, as with other aspects of the relation of states and politics to ideology, it is at least as much political interest that shapes ideology as the other way around. To put it more concretely: the religious, cultural and historical reserves of Islam allow for both the legitimation and the delegitimation of monarchs. It depends on who is doing the interpreting. As Bernard Lewis and others point out, monarchy is not an intrinsic part of the Islamic faith. The term *malik* is used both in a pejorative and in an approving sense. The contrast with Christianity and other religions is clear: Christ was the King, and in the early modern period monarchs claimed divine right, if not directly then through

Christ's annointed vicar, the Pope of Rome.[7] Elsewhere, further east, divinity has until very recently been even more central: the kings of Nepal and Thailand retain semi-divine status, the very term 'divine' having a different shade of meaning outside the monotheistic world; while those of Japan, China, Vietnam and Cambodia were to lose it in the course of the twentieth century. Muhammad and God were not normally characterized as kings in Islam, though there are some references to God as *malik* in the Quran. Islamic tradition has not even been able to bestow the kind of religious legitimation that was obtained by early modern European monarchs with the 'divine right of kings'.

Monarchy is not part of the five *arkan* or pillars of Islam and comes nowhere near it. From the Quran, the *hadith* and the broader traditions of law and custom it is possible to derive a justification for monarchy, and this has been assiduously done over the centuries. Thus the status of *sharif*, or descent from the prophet, is one available mechanism, although only the preserve of two of the eight Arab monarchies today – the Jordanian and the Moroccan.[8] The Ottomans did not claim to be descendants of the Prophet, but the Safavids in Iran did (as did Khomeini). Another means of deploying religion is to make the claim that monarchs preserve an Islamic polity – long argued by the Ottomans, and now most obviously by the Saudis: the easiest texts to use being that which enjoins the good and forbids the evil, and that which instructs the faithful to 'obey God, the Prophet and those in authority over you'.[9] Another legitimate argument is that other forms of rule, including republicanism or democracy, are anti-Islamic. The history of the term *malik* with its various cognate terms *(malakia* is the Arabic for monarchy) illustrates the process whereby a secular term is given, when deemed appropriate, religious sanction.[10]

The word 'Imam', associated in modern times with religious authority, was distinct from the religious *ulema* in the case of eighteenth-century Oman. Equally, monarchs can be delegitimated: the terms *dhulm*, (oppression) and *istibdad* (tyranny) are available from tradition, as are the figures denounced in the Quran, of the pre-Islamic tyrants, Pharaoh and Croesus. In the campaigns against the Imams of Yemen in the 1930s and 1940s the opposition *al-yamaniin al-ahrar* used traditional Islamic vocabulary to challenge the Imams.[11] In Iran Khomeini termed the Shah Yazid, the name of the Ummayyad Caliph who killed Hussein, the founder of Shi'ism, and hence a term of significance for Shi'is, and the all-purpose *taghut*.[12] One of the most potent cultural dimensions of the Iranian revolution was the resonance of the slogan that came to dominate in the latter part of 1978, *marg bar shah*, 'Death to the Shah'. That this could be enunciated was itself a powerful element in the delegitimation of the monarch in a country that had seen more than two millennia of monarchy.

Thus, if it is possible to trace monarchy in the Muslim world from the seventh century on, and legitimate it through the texts of the religion, it is equally possible to tell the different, less doctrinal story of how political and social power moulded and used the texts. From this story one could even say that the greatest exponents of secularism were the Muslim monarchies of the past fourteen centuries. Studies of kingship in earlier Islamic periods and of particular Islamic states do not suggest that the monarchs and their ideologists were confused on this issue.[13] While Islam may provide a necessary part of the legitimation of monarchical rule, it cannot provide an explanation for it, any more than it can for other forms of social activity – the family, the economy that also get legitimated in such terms. When, in the twentieth century, it came to formulating official titles for these monarchs, the terms used once again reflected contemporary concerns: *khadim al-haramain* (servant of the holy places), *aryamehr* (light of the Aryans) and so forth. Such choices often reflected not only the wish to appropriate some earlier symbol of legitimacy, but also the desire to assert who one was not: thus the Pahlavi adoption of Sassanian titles was designed to contrast them to the Safavids and Qajars who had preceded them. Jordanian and Saudi royal nomenclature also stresses a legitimacy that neither in fact has.

A third conclusion which arises from a closer look at Middle Eastern monarchy is the modernity of the institution. By this is meant both the recent origin of most monarchies, and, more importantly, the way in which, in addition to direct political or military support from abroad, it is the constraints and influence of the modern world that explain their emergence and endurance. The historical record is clear enough: of the eight Arab monarchies only two, those of Oman and Morocco, predate the twentieth century. Their survival has, moreover, much to do with the use of violence, political calculation and foreign backing: as I have argued, all important is how these monarchs have managed to combine domestic and international support. For example when the Sultanate of Morocco nearly fell to internal revolt and financial crisis in 1912, it only survived because the ruler, Moulay Hafiz, invited in French troops and agreed to a protectorate. Later it owed its survival to the way in which Muhammad V adapted to and used the national confrontation with the French. Still later, Hassan confronted the

Spanish over Sahara, to consolidate his position against the left wing opposition. At the same time Hassan II inherited from the French a state, and an external support, which allowed him to confirm his power. Even more so the state system, the economic and social foundations, and the international context are at different times distinct. The symbols may appear continuous but even here memory can mislead. Morocco only acquired a king, as distinct from a Sultan, in 1957. Egypt's *khediv* became a king only in 1922.

Elsewhere we see the emergence of monarchies in the context of state-building and state consolidation in the broader Middle East context after World War I: the imposition of the Hashemites on Jordan by the British; the victory of the tribal coalition of the Saudis in Arabia in the 1920s; and the evolution under British tutelage of Persian Gulf rulers from being *amirs* of small coastal villages to rulers, endowed with oil, of modern states. Oman is a story apart: one of the longest surviving Arab states, along with Egypt, Yemen and Oman, it saw the conflict between two power centres, the Imam of the interior and the Sultan of the coast, resolved by British intervention in the 1950s. Here again, however, an apparent continuity masks major changes: the administrative and military system, the territory controlled, the relation with the tribes of the interior, even the name (from Sultan of Muscat, up to 1970, to Sultan of Oman thereafter) involved adjustment to change. The shortest lived monarchy of all was that of Libya: in 1951 the British had Sayyid Idris al-Sanusi, the ruler of their zone of control, Cyrenaica, proclaimed king, only to see him despatched into exile eighteen years later.

The modernity of these monarchies is evident in the broader international context. In reorganization after World War I, choices were made as to the form of state being established in the region. The British favoured monarchy, in Iraq and Jordan, as they later did in Libya, while the French favoured republics. This had little to do with the countries concerned, and much to do with the constitutions of the metropolitan countries at the time – the French, it should be remembered, had not been loath to take over or create monarchies in Indo-China and Mexico in the nineteenth century. The decision in 1922, at the time when Egypt became formally independent, for the Egyptian ruler, Sultan Ahmad Fuad, to become a king, reflected a contemporary choice. In two other cases newly established militarized regimes chose monarchy – in Iran, Reza Khan had initially favoured a republic, following Turkey, but changed his mind at least partly under pressure from the clerical establishment who associated republicanism with the negative example of secularism in Turkey. Meanwhile, in Saudi Arabia the tribal *amir* of the Al Saud decided, also for tactical reasons and mainly to deny the claims of the Hashmite King of Hijaz, to proclaim himself *malik* in 1926.[14] The impulse for Arab rulers to do so at that time was all the greater because of the uncertainty caused by the abolition of the Ottoman caliphate in 1924. Such was the contemporary vogue for monarchy that even Sheikh Mahmud Barzinji, initially denominated by the British as *hokemdar* of the Kurds and subsequently leader of the Kurdish revolt in northern Iraq, called himself 'King of the Kurds'.[15] Turkey chose a republic, but we know from the evidence of the time that this was quite a close thing: Atatürk consulted on what path to take and found opinion divided. He did not at first abolish the caliphate, only the sultanate: the decisive factor was that these old institutions were seen as unable to fulfill the national role of defending the interests of the people against foreign attack.[16]

These choices reflected, therefore, not continuity, but the combination of domestic calculation and international conformity to which these states were subjected at the time. In cases where monarchy fails, one can see how the factor of external defeat and challenge plays such a central role. The European and Far Eastern monarchies fell in the twentieth century largely due to defeat in war: Russia, Austro-Hungary, Italy, China and Japan all provide instances of this. And so, too, do the Ottoman empire, Egypt and Libya. The one exception was Iran in 1979: here it was a set of powerful internal tensions, augmented by external financial inflows, that undermined the Pahlavi regime. Yet while tension between the Pahlavis and the Iranian society had endured for decades, it was only in 1978 that the Islamist opposition started to call for a *jumhuri-yi islami,* an Islamic republic, the only political force calling for a republic prior to that had been the *Tudeh* party. It would seem that Khomeini took his lead from them.

### Regional and international comparisons

The analysis of different origins and of the broader Middle Eastern context leads to the question of comparison, both of monarchies with each other and of these monarchies with republican regimes. Examination of these eight cases, and of the conditions of their emergence and consolidation, raises the question of how far we are talking about similar institutions. The answer can only be that to some extent we are, but that in many respects we are not. The demonstration effect has meant that the fact of there being other monarchies in the region has to some degree had a consolidating effect: the Middle Eastern monarchs were disturbed by the fall of monarchs elsewhere and must retain the hope that those now surviving will continue. Yet by dint of their shared monarchical claims to legitimation there are also problems: the Saudis have their frictions with the other monarchs of the Gulf, especially when, as in the case of Kuwait, these monarchs allow in a limited way elections. The Saudis had greater frictions with King Hussein of Jordan, descendent of a family with alternative claims in the Western peninsula. This kind of jostling was also evident in the claims of each to the role of protector of the holy places – King Hussein's attempt, in regard to his claims on the West Bank, to assert responsibility through the Jordanian-Palestinian agreement of 1985 for Jerusalem led the Saudi monarch, in 1986, to proclaim himself *khadim al-haramain*, custodian of Mecca and Medina.

In terms of origin and internal constitution, however, there are great differences between the Arab monarchies. Morocco and Oman are comparable, as traditional sultanates turned into modern states by colonial support. Jordan is a praetorian monarchy, created *ex nihilo* or at least *ex deserto*, by Britain after World War I. Saudi Arabia is a product of tribal conquest, while the smaller Gulf states are towns that became states because of colonialism and oil. The eight Arab monarchies therefore constitute not one but four different types of regime: transformed sultanate, praetorian monarchy, tribal military oligarchy, monarchical city state. This is as true in terms of how they were established, and the forms of legitimation they claim, as it is in terms of how they maintain themselves in power.

On the other hand, there is the question of how far the monarchies of the Arab world can be compared with other non-Arab monarchs. Here again the answer has to be mixed. A brief glance at the broader pattern of colonial relationship to monarchy in Asia and Africa during the nineteenth and twentieth centuries shows that it often suited the European powers – British, French, Dutch – to maintain or create monarchies. This was as true in Southeast Asia as in India or parts of Africa, such as Uganda, Lesotho and Kano. The Middle East came under imperial control later but when it did it was also favoured, when deemed appropriate, with monarchical collaborators.

The evolution of the Moroccan state is one that also bears some comparison with other third world monarchies – Nepal and Thailand, in particular – that arose in non-colonial countries. Although distinct in not having been subject to colonial rule, these two Asian states were ones in which religion (Hinduism and Buddhism respectively) provided the legiti-mation for autocracies that survived thanks to coalitions built with the armed forces and foreign support. The Thai monarch ruled as absolute autocrat till 1932, and that of Nepal until 1990. The oil-dependent smaller emirs of the Gulf have an almost exact counterpart in the Southeast Asian Sultanate of Brunei, an oil-producing state, long protected by Britain, where an early experiment in parliamentary government was stopped in 1962 by Sultan Omar Ali Saifuddin III: when it became independent in 1984, this state with a population of 230,000 had an absolute monarchy under Sultan Hassanal Bolkiah, legitimated by Islam and the ideology of Malayan monarchy. As in the Gulf, oil and foreign support against larger predatory neighbours go a long way to explaining the survival of the monarchical regime in Brunei. Jordan's monarchy was, in effect, a praetorian state established by European colonial powers with an imported ruling family: it is unique in its survival but not as a model – the French tried the same model in Mexico in the 1860s and the British promoted and, in 1944, reinstalled such an exogenous monarchy in Greece. It has been the Jordanian monarch's survival as a result of astute politics and international support, rather than its origins or the character of the regime, that requires explanation.

The Arab monarchies are, however, rather distinct in two other respects. One, which is more than casual and raises interesting questions about the solidity of monarchy in the Middle East, is the remarkably high incidence of deposition, where one member of a ruling family is replaced by another. The assumption of monarchies outside the Middle East has been that succession is clear and once installed the monarch remains until death or there is a regency in the event of illness. This has not been the pattern in the modern Middle East: time and again we see the removal of reigning monarchs by relatives, often with foreign encouragement, for reasons other than ill health. Thus in Saudi Arabia Ibn Saud's first successor, Saud, was effectively removed in 1962 after the Yemen revolution. In Jordan, Abdullah's son, Talal, was prevented from taking office and despatched to a sanatorium in Istanbul in 1952, to be replaced by his son: it was not at the time clear how far this was a result of medical factors and how far a result of Talal's anti-British sentiments. In Oman, Said bin Taimur, who himself had come to power in 1932 by deposing his father, was ousted in 1970 by his son Qabus. In Abu Dhabi, Shakhbut was ousted in 1966; in Qatar Hamad al-Thani was removed in 1972, and his successor Khalifa al-Thani deposed in 1995. In Bahrain, Isa al-Khalifa was deposed in 1923. The most spectacular case of deposition occured in Iran, in 1941, accompanied as it was by an invasion from north and south. In most cases there was, of course, a foreign role, if not a foreign hand: one need not lapse into conspiracy theory to note that external, imperial interest played this part. This suggests that Middle Eastern monarchies are less absolute and less above manipulation, than those of other countries. Put another way, and drawing a distinction between monarchy and dynasty, the political systems being discussed here bear a close resemblance to ruling families whose rulers may change than to monarchies in the sense of consolidated single rulers.

The other distinctive feature about Arab monarchies is the fact that they reveal the significant lack of real constitutional evolution in their countries in the sense that there is little effective limitation of the monarch's power. The monarchies of Europe and, more recently, those of Nepal and Thailand have under internal and international pressure come to accept the growth of parliamentary systems. The most liberalized monarchies – in Britain, Spain, Holland, Sweden, Denmark and Norway – are modernized constitutional monarchies. Parliamentary developments have occurred under all Arab monarchies, with the exception of the Emirates. But in some of these (Oman, Saudi Arabia, Qatar) these consultative councils amount, as yet, to very little. In Bahrain the parliament was suppressed in 1975. In Kuwait, Jordan and Morocco a parliamentary politics does operate, but within limits very clearly set by the monarchy: in contrast to the constitutional monarchies of Europe the monarch, backed by the armed forces, remains very much in charge. He defines what the political parties can, and cannot, do. When considering the specific character of the Arab monarchies, however, we must consider the pattern of rule in the non-monarchical states of the region. For it must be the case that one of the reasons for the survival of monarchy is the contrary demonstration effect, the fate of the countries where republics have been established. Egypt's defeat in 1967, the instability and later extreme authoritarianism of Iraq and the turmoil of Iran have all served as negative examples. The specificity of Arab monarchies is therefore part of the broader resistance to democracy by established states in the Middle East as a whole.

Yet while this is the case, there are limits to how far the monarchies can be regarded as similar to the republican regimes. Frequent use has been made of the term 'presidential monarchy' to refer to Nasser, Saddam, Qaddafi, Ali Abdullah Salih and others.[17] It has, in four respects, some analytic force: each of these rulers has in terms of policy-making been an autocrat like the monarchs; each has appointed relatives and friends to positions of power;

none has been financially accountable, taking a significant percentage of state revenues for undisclosed purposes; each has promoted a cult of personality to mobilize support. However, the force of the comparison is above all a critical one, designed to trim the republican presidents of some of their illusions. As such it is valid. In the novel, *An Apartment Called Freedom*, of the Saudi intellectual and diplomat, Ghazi Algosaibi, we find a sympathetic account of the Arab nationalist intelligentsia of the 1950s, but also scorn for the pretensions of the new rulers of Egypt.[18] We see the same critical and comparative point made in other societies: in Russia the Soviet leaders were denounced as Tsars, in China, Mao was seen as an 'Emperor', and even in countries that never had a monarchy this delegitimation can occur, as references in the USA to the 'imperial' presidency of George Bush or to George III indicate.

Yet there are also important differences. In the first place, and this is not a trivial point, the autocrats have not been able to appoint their family, let alone their eldest sons, to succeed them or to serve as prime minister. The democracies of South Asia (India, Pakistan, Sri Lanka, Bangladesh) have gone much further in the creation of such dynasties than have the republics of the Arab world. It is indeed worth noting what did happen to the sons of Middle Eastern heads of state: one of Nasser's sons, Khalid, went first into opposition and then into business, the other, Abd al-Hakim, is also a businessman; of his two daughters, Huda married Hatem Sadiq a researcher at *al-Ahram*, and Muna married a controversial businessman, Ashraf Marwan, and both daughters have kept away from politics. Khomeini's son, Ahmad, led a quiet clerical opposition until his death in 1995; İnönü's son, Erdal, became head of a small left-of-centre party; Habib Bourguiba II lives in retirement in a Tunis suburb. Some Middle Eastern rulers – Saddam, Hafez al-Asad and Qaddafi – have been grooming sons for some kind of influential role, but this would appear to be more as trusted supporters of their own rule. In other cases, most notably that of the sons of Husni Mubarak of Egypt, Alaa and Jamal, it appears to be more a case of them enjoying their father's standing as they develop their own interests. There is no sign of an effective hereditary principle here.[19] Ironically, the Arab country where sons were most prominent as successors to fathers was Lebanon: the names of Chamoun, Franjieh, Jimayyil, Jumblatt and others illustrate the point. In the Iranian case it is particularly inapposite to compare Rafsanjani to the Shah: whatever his informal influence before and after his two periods of presidency (1989-

97), Rafsanjani had a limited term in office and, within the pluralism of the Islamic Republic, limited powers.

There are, moreover, differences in the ways in which monarchs and presidents can seek to mobilize support and implement policies. Presidents can create ruling parties, but monarchs have more difficulty – few remember the *Rastkhiz* party of the Shah.[20] The contrasted interventions of monarch and presidents on the sensitive issue of birth control are also illustrative only republics limit population. This argument may be strengthened by a counter-factual one: if monarchy conveyed such benefits and was so attractive to presidents, surely there would have been more attempts made to restore or recreate it. Saddam's flirtations with the Hashemite legacy aside, we have to go back to Reza Khan in 1925 to find a case of a republican ruler crowning himself.[21]

We can take many indices of contrasting means of legitimation and use or abuse of power: economic policy is one, population policy another. Amongst the most important, however, is that of the use of repression. The monarchs ruled autocratically and where they deemed it necessary they killed their opponents – as Fahd in Iraq, Ben Barka in Morocco, Fatemi in Iran, Nasir Said in Saudi Arabia and successive generations of protesters in Bahrain have found out. The Moroccan regime has repeatedly resorted to violence against the demonstrations and insurrections it has faced.

But not all the monarchies have killed their opponents in extra-judicial ways: Kuwait, Qatar and the Emirates have clean hands in this regard, and Jordan resorted to mass repression only when challenged with overthrow in 1970. Oman suppressed insurrections in the 1950s and 1970s: but once they were defeated or fighters changed sides, it pursued a remarkable policy of reconciliation towards its former opponents, providing them with employ-ment and drawing them into the political apparatus of the state. Oman in the 1990s showed far less division resulting from its civil wars of two and four decades before than modern European states in the aftermath of their conflicts – Ireland, Spain, Greece, Finland. By contrast some republics have resorted to violence, repeatedly and on a scale far greater than that of their monarchical predecessors: Nasser and Qaddafi have been relatively low scorers in this regard, though both regimes saw judicial and extra-judicial killings. One other moderate case which has been given too little credit is that of Ali Abdullah Salih of Yemen, no friend of democracy but not a Saddam or Hafiz al-Asad either. When it comes to the Ba'thi regime in Iraq, to Ba'thist Syria and, to a significantly lesser extent, the Khomeini regime in

Iran, then the contrast with monarchies comes to the disadvantage of the republics. Having mobilized the people into politics, and having thrown away an established system of legitimacy, various republican regimes have had to resort to violence to protect and legitimate themselves. Saddam has certainly scored higher than anyone else and seems to feel he has to continue to do so.

This high incidence of violence applies to the policies pursued after the seizure of power: the contrast between republics and monarchies looks rather different if what is assessed are the costs of the seizure of power itself. The establishment of the kingdoms of Saudi Arabia, Iraq and Iran, however, were marked by widespread violence. The costs of republican regime maintenance have proved much higher than the costs of establishing the regimes: the coups that brought Nasser, Hafiz al-Asad, Qaddafi, even Saddam (in 1968, if not 1963) to power were relatively bloodless.

*Prospects*

The endurance of the Middle Eastern monarchs is not just a historical question. What does the future hold? Here we should be cautious. The most pragmatic answer is that if we rid ourselves of any deterministic view of how Middle Eastern society will progress, be it towards republics, or chaos, or 'Islam', then the question of the survival of the monarchies is contingent. Insofar as they continue to meet the three criteria of survival – mobilization of economic resources, maintenance of a domestic support coalition and management of international alliances – they may continue. By contrast, economic collapse, the antagonism of the armed forces or other powerful domestic social interests, or confrontation with powerful regional or global forces, could spell their end. In all of this chance plays a role – be it in the vagaries of the international economic system, not least of oil prices, or in the personalities of rulers. The latter is not all-important, nor is it trivial, any more than it is in the context of the republican leaderships. An account of the conditions needed for the perpetuation of the monarchies perhaps indicates where future difficulties may lie. One is delegitimation on nationalist grounds: King Hussein balanced this most shrewdly over the years, as did Hassan II, but their successors will have to go on doing so. The Saudis are confronting Saddam, but they run the risks of appearing to be clients of

Washington. In economic matters the fact is that both the oil-producing and the non-oil producing states face difficulties.

It is easy and true to say that Jordan and Morocco are better of by dint of not having oil: but they need money, and they need to find employment for their younger population. Per capita income is low, if not by Arab then by Mediterranean standards, and population pressure is rising. In the oil-producers the era of money and security is over, even if there is oil in the ground for many decades to come. The issue of taxation, reduction of free services and an end to gross corruption are unavoidable and very difficult to confront. As for domestic coalitions, not least the relationship with the armed forces, this too hangs in the balance: rapacious Saudi princes, already in receipt of their *khususiat* estimated to average $500,000 per year, do not win the hearts of Hijazi merchants or Najdi tribal recruits to the armed forces, let alone Shi'ites; merchants in Kuwait and Bahrain resent the mismanagement of their oil revenues by the al-Sabah and the al-Khalifa; all is far from being well in Oman, both because of allegations of profligacy and because of declining revenues. These societies, like many of the republics, are states run by a self-appointed elite who treat the state's finances as their own. Some use this power and wealth better than others, but none are accountable.

The question of the future also relates to the possibility of the restoration of monarchy. Here comparison may be the best place to start. Monarchies can be restored in some circumstances: when they return from exile after war and occupation (as in Holland, Denmark and Norway after World War II), or when they are associated with the restoration of democracy (Spain after 1975). But a certain republican inevitability does prevail at least here: the overall record of monarchies returning is not a strong one, even where there is a clear royalist party within the country. In Greece and in the Eastern European countries where monarchs were ousted by communism (Russia, Serbia, Rumania, Bulgaria, Albania) the monarchs have some support but they are not serious contenders for power. The same would apply to other countries where monarchy has disappeared in this century: there is little clamour in China for the return of the Manchus, in Vietnam for the return of the Hue dynasty, or in Ethiopia for the return of the Solomonic family. Respect, interest, nostalgia, yes, but not restoration, and when restored, as in Spain, not with the powers that were previously those of the monarchy. If some of the Eastern European monarchies do get re-established, Serbia being the most likely candidate, then this will almost certainly also be the case.

If we look at Middle Eastern societies today there are cases where an element of nostalgia, in some cases from independent sources and in some cases from on top, is detectable. Thus in Iraq Saddam sought to recruit the Hashemite past to his purposes, as he did Hamurrabi and the Quran; in Egypt the view of Farouk mellowed;[22] and in Iran people began to repeat the old saying *nur az maqbare miayad* – 'light comes from his grave'. In Turkey the political logic is the opposite of that in Iran: where in the latter Islamism is republican, in hostility to the secular monarchy, in Turkey it is monarchical, in opposition to the secularism of the Kemalist republic. Turkish Islamist publishing houses produce books on great Ottoman victories, and on the glories of the 'Tulip Age', the high point of the Ottoman rulers. There are articles in the press by writers evoking the benefits of the Ottoman period and the peace it brought, part of a trend termed 'New Ottomanism', *Yeni Osmanlik*. In Yemen today the figure of the Imam is, as in his own time, both feared and respected, though this is not to say that one might return. In Afghanistan there has been much speculation, ever since the process of 'national reconciliation' under the communist regime began in the mid-1980s, of a return of King Zahir from his exile in Rome: but this has not happened, and were he to go back he would find a country so transformed, and so lacking in the levers of power and attendant balances with which he and his predecessors had ruled, that he would be unable to bring about peace. Echoes of monarchy emerge elsewhere: in the Afghan Taliban use of *amir al-mu'min*, in the Islamist interest promoted by *Hizb al-Tahrir* in the caliphate, and even in Israeli right-wing salutations to Ariel Sharon as 'king'.[23] There is certainly a study to be done of how the deposed monarchies are viewed in contemporary literature, symbolism and state presentation, and we can note than in almost all cases a mellowing is taking place. This mellowing reflects both the passage of time and political calculation, as well as the disappointments of the republican period. It does not seem to suggest that monarchy, in the sense of a dynastic autocracy, can return in any of these states or that there is some cultural essence, inherent in the society and reproduced, which will lead them back to this institution. This is especially so in the country with the deepest and most continuous of monarchical traditions, namely Iran. Nor, of course, does it apply to Israel, the one country in the Middle East which has based its legitimacy and claim to land on the state established by a divinely sanctioned king, David.

For social scientists and historians of the Middle East the challenge of reflecting on monarchy is essentially two-fold. The first is to provide, as carefully as possible, an account of how the contemporary monarchical system emerged: monarchy, like nationalism or religion, provides its own ideological account of its origins and of how it came to be, but such narratives usually involve an overstatement of historical continuity and mask the changes of symbol, power and function which monarchies perform. The second challenge is that of analysing how the societies in question function, and to include in this an account of the ways in which monarchs have been able to manipulate domestic and international factors to maintain their position. There are no certainties here and each society has elements which distinguish it from others. The twentieth century has both created and destroyed monarchies, for reasons that historical and political analysis seeks to explain. It is questionable whether the twenty-first century will see the creation, or the restoration, of those that have gone. Even if it does not, the challenge of analysis of how these rulers and their relatives maintain their positions will remain. The analytic challenge, if not the light, shines from the grave.

### CHAPTER 6

# A Contemporary Confrontation: The Conflict of Arabs and Persians

If the Iranians had not tried to establish the Abbassid Government and culture in Baghdad, or their great thinkers and volunteers had not striven and even sacrificed their lives in 1920 for the independence of Iraq, the Iraqis could not now pride themselves on their past history. Iranian Foreign Minister, 1965, quoted in Jasim Abdulghani, *Iraq and Iran* (London, 1984), p. 21.

What are these Persians shouting about all the time? We were Shi'ites before they were Shi'ites. We had a revolution before they had a revolution. Author's conversation in the Baghdad *suq*, April 1980.

The geopolitics of the contemporary Gulf are dominated by a triangular conflict between the three most powerful states of the region – Iran, Iraq and Saudi Arabia. Emerging from an earlier history of Western intervention, and from the process of state building within Gulf states in the post-1918 period, this conflict has dominated the region for the past quarter of a century and shows no sign of abating: no stable resolution of the conflict, in which each state feels itself to be at a potential disadvantage, has yet been achieved. Yet if this instability is evident to all, the causes of it remain less evident. There is, at first sight, no insuperable international obstacle to peace between these three states; there are plenty of mechanisms that could resolve those issues – territorial, economic, political – that divide them. It is the apparent conundrum of how this apparently factitious conflict came about, and what its underlying determinants are, that the chapter which follows seeks to examine. The central thesis is that the causes of instability in the Gulf, of past conflicts and probable future ones, lie much less in the geopolitics itself, in external intervention or relations between local states, and much more in the domestic politics of these countries. In the modern period politics has both created linkages between the two peoples that hitherto did not exist, and at the same time constituted new barriers between them, as well as between the two major Arab states of the Gulf themselves.

The conflict between Gulf states, and between Arabs and Persians, is a product not so much of imperialist interference or of millennial and atavistic historical antagonisms, but of the two interrelated modern processes of state formation and the rise of nationalism. One of the most enduring features of the strategic situation in the Persian Gulf is the gap, as much psychological and cultural as economic, military or political, between the Arab and Iranian perceptions of the region. To illustrate the point with an anecdote, I remember in the spring of 1980, visiting the Centre for Arab Gulf Studies at the University of Basra. The Centre was situated in the university campus on the outskirts of Basra, a few miles from the frontier with Iran. It would have taken little more than an hour or two to walk to Iran. (Only a few months later the area was to be convulsed by a war which was to last for the following eight years.) In the course of the discussion with faculty members I asked whether any of them had ever been to Iran. The answer was no. I asked to see the Iranian newspapers that they had in their library. Some old copies of the English edition of *Kayhan*, from the time of the Shah, were produced. I asked if anyone spoke Persian. A junior colleague was produced: a Palestinian, who was an expert on Hafez and Sa'adi. This academic centre, closely tied to the party and state structures in Iraq, had no resources with which to evaluate, let alone understand, the powerful neighbour lying nearby.

The purpose of this story is not to single out the faculty of the Centre for Arab Gulf Studies in Basra. It illustrates a broader characteristic of relations between the two communities, and one that could certainly be replicated on the Iranian side as well. The Arab world occupies a place in the consciousness and history of modern Iran, but very much as a symbolic point of reference, negative for Iranian secular nationalists, selectively positive for Islamists. Iraq has always been important as the site of the holiest cities of Shi'ite Islam, Najaf and Karbala, and networks of clerics and traders have grown around these pilgrimage routes. But in the modern period such connections have, largely, been without political import. Thus, while references to Russia and Britain, America and Germany would be mandatory, one could write the modern political history of Iran up to the time of the revolution without mentioning Iraq or the Arab world at all. The same applies, *grosso modo*, to Iraq up to the fall of the Hashemite monarchy.[1] Arabs and Persians are aware of each other's existence and of the long history of culture, religion and politics that has linked them. There is not between them the complete chasm that, until at least very recently, separated Arabs and Israelis. Yet proximity has not produced, and is not producing, greater knowledge or understanding. The antagonism and lack of shared perception between the two sides is enduring, and an important constitutive element in the unstable strategic situation in the Gulf.

It is easy in such circumstances to fall back as an explanation on 'history': there is plenty of history to invoke, above all because the dividing lines have been, if not uninterrupted, then certainly recurrent. From pre-Islamic times one can cite the conflicts between the Persians and their Western neighbours, the Mesopotamians and Medes: during the Iran-Iraq war Iraqi propaganda made much of the claim that Khomeini was a *magus*, a Zoroastrian priest. Iraqi and other Arab nationalist denunciations of Iranian expansionism, *al-tawassu' al-irani*, make much of this connection. The conquest of Iran by the Arab armies and the victory of Qadissiya have often been invoked by modern politicians: if Iranian secular nationalists denounced the Arab conquest and sought to claim legitimacy from pre-Islamic times, Saddam was quick to invoke Qadissiya as a mobilizing symbol in his war with the Islamic Republic.[2] The earlier history had its own themes, appropriate for defining difference: Arab hostility to the Persians traditionally denoted by the contemptuous term *'ajam*, was matched by Ferdousi's characterization of the Arabs as 'eaters of lizard'.[3] The re-emergence of distinct Iranian states in the mediaeval period is associated with a reassertion of a distinct Persian culture and political interest. This was to culminate in the establishment of the Safavid dynasty in 1501: in addition to creating a strong Iranian state, which on several occasions invaded Ottoman Iraq, the Safavids continued to clash with the Ottomans over the frontier between the two states, and in particular over the delimitation of the Shatt al-Arab river. A series of treaties did succeed in defining most of the land boundary between the Iranian and Ottoman empires, but the issue of the Shatt, and the related issue of the loyalties of groups living across the frontiers, remained unresolved.[4] The Safavids also institutionalized what was to be another central defining difference between Arabs and Persians, the predominance of Shi'ite Islam in Iran. This made formal the religious difference between Arabs and Persians that had been smouldering since the early years of Islam. In subsequent nationalist rhetoric the Iranians could be seen as *shu'ubiin*, defectors from both Arabism and the faith,[5] while in Khomeini's rhetoric Saddam was associated with Yazid, the Ummayyad tyrant who killed Hussein at Karbala in 680 AD.[6]

In this perspective, hostility between Arabs and Iranians has been an enduring feature of the Gulf for centuries, if not millennia. It is in this way that contemporary nationalists, and those who see the region in terms of timeless cultural forces, often present current conflicts. But such an approach is questionable. History is not univocal: for all the conflicts and conquests and insults and divergences there has been at least as much to unite and bring together the Arabs and Iranians as there has to unite them. Language, religion, migration and trade have tied the regions of both peoples together for all of history. For much of the time they have lived in peace, not war. Moreover, the very formulation of the issue in terms of two opposed, conflicting 'nations' is misleading: the political boundaries have not corresponded to neat ethnic and linguistic divisions. Within what is today the Arab domains there have always been communities with Iranian character-istics; in Iraq, open for centuries to Iranian influence, not least in the period of the Persian-influenced Abbasid empire, the very culture of the Arab speakers is suffused with Iranian influence. One only has to listen to spoken Iraqi,[7] or look at the turquoise domes of the mosques of Iraqi cities, to see how strong the Iranian influence is, not forgetting the fact that half of the whole population of Iraq are Shi'ites, while another quarter are Kurds who, by language and culture, fall very much within the Iranian cultural sphere.[8] On the Iranian side, script, vocabulary and religion are all of Arab origin. If one ventures into the difficult and often tendentious domain of anthropological characteristics, the situation is clear enough: the faces, physical characteristics, body language in Baghdad and Basra differ little if at all from those in Tehran and Isfahan. The 'we' and the 'they' are not given by history but are the products of specific, often conscious, political interventions.

To answer the question of where this misperception comes from it is not, therefore, sufficient to invoke history: indeed far from history being an explanatory factor or a cause, it would be better to see history, or more precisely the contemporary interpretation of it, as itself a result of other factors. To restate the argument made in chapter 2, nationalisms and all official ideologies of 'historic' national conflict are modern products, the result of the intellectual and economic processes of the past two centuries and, in particular, of the rise of modern forms of communication and of the state.[9] This applies to the Gulf as to anywhere else. If we are to ask what it is that has constituted the current divisions within the Gulf, including the misperceptions, the answer is to be found in the forms of state produced in the region in the modern period and in the way in which two groups of people, previously almost completely separated from each other, came to be brought into contact by modern political forces, in particular by initial imperial intervention and then by the rise of nationalism. Here we have to look at the formation and interests of states and at the mechanisms – education, socialisation in the armed forces, the writings of nationalists, stereotyping fiction, print and electronic media – that served to constitute and diffuse such ideas. The form that relations between Arabs and Iranians take today has much to do with these two factors and much less to do with Medes or Persians, Sunnis or Shi'ites, Ottomans or Safavids. To illustrate this argument, one may divide the modern history of the Gulf into three periods: 1921-58, 1958-79 and 1979 to the present day.

### 1921-58: Compartmentalized state building

The emergence of the contemporary inter-state system in the Gulf and of the antagonisms underlying it can be seen as a product of the imposition of modern state formation, and of the nationalist or revolutionary ideologies associated with it, upon the pre-existing mosaic of peoples, languages and beliefs in this area of West Asia. The initial territorial divisions were a result of imperial state formation from the fifteenth to the early twentieth centuries. The boundary between Safavids and Ottomans was the site of substantial wars in the sixteenth to eighteenth centuries but was gradually stabilised through treaties, beginning with that of Zuhab (Qasr-i Shirin) in 1639 and culminating in the Treaty of Erzurum of 1847. The boundary between the two encroaching modern empires, the Russian and the British, was gradually drawn from the late eighteenth century onwards: the Romanovs took Iranian territory in the Transcaucasus, while the British pushed against Iran's eastern frontier, through India (now Pakistan) and Afghanistan, and from the late nineteenth century also encroached on the Arab territories lying on the southern side of the Gulf.

World War I was to produce a new strategic situation, which led to the creation of the structure of inter-state relations that has continued thereafter. The frontiers of Iran with the Russian (now Bolshevik) states and with British India remained constant, but the territories formerly occupied by the

Ottomans were divided into a now independent Turkey to the north-east and the new states of Iraq, formed from three Ottoman *vilayet*, to the West and south-West. In the aftermath of the Ottoman collapse, one further change was to occur: in the oases of central and eastern Arabia, regions only vaguely influenced by either Ottomans or British, a tribal confederacy led by the Saud family, and proclaiming a revival of the Wahhabi sect first seen in the eighteenth century, seized large areas of territory (including two thirds of Kuwait) and established, in 1926, the Kingdom of Saudi Arabia. Thus one year after Reza Khan established a new dynasty in Iran, the Saudi dynasty had emerged in the Arabian Peninsula. Though this probably caused little concern in Tehran at the time, it was later to do so; for the Iraqis, on the other hand, this rebel regime which had ousted the Hashemites from the Arabian Peninsula, was from the start a rival, or at best an uneasy ally, and would remain so for decades to come.

For the following four decades the dominant power in the Gulf was neither Arab nor Persian, but Britain, which formally controlled Iraq and much of the peninsula's coastline, from Kuwait to Aden. While Britain maintained its military and administrative dominance, local states, Iran included, conducted their relations largely with Britain and other major powers. There was very little contact of substance between the regional states. Iran and Saudi Arabia formally recognized each other. At first, however, Iran refused to recognize Iraq, since Baghdad refused to provide suitable guarantees to Persians living in its territory. Later Reza Khan was drawn into a loose, sympathetic relationship with Atatürk, and with Iraq and Afghanistan, and formalized in the Saadabad Pact of 1937: but these were secondary, largely ineffectual, activities. Real business was conducted with the great powers. The frontier between Iraq and Iran itself, particularly that along the Shatt al-Arab, remained contested.

Where there was nationalist and social upheaval in these states it had little to do with other regional peoples and much to do with external imperial domination. Thus the 1920 revolt in Iraq, or the mobilizations in Iran between 1941 and 1953, were not to any significant extent influenced by events elsewhere in the Middle East. Indeed in accounts of the politics of these countries there is little or no mention of this dimension. This was most evident in the case of the Mosadeq period in Iran itself: Iran's challenge to the Western states, and to the oil companies, took place in the aftermath of the first war over Palestine and coincided with the Egyptian revolution of 1952. Yet there was little echo in the Arab world of what was happening in Iran, and the Arab upheavals had little influence on Iran. If there was an interaction, it was a negative one: Iran's nationalization of oil and the embargo on oil exports subsequently imposed by western states provided an opportunity to the Arab world to promote its own interests. Kuwait increased its production to fill the gap left by Iran, while in the British colony of Aden British Petroleum (BP) constructed a refinery to replace the one lost at Abadan. The Arab world's exploitation of Iran's difficulties confirmed the gap between the two regional blocs, and was to leave some bitterness in Iran in subsequent years.

Following the restoration of the Shah to power in August 1953, the US began to encourage the formation of a regional military bloc, and this led in 1955 to the signing of the Baghdad Pact, comprising Iran, Iraq and Turkey. While this very much reflected the continued dominance of external, Western strategic concerns, it also reflected the shared interests which the monarchies of Iran and Iraq had in facing a rising nationalist tide in the region: the Shah had already weathered the storm of the Mosadeq years, the Hashemites in Iraq were increasingly anxious about the challenge from Egypt. On this basis the first clear Gulf alliance was formed. All was to change in 1958, however, when the Iraqi monarchy was overthrown and Iraq became an unstable revolutionary republic, the site of successive nationalistic military regimes that were seen as a challenge to Iran's political system and regional influence. Equally, the Iraqi revolution re-opened two other issues that were to have a permanent destabilizing impact on the region – territorial claims on neighbouring states (Kuwait and Iran's Khuzestan province) and the Kurdish question.

This picture of an apparently compartmentalized Iran and Arab world in the period up to 1958 requires, however, one important qualification, one that was to have an important function in later periods. For if external relations were largely conducted without reference to each other, Iran and the Arabs, and particularly Iran and Iraq, used perceptions of the other as an important element in one central component of the new process of state formation, namely the education system. The post-World War I states in both Iran and Iraq sought to consolidate their hold on society by the development of education systems and by the diffusion of a state ideology of national identity: as elsewhere, such an identity involved both a recuperation of the past, sifted or even invented to suit present purposes, and the identification of what distinguished their own people or 'nation' from others. It was here above all, in the requirements of national state building, that ideologies of antagonism were born. On the Iranian side, the Pahlavi monarchy sought to distinguish Iran from the Arabs by highlighting the glories of the pre-Islamic past, by promoting changes in symbolism, vocabulary and personal names, and by identifying Iran as an 'Aryan' as distinct from a Semitic culture and people. In both official and unofficial nationalism, and a disgracefully large amount of Persian literature, the Arab world became identified with what Iran was not, with what had weakened it in the past.[10] On the Iraqi side a comparable process took place, with an educational programme that drew heavily on the writings of the Syrian nationalist, Sati' al-Husri. Al-Husri, who worked in Iraq and wrote fictional stories that focussed on the suspicious influence of Iran on the Arabs, not only played up the unique national characteristics of the Arabs, but also identified Persia as the great enemy of the Arab people.[11] To ascribe subsequent hostilities between Iran and Iraq simply to such ideologies would be simplistic: but the diffusion of such ideas by states intent on mobilizing their populations through nationalist ideology was an important precondition for later inter-state conflicts.

### 1958-79: Arab nationalism confronts imperial Iran

If there was one event that served to break the mould of previous Gulf politics and lay the foundations for the later decades of instability and rivalry in the Gulf, it was the Iraqi revolution of 1958. This for the first time breached the compartmentalization which had separated the domestic politics of the Arab world from those of Iran, and provoked considerable anxiety within the Iranian regime itself.[12] In the first place, the fall of the Hashemite monarchy in Iraq marked the beginning of the end for British influence in the Gulf, coming as it did a year and a half after the Anglo-French debacle at Suez: decolonization was already in the air, yet the fall of the Baghdad monarchy, albeit in a country formally independent since 1932, was a serious additional blow to British influence and prestige. The withdrawals from other comparatively less important states followed: from Kuwait in 1961, South Yemen in 1967, Bahrain, Qatar and the Emirates in 1971 and Oman in 1977. In part, the military, political and economic role of the British was being taken over by the USA, which had begun developing its position in the peninsula in the 1940s and which had taken advantage of the crisis in Iran to displace Britain as the Shah's major ally. But the USA, while increasing its naval presence and becoming the main arms supplier to pro-Western regional states, was not willing to duplicate the British presence. The result was that Iran came, increasingly, to present itself as the dominant power in the Gulf: it developed its navy and, especially after 1971, insisted that the Gulf be known by the name 'Persian Gulf'. During the 1970s this assertion of Iranian hegemony was reinforced by the Shah's desire to make Iran a great economic power, a 'second Japan': this imperial project was conceived of as a counter-weight to the Arab world as a whole, and Iran sought to develop its military and economic ties with a bloc of non-Arab states – Turkey, Pakistan, Afghanistan and India – as a counter-weight to the Arabs.

This assertion of Iranian influence in the Gulf resulted, however, from the other factor of improved relations with the USSR. If after the 1953 coup relations between Tehran and Moscow had been cool, reaching a critical point in 1959, there was thereafter a significant improvement, such that by the middle 1960s Iran felt that it did not face a major threat to the north. This meant, in effect, that Iran could refocus its forces to face a possible challenge in the south, from Iraq, and to promote its presence in the Gulf. On the Iraqi side, the revolution of 1958 also opened the way for increased confrontation with Iran: the assertion of Iraqi nationalist aspirations on the one hand, and the real or imagined involvement of Iran in the now fragmented domestic politics of Iraq, made the connection with Iran for the first time a factor in Iraqi politics.[13] This was all the more so because onto the regional conflict was now superimposed the longer conflict of the Cold War: Iraq, allied with the USSR, faced Iran, an ally of the USA. Iran was seen as a potential supporter both of Kurdish and Shiʻite movements. As a result the tone of Arab nationalist reference to Iran became much more assertive and critical: Iran was accused of expansionism, of using Iranian migrants in the Gulf as agents, of infiltrating the Iraqi educational system and so forth. These themes were particularly present in Baʻthist ideology where, under the influence of al-Husri, Iran was presented as the age-old enemy of the Arabs.

Al-Husri's impact on the Iraqi education system was made during the period of the monarchy, but it was the Baʻthists, trained in that period and destined to take power later, who brought his ideas to their full official and racist culmination. For the Baʻthists their pan-Arab ideology was laced with anti-Persian racism, just as their interpretation of Iraq's international role and of the character of Iraqi society rested on the pursuit of anti-Persian themes. Thus over the decade and a half after coming to power, the Baʻth party organized the expulsion of Iraqis of Persian origin, beginning with 40,000

Fayli Kurds, but totalling up to 200,000 or more by the early years of the war itself. Such racist policies were reinforced by ideology: in 1981, a year after the start of the Iran-Iraq war, Dar al-Hurriya, the government publishing house, issued *Three Whom God Should Not Have Created: Persians, Jews and Flies*. The author, Khairallah Tulfah, was the foster-father and father-in-law of Saddam Hussein.[14] It was the Ba'thists too who, claiming to be the defenders of 'Arabism' on the eastern frontiers, brought to the fore the chauvinist myth of Persian migrants and communities in the Gulf being comparable to the Zionist settlers in Palestine.[15]

The stage was therefore set for the protracted military rivalry between Iran and the Arab states that lasted for the two decades between the overthrow of the Hashemites in Baghdad and the fall of the Pahlavis in Tehran. Following the revolution of 1958, Iran began to support the Kurds in northern Iraq, a commitment that reached its peak in the period 1969-75 when Iran and Iraq fought a controlled but at times intense border war. Iraq, for its part, provided some assistance to Kurdish groups inside Iran, and from 1965 began to champion the cause of the Arab population of south-West Iran. Much of the overt conflict between the two states involved the question of the frontier: an unfavourable settlement imposed by Britain on Iran was rejected by Iran in 1969, but this border question was less an issue of substance in itself, a reasonable compromise being possible at any time, and more a symbol around which inter-state and nationalist mobilization could occur. The settlement reached by Iran and Iraq at Algiers in 1975, an agreement made possible because of Iraq's exhaustion and Soviet withholding of arms supplies to Baghdad, contained three elements: an agreement on the disputed land frontier, an agreement on the Shatt al-Arab water frontier, and, most importantly, an agreement on non-interference in each other's internal affairs. It was around this third issue that the conflict had raged since 1958 and which was to occasion the next, and far bloodier, confrontation after the Iranian revolution.

The concentration on conflict with Iraq did not prevent Iran from asserting its position vis-à-vis other states in the region. Relations with the third powerful state in the Gulf, the fellow monarch Saudi Arabia, remained correct, but there was suspicion between the two royal families, not least because of Tehran's perceived closeness to the Hashemites in Baghdad. As the British withdrew, the USA tried to promote a loose alliance, the 'twin pillar' policy, involving Iran and Saudi Arabia in a formal 'Gulf Pact', but this never reached formal status and the Saudis, lacking a significant military capability, were suspicious of the Iranians. For its part, Iran continued to press for recognition of the 'Persian' character of the Gulf, and was to a considerable extent hostile to the constitutional plans made for the British withdrawal from the smaller Gulf states between 1968 and 1971. Thus Iran at first opposed the independence of Bahrain, and only accepted its sovereignty after a UN 'consultation' of the islands' population. Less officially, it also insisted that its yielding on Bahrain should be compensated for by the acquisition of three small islands, the Tumbs and Abu Musa, belonging to the Emirates: when no agreement was forthcoming Britain acquiesced in the Iranian seizure of the islands in November 1971, on the eve of the British withdrawal. Iran also took advantage of crises in other regional states to assert its military influence: thus it sent support to the royalist forces in North Yemen after 1962; despatched several thousand troops to assist the Sultan of Oman against the Marxist guerrillas in his southern Dhofar province between 1973 and 1975; and provided the Bhutto government in Pakistan with helicopter gunships to help suppress the guerrillas operating, with some Iraqi support, in Baluchistan in the early 1970s.[16]

These conflicts over influence, nomenclature and military influence opposing Iran to the Arab states were not, however, the only side of the picture. In the other, very significant arena of oil a different pattern emerged, one in which the dividing line conformed not to the Arab-Iranian distinction, but to demography and economic logic. Iran and the Arab states had been members of OPEC since its founding in 1960, but from the early 1970s divergences began to emerge with the Iranians forming an alliance with Arab states, including radical ones, to increase prices. Here Iran and Iraq had a common cause, and one that pitted them against the Saudis and other Arab Gulf states, even as the latter benefited from higher prices. Throughout the ensuing two and a half decades, for all their other differences, Iran and Iraq shared a broadly common position on oil prices and quotas: whatever else, their disagreements were not a result of a divergence on economic interest.

The conflicts unleashed by the Iraqi revolution of 1958 lasted for nearly twenty years and produced a linkage between the politics of Iran and the Arab states that had previously been absent. Yet by 1975 it appeared that these tensions had abated: Iran and Iraq settled their disagreements in Algiers, with Iraq recognizing the *thalweg* or middle course principle in division of the Shatt al-Arab river; the revolutionary movement in Dhofar had been defeated; and the Iranians and Saudis, though suspicious of each other, had learned to live together. For their part, the Russians and the Americans had, in the spirit of negotiation then prevailing, agreed to reduce their rivalry in the West Asian and Indian Ocean regions. They did not want trouble. All this however, was to last for only a rather short time: four years later the politics of the Gulf were to be convulsed by another upheaval, as sudden and dramatic as that which had convulsed Iraq in 1958, namely the Iranian revolution of 1978-79.

### 1979-95: Revolutionary Iran, aggressive Iraq

The fragile understandings of the mid-1970s were overturned by the Iranian revolution and its impact on the Arab states of the Gulf. As in the case of all revolutions, interpretations tend to diverge as to whether the subsequent worsening of relations was a result of the actions, based on various forms of internationalist appeal, of the revolutionary regime, or whether the prime responsibility lies with the states opposed to the revolution, who used the supposed 'threat' from Tehran as a reason to pursue their own political goals, domestically and in the region. The reality, in the case of the Iranian revolution, as much as in that of other revolutions caught up in such conflicts (France after 1789, Russia after 1917, China after 1949, Nicaragua after 1979 and so on) is that both factors operated. No objective reader of the record can doubt that Iranian leaders did appeal to fellow revolutionaries and, in particular, to Shi'ites beyond their own frontiers, and that at least some sections of the Iranian state gave active financial and military support to such forces. No one can doubt too that on occasion Iranian leaders challenged frontiers: they allowed clashes to develop along the land frontier with Iraq and some sought to revise the agreement on Bahrain which the Shah had concluded in 1971.[17] At the same time, it is equally evident that Arab regimes, and the Iraqi regime in particular, responded to the Iranian revolution by seeking to promote their own interests in the Gulf: in other words, beyond a very real apprehension about the potential impact of the Iranian revolution on their own people, and above all on the Kurds and the Shi'ites, the Baghdad regime believed it had an opportunity to wrest dominance of the Gulf from Iran and to push its territorial and other claims against Iran itself. We may never know the full story, but it would seem likely that, in part influenced by the exaggerated reports of Iranian exiles, in part deluded by their own fantasies and lack of information, the Iraqi regime believed that by attacking Iran it could bring about the fall of the Khomeini regime itself.[18] The result of these multiple factors was the Iraqi attack on Iran in September 1980 and the ensuing eight-year war, the second longest war between states in the entire twentieth century.[19]

As with any war, it is too easy to identify one single cause: both sides contributed to the outbreak of hostilities in September 1980, which was preceded by months of recrimination and border clashes, and in each case several factors seem to have operated. International factors were certainly present: Iran saw an opportunity to promote its revolutionary message against Iraqi and other Arab leaders; Iraq believed it could reverse its 1975 acceptance of the *thalweg* division of the Shatt al-Arab and project its power in the Gulf. In both states there were groups who saw the Iranian revolution as an opportunity to revive their causes and become politically active – the Kurds and Shi'ites in Iraq, the Kurds and Arabs in Iran. The old fear which both states had of external support for domestic opposition had returned.

However, on their own these causes could hardly have led to war. The decisive factors were in each case internal. On the Iranian side, the revolution, like all such processes, unleashed a political system in which calls for revolution abroad and assertions of the importance which the new regime had in other countries were part of the domestic legitimacy of the state itself. In addition, in the Iranian as in other revolutions the ideology of the revolution led its exponents to deny the very legitimacy or importance of inter-state frontiers: when Khomeini proclaimed 'Islam has no frontiers', he was merely repeating, in altered form, what revolutionaries of the past two centuries had proclaimed.[20] The reason for this was primarily the logic of the ideology itself: the ideals in the name of which the old regime had been overthrown and a new regime was being created could not be legitimated simply by reference to what was occurring within Iran. If they had any relevance, it had to be an international one. On the Iraqi side two very important factors operated: on the one hand, the fear of domestic challenge, encouraged to a greater or lesser extent officially by Iran, on the other, the temptation to consolidate domestic legitimacy by an act of international bravado that would mobilize patriotic sentiment within.[21] No explanation of the outbreak of the war can omit the role played by these domestic factors, products of the contrasted priorities of the two states involved.

The consequences of the war were three. In the first place, the Iraqi attack, far from leading to the collapse of the Iranian regime, enabled the Islamic Republic to consolidate its political and administrative hold on the country. Within three years of the war having started, and most spectacularly in the confrontation with the Mujahidin-i Khalq in July 1981, the regime had confronted and defeated all the main opposition currents in the country. At the same time it not only rebuilt the regular army, but developed paramilitary institutions, the *basij* and the *pasdaran*, that served both internal political as well as front-line functions. The long-term cost of the war to Iran in terms of destruction and lost opportunities was enormous, but the immediate result was to give the regime a patriotic legitimacy it had sorely lacked, not least because of the widespread sense in 1978 and 1979 that Khomeini was too influenced by the Arabs. Within a short time Iran had reconstructed an army and air force; in the longer run the war led to the mobilization of large numbers of young people into military and paramilitary units.[22] At the level of ideology, the regime also adjusted its message to introduce patriotic, as well as strictly Islamic, elements into its repertoire: Khomeini in the initial days of the revolution had spoken only of the 'people of Islam' and now began to talk of Iran and of the need to defend this particular fatherland (*mihan*).

Secondly, the Iraqi attack on Iran led to an realignment of the other Arab Gulf states. To say that they simply supported Iraq would be mistaken. They continued to fear Iraq and, in varying measures, maintained relations with Iran: while Saudi Arabia and Kuwait were closest to Iraq, and provided substantial financial support to Baghdad, estimated at around $30 billion by the end of the war, some lower Gulf states, notably Dubai and Oman, maintained commercial and diplomatic links to Tehran. One of the most striking indices of this dual concern, directed both at Baghdad and Tehran, was the founding of the Gulf Cooperation Council. For years prior to the Iranian revolution there had been calls, most notably from the USA and Iran, for the establishment of a Gulf alliance or pact: the reason it was not set up was that the Arabs, and particularly Saudi Arabia, feared Iranian dominance. At the same time, the Arab monarchies feared Iraq, just as to a lesser extent they feared Yemen. Rich monarchies with small populations feared larger states, not least Arab republics with large populations and comparatively lesser oil resources. It is this dual concern which explains the timing of the establishment of the GCC in March 1981. It was only possible to establish this union of Arab monarchs once both Iran and Iraq were otherwise distracted. The main function of the GCC was not, as it might have appeared at the time, to control Iranian influence but rather to protect the Arab monarchies from the influence of Iraq. Its correct title – as 1990 was to show – might have been the 'Keep Saddam Hussein Out of the Gulf Council'.

The timing of the founding of the GCC is important, however, because it occurred at a point when Iraq was in a stronger military situation and appeared to he capable of winning victory over Iran. The other Gulf states understood very well what this could mean for them. They provided aid to Iraq, but at the same time feared its triumph. From the middle of 1982, when the tide of war swung against Iraq and it appeared that Iran might win, their problem was to a large extent resolved: they could now support Iraq without fearing negative consequences for themselves. In 1984 this alignment with Iraq went a stage further when Iraq, seeking to internationalize the war, began attacking Iranian shipping: since, because of the Iranian blockade of Iraqi ports, there was no Iraqi shipping for Iran to retaliate against, Iran began attacking the ships of Iraq's closest allies, Saudi Arabia and Kuwait. The 'tanker war', which the USA and other navies were eventually drawn into on Iraq's side, had begun.

The third consequence of the war was a gradual alienation of Iran from the populations of the Arab Gulf states. This is not an issue about which it is easy to be precise, and there is a need to be sceptical about claims either that there was great sympathy for Iran immediately after Khomeini's advent to power, or that subsequent events completely alienated Arab popular opinion. The reality is that, given the undemocratic nature of these states, no-one can be sure and in any case sentiment on such issues was probably confused. The Iranians hoped that as elsewhere the oppressed masses, the *mostazafin*, of the Gulf would support the Iranian revolution. They must also have hoped that where there was a Shi'ite population this would play a leading role in opposing existing governments. There was considerable validity to this latter point of view: in Iraq, support for the underground *al-da'wa al-islamiyya* rose in 1979 and 1980, and the low-level guerrilla war being waged in Iraqi cities must have been a contributing factor to Saddam's decision to go to war with Iran; in Bahrain, an underground Shi'ite organization came quite near to staging an uprising in 1981; in Kuwait, a bombing campaign by non-Kuwaitis, with some support from Shi'ites in Kuwait, was waged from 1983 to 1985.[23] However, not only did these movements not succeed, but there is also considerable evidence that even among Shi'ites support for the Iranian revolution was qualified. In Kuwait, the majority of the Shi'ites, a community comprising around a quarter of the population, remained supportive of the Kuwaiti state. In Bahrain, the Shi'ites, while sympathetic to Iran, continued to work within a Bahraini political framework, calling for the restoration of the constitution abrogated in 1975.

Above all, in Iraq the mass of the Shi'ite population, while resenting Saddam, remained supportive and did not seek to rise in response to Iranian appeals. It would be too simple to say that the Iranian revolution was perceived simply as a Shi'ite revolution, or as yet another chapter in the history of Iranian expansionism. But some suspicion of Tehran, and some support for an Arab or Iraqi patriotism, seems to have been evident.[24] The result of the war was, therefore, far from creating more links or solidarity between Arabs and Persians to compound those divisions which earlier state policies and nationalist movements had created.

The end of the Gulf war led to some improvement in relations between Iran and the GCC countries, yet suspicions remained. Tensions continued over the Iranian participation in the *hajj*, the Saudi organizers believing that the Iranian pilgrims were using their visit to Mecca and Medina for political purposes. Relations with the Emirates remained difficult because of the unresolved issue of Tumbs and Abu Musa: Iranian moves to reinforce their position on these islands led to protests from Arab countries. Above all, however, the cease-fire between Iran and Iraq in August 1988 did not lead to a new period of stability in the Gulf but rather, after a year and a half of apparent calm, to a new crisis between Iraq and Kuwait, culminating in the Iraqi occupation of the Kuwaiti state in August 1990.

There is as little agreement on the causes of the Iraqi invasion of Kuwait in 1990 as there is on its invasion of Iran in 1980.[25] One contrast is obvious enough: if in the case of Iran in 1980 it could at least be argued that the Iranian revolution presented a political and military threat to the Iraqi regime, this was not so in 1990. Iraq's attack on Kuwait can, however, be seen as following a comparable logic to its earlier assault on Iran. There were international causes, in particular Iraq's sense, shared in this instance by Iran, that its economic strength was being undermined by lower oil prices, a trend encouraged by Kuwaiti and Abu Dhabi exports above their OPEC quotas. The fear that the GCC states were overproducing to keep both Iran and Iraq weak was evident in both Baghdad and Tehran. At the same time, Iraq may have felt that there was a political vacuum in the Middle East caused by the lack of progress in the Arab-Israeli context, which Iraq could fill by a dynamic move. But as in 1980 the domestic factors were important, and in particular the link between the impasse vis-à-vis Tehran and domestic sentiment: Saddam had fought the eight-year war with Iran, and had survived, but he had little to show for it. Hundreds of thousands of Iraqis had died, tens of thousands were held prisoner by the Iranians and the national debt had risen to an estimated $80 billion.[26] Immediately after the cease-fire he may have felt that he could impose an unfavourable peace on Iran and he seems to have wanted to wait to see how Tehran would react. But events following the death of Khomeini, in June 1989, followed by mass outpourings of grief and support for the regime, and by the rapid reorganization of the Iranian government, may have convinced him that he would not wring more concessions from Iran. It can be argued that the attack on Kuwait had less to do with conflict with the Arab world, and more to do with the inability of Saddam to force the Islamic Republic to its knees. In these circumstances, he appears to have felt that, failing any breakthrough on the east, Iraq should try instead to attack Kuwait as a compensation. The domestic cost of inaction was too high; the prospects of international benefit were too great.

The events following this Iraqi invasion of Kuwait do not need detailed repetition here: suffice it to say that despite its hostility to any external intervention in the Gulf region, Iran did not oppose the US-led coalition in its war with Iraq.[27] Yet the war, while it reversed the Iraqi annexation of Kuwait and reduced Iraq's power, did not resolve the most important issues in the Gulf itself that had led to the crisis in the first place. As far as the international issues were concerned, there was no progress: Iraq continued to dispute the frontier with Kuwait, especially after it was redrawn in Kuwait's favour by the UN; there was no progress on the issue of 'unitization', concerning oil fields that lay beneath their common frontier; the issue of oil prices remained beyond any diplomatic or negotiating process, with Iraq remaining under a complete embargo; beyond the specific limits imposed on Iraq's weapons of mass destruction, there was no discussion of multilateral arms control measures for the Gulf states as a whole, and an arms race continued apace.[28] Most importantly, the underlying political causes of both wars, the character of the political regimes in Iran and Iraq and, by extension, in other states remained fundamentally unchanged. If anything, the situation got worse: while in Kuwait there was some political improvement, associated with the parliamentary elections of October 1992, the Saudi elite remained anxious about nationalist and religious discontent, and its constitutional reforms had little effect; in Iran, the regime, buffeted by economic and social pressures, and facing continued difficulties abroad, was more beleaguered than at any time since the crisis of 1981. The difficulties of regional accommodation and the temptations of external confrontation therefore remained.

To a considerable extent the drama of 1990-91 was therefore followed by a return to the uneasy status quo ante, with the difference that Iraq was, for some time at least, reduced in power. Iran's acceptance of the GCC and US response to Iraq did not lead to any improvement in relations with Saudi Arabia, or in relations with Iraq: on the contrary, at least two issues emerged following the Kuwait war to make relations with Saudi Arabia and other states more difficult. One was the continued conflict between Iran and the West, and in particular the USA. Any prospects of improved Tehran-Washington relations that had existed in the immediate aftermath of the Kuwait war were soon dissipated: by the early months of the Clinton administration, Iran and the USA were once again on a collision course and Washington evolved a policy of 'dual containment' designed to limit and weaken both Iran and Iraq. Although it was not able to get complete Western and Japanese support for this policy, Washington was able to put significant economic pressure on Iran. For their part, the GCC states rejected Iran's insistence that the security problems of the Gulf should be solved without external involvement, and in particular without the involvement of the USA. For Saudi Arabia and Kuwait, whose whole security policy rested upon a US guarantee, this was unacceptable. The USA justified its containment of Iran by reference to four issues: Iran's opposition to the Arab-Israeli peace process, Iranian support for 'terrorism', including its call for the killing of Salman Rushdie, its alleged plans for nuclear weapons, and its domestic human rights record. As in the case of the earlier policy of 'containment' towards the USSR, first enunciated in the 1940s, the apparent goal of the policy to contain the expansion of the revolutionary state concealed the other goal of undermining it altogether by depriving it of its international ideological legitimation, the spread of revolution.[29]

The other issue that divided Iran from the GCC, less obviously spelt out but present in the minds of Gulf rulers, was the fear that if there were a crisis in Iraq and if the regime was foundering under international or domestic pressure the Iranians would take advantage of it and install their own supporters in Baghdad. Iran had failed to promote an uprising in Iraq during the eight year war, and had been indecisive in the opportunity opened up by the Iraqi uprising of March 1991. But Iran obviously also retained a long-term interest in the political future of Iraq and could be expected to take advantage of any new crisis to promote its own interests through both its Kurdish and Shi'ite associates. For the Saudis, and probably for the others, a weakened Ba'thist regime, even with Saddam in charge, was thought preferable to the creation of a pro-Iranian Islamic Republic of Iraq.[30]

*Gulf geopolitics in the 1990s: the issues*

From the perspective of the mid-1990s the Gulf would appear to be one of the potentially most unstable regions of the world, given the combination of economic resources, militarized tension and internal political instability. Yet beyond this evident instability it is worth examining what the difficulties consist of. As far as international questions are concerned, one can identify at least six areas of tension: territory, ethnic and religious minorities, oil, arms races, conflicts in foreign policy orientation, and interference in each other's internal affairs. Yet the sheer accumulation of these issues need not lead to alarmist conclusions. The territorial issues, if properly addressed, can be resolved by compromise, be they the Shatt al-Arab or the Tumbs and Abu Musa: by the standards of other border disputes, these are relatively minor issues. The question of minorities is again something that can, when not enflamed by external factors, be resolved. Iraq has no formal claim on Khuzistan; Iran accepts the sovereignty of the Gulf states in which Iranian minorities live. These communities only become a major international problem when states for other reasons chose to make them so. As far as oil is concerned, there are differences of opinion and interest but, as in the 1970s, these correspond not to any Iranian-Arab division but to the division that underlay the Iraqi attack on Kuwait in 1990, namely that between oil-producing states with larger and small populations, and between states which are disputing a restricted world market. It is commercial and demographic factors, not religion or history, that explain this issue, which is one that can also be resolved by multilateral negotiation: for this, OPEC remains the obvious forum. The issue of the arms race is, equally, one that under suitable political conditions should be open to resolution: for all that arms races are seen as having an autonomy of their own, beyond political rationale or control, that in the Gulf is born of the evident political suspicions of the three major states of each other and of the sense that each may be tempted, for reasons of political calculation, to engage in further military adventures in the future. The same applies, *a fortiori*, to the two final issues mentioned above, foreign policy coordination and non-interference: the latter is a pure function of political will, of calculation by regimes of where their state and national interest lies; the former is something which could easily be resolved, through a combination of tolerated diversity, as on the Arab-Israeli question, and broad consultation.

It is not the issues themselves that pose the greatest problems, but rather the insecurity of the three major regimes vis-à-vis their own peoples and their fears as to what others will seek to exploit. In such circumstances relations between Iran and the Arabs, and the ideologies of rivalry and suspicion which Gulf states generate, reflect the political character of these states themselves. What we see in the 1990s is what has been the pattern since the collision of Arab nationalism with Iranian state interests first emerged in 1958: the upheavals in both Arab states and in Iran have produced a situation in which the politics of all countries are now interconnected, but this interconnection has been accompanied by the intervention of states whose ideologies stress the differences, and reinforce the psychological gaps, between Iranians and Arabs. The rise of the modern state, and of forms of radical nationalism and revolutionary ideology associated with it, has, therefore, in addition to dividing Iraq from the Arab monarchies of the Gulf, served to drive a deeper wedge than ever before between the Arab world and Iran.

### CHAPTER 7

# Fundamentalism and the State: Iran and Tunisia

The rise of Islamic fundamentalism has occasioned many, often contradictory claims as to its significance for the contemporary world. Within the Islamic countries themselves there are those who argue that a new era of Islamic power is dawning – present in the rhetoric of the Iranian revolution, this theme has acquired apparent confirmation from the collapse of the Soviet Union a decade later, interpreted by some Islamists to show that the only contestatory ideology with a global potential is Islam. In the West, the 'challenge' of Islamic movements has been variously construed as the rise of a new threat equal to communism or as part of a new pattern of world politics dominated by the 'clash of civilizations'.[1] For others, Islamic movements correspond to some new conceptual and even ethical epoch termed 'post-modernity' in which the claims of rationalist discourse derived from the European enlightenment are no longer valid either as analytic tools or moral guidelines.

The analysis that follows corresponds to none of these interpretations. There is no sense in the argument, whether made by Islamists or their enemies, that 'Islam' constitutes a strategic challenge to the West – not least because of the weak economic condition of the supposedly menacing countries. The theory of a clash of civilizations operates with a deterministic concept of 'civilization', and understates the degree to which conflict is within peoples of similar orientation. As for the claim that the enlightenment project should be abandoned, there is in this a high degree of exaggeration and projection – exaggeration of how supposedly 'new' much of the contemporary world is, and projection of what may be valid forms of literary analysis onto the very different terrain of social and political reality. The analysis that follows is by contrast neither apocalyptic nor 'post-modern': it is rather an attempt, using decidedly traditional and rational categories of analysis, to grasp the contingency, variety and indeed modernity of the Islamist upsurge. In this vein, I will begin with the most traditional approach of all, a dose of historical perspective.

The past decade or two have not been the first occasion on which forces claiming to represent 'Islam' have adopted an assertive international stance. The dynamic unleashed in Arabia in the seventh century of the Christian epoch took more than a millennium to spend itself and for today's boundaries to be drawn: if the Arabs were expelled from Spain at the end of the fifteenth century, the Ottomans sought to counter-attack in the sixteenth and subjected much of the Eastern Mediterranean and North Africa to their control. The siege of Malta in the mid-sixteenth century failed; that of Crete, over a century later, succeeded. Where Vittoriosa, Cospicua and Senglea held out, Chania, Rethimno and Heraklion succumbed – not least because of shorter Ottoman lines of communication. The Ottoman empire ruled Crete until 1898. Only at the end of World War I, when other empires had obtruded into the Mediterranean, did the last of the Islamic empires collapse. To the south-east a similarly long confrontation was fought out between the Muslim and Hindu worlds, one that culminated in the establishment of the Moghul empire in northern India.

In this, as in so many other cases of international and confessional conflict, the past provides a reserve of symbols and fears, even if it does little to explain the resurgence of religious and ethnic identities. Both Muslims and their non-Muslim neighbours in the Mediterranean and elsewhere are aware of and frequently invoke these precedents, to legitimate or discredit more recent manifestations of Islamic assertion.[2] But the earlier expansions of Islam – in the seventh to tenth centuries AD with the Arab conquests, and in the sixteenth and seventeenth centuries with the Ottomans – took place in a very different context for two evident reasons. First the historical context was one in which the industrial and military supremacy of the West had not yet been assured. Today the Islamic states may present a rhetorical threat to the West, and may engage in individual acts of military or economic pressure against it, but the strategic situation has changed. Muslim states are incapable of mounting a concerted challenge, let alone of redrawing boundaries. In this sense, those areas of Europe once occupied by or threatened from the south are to a considerable degree immune – the flow of migrant workers and the incidence of terrorism by Middle East groups being very different from the military and piratical attacks of previous centuries.

Secondly, the contemporary challenge of 'Islam' is, demagogy on both sides apart, not about inter-state relations at all. It is about how these Islamic societies and states will organize themselves and what the implications of such organization for their relations with the outside world will be.[3] The dynamic is an internal, often destructively involutionary, one rather than a continuation, however remote, of the Arab and Ottoman conquests. As will be argued below, the more recent rise of Islamic politics in the states and popular movements of the Muslim world poses little threat to the non-Muslim world without; it is primarily a response to the perceived weakness and subjugation of the Islamic world and is most concerned with internal regeneration. That this process is accompanied by much denunciation of the outside world and the occasional act of violence against it should not obscure the fact that the Islamic revival concerns above all the Muslim world itself. The question it poses is not, therefore, whether it threatens the outside world – which, broadly speaking, it does not – but whether, in any of its variants, it can provide a solution to the problems which Muslim societies face today.

The 1990s provide a reasonably advantageous position from which to assess the causes and consequences of the rise of what is termed Islamic fundamentalism or 'Islamism'.[4] Two decades have passed since the most spectacular success of this movement, the advent to power of Ayatollah Khomeini in February 1979 and the establishment of the Islamic Republic of Iran. The passage of time allows for assessment of its achievement in constructing a post-revolutionary state and a consideration of the impact of the revolution internationally. The years since then have also seen the growth of fundamentalist movements in a number of countries, notably Algeria, Egypt, Jordan and Afghanistan.[5] The Iraqi invasion of Kuwait in August 1990, while initiated by a regime of decidedly secular and anti-clerical orientation, nonetheless served to mobilize Islamist sentiment in a range of countries in support of Saddam Hussein.[6] They have also been ones in which the several million Muslims of Western Europe have become more organized and explicit in their Islamic identity. The Rushdie affair, which exploded in 1989 with Khomeini's condemnation of the writer to death, became a particular source of conflict and resentment.[7] Earlier emphases have now given way to a pursuit of identity, community and continued distinctness.

## Disaggregating 'Islam': four guidelines

This overview of developments since the 1970s may serve to illustrate some of the features of this international trend, but also to underline the dangers of simplification with regard to it. In the light of the diversity and the record of the past two decades, it is possible to make some general remarks about this current and to place it in some broader perspective. Four of these guidelines are especially relevant to any assessment of the current stage of Islamic movements.[8]

First, let us look at Islamism as politics. The terms 'revival' and 'fundamentalist' are misleading, since both refer to trends within a religion. This Islamic current involves not a revival of religious belief, but an assertion of the relevance of this belief, selectively interpreted, to politics. The Islamic movement has had a strong religious character, but it has not involved a movement of conversion from other religions or a return to belief by formerly Muslim communities who had abandoned their faith. Rather it involves the assertion that, in the face of secular, modern and European ideas, Islamic values should play a dominant role in political and social life and should define the identity of the Islamic peoples. If there is one common thread running through the multiple movements characterized as 'fundamentalist' it is not related to their interpretation of the Islamic 'foundations' – the Quran or *hadith* – but rather their claim to be able to determine a politics for Muslim peoples. The central concern of Islamist movements is the state, how to resist what is seen as an alien and oppressive institution and how, through a variety of tactics, to obtain and maintain control of it. In this perspective the rise of Islamist movements in the 1970s and 1980s bears comparison with that of tendencies elsewhere that deploy religious ideology in pursuit of nationalist and populist political goals – in Christianity, Judaism, Hinduism and Buddhism.[9] Given the tendency of both Muslims themselves and those who write about 'Islam' to treat it as both a unitary and unique phenomenon, it would be prudent henceforth to check any generalization about Islam against the practices of those using other, non-Islamic, religions in a similarly political manner.

Secondly, let us consider the variants of Islamism. Once their essentially political character becomes clear, then it is more possible to identify and explain the variety of Islamist movements and ideas. For Islamist movements vary according to the political and social context in which they arise.[10] Broadly speaking, there are three such contexts. The first is Islamic populist revolt.[11] This is where a populist movement within an Islamic country challenges a secular state or one that is regarded as insufficiently Islamic, for political power: this was classically the case in Iran in 1978-79, and it also applies in Algeria, Tunisia, Egypt, Turkey and, in very different circumstances, Afghanistan. It involves a revolt against the modernizing, centralizing state. The second form of Islamic politics is where Islam is used by a state itself to legitimate and consolidate its position. Here there exists a spectrum, from the very token invocation of Islamic identity by what are in effect secular rulers (Nasser in Egypt, Morocco, the FLN in Algeria, the Ba'th in Syria and Iraq) through to the use of Islam as a more central part of the state's authority and power. Even this category permits of no simple definition, since regimes that proclaim themselves as legitimated by Islam range across the gamut of political options: military dictatorships (Libya, Pakistan, and now Sudan); tribal oligarchies (Saudi Arabia); clerical dictatorship (Iran). Nothing could make clearer the extent to which Islamic politics is dependent on the pre-existing context and serves as the instrument of state power.

The last variant of Islamic politics is in contexts of confessional or ethnic conflict. Here Islamism serves to articulate the interests and identity of groups that form part of a broader political community that is heterogeneous along religious lines, that is to say a political community that may include Muslims and non-Muslims or, even where all are Muslims, includes divergent sects of Islam or different linguistic and ethnic groups. This has received less attention on the international level, but it is a major part of the picture of Islamic politics in the contemporary world. Long-established variants of this are to be found in Lebanon and the Caucasus, and in the case of the Islamic-Coptic conflict in Egypt. Modern developments have created new contexts in which such tendencies can now develop as part of conflicts within specific states. This is, after all, the context in which Islamism is spreading in Western Europe, as part of a self-definition of new communities within a secular, post-Christian society. It is equally so in the Balkans: for all the talk, mainly from Orthodox Christians in Serbia and Greece, of a 'Muslim' challenge to the Balkans, it is the non-Muslims who have accentuated the situation there and in so doing have led some Muslims, in Bosnia and in Albania, to adopt more fundamentalist positions. This communal context is part, too, of the explanation for the role of Islamist ideas amongst the Palestinians, since they are, in effect, a subordinated part of a broader non-Muslim Israeli society. Equally a part of the Islamist movement in Algeria can be seen in this light: as the expression of Arab hostility to the Kabyle minority for whom the French language and a more secular order provide an alternative to domination by the Arab majority. The issue of Arabic within Algeria, therefore, has several layers of significance: as a cultural assertion against

French, as an Islamic assertion against non-Islamic values, and as an Arab assertion against the Kabyles. The close association of the Arabic language with Islamic identity enables this campaign for Arabic to bear these multiple, ethno-religious meanings. To take an example from the non-Arab world, that of Malaysia: in a society divided between Muslim Malays and non-Muslim Chinese, and some resentment by the former of the latter, Islamism serves amongst the Malays to express an ethnic and confessional interest.

This picture of the variant roles of Islam in politics can illuminate the degree to which 'Islam' itself is open to differing interpretations, how the particular use made of its traditions and texts is variable and contingent on contemporary, rather more material and political concerns. It is this issue of the contingency of interpretation that constitutes the third guideline for assessing Islamist movements. In the hypostatization of doctrine this is a point that is too often obscured in discussions, by both Muslims and non-Muslims alike, of the role of 'Islam' itself in political life. The presupposition upon which much discussion of the question rests is that there exists one, unified and clear, tradition to which contemporary believers and political forces may relate. Many of the discussions that have taken place in the Islamic world have rested on this assumption of an essential Islam. This was the case in the 1960s in the debate about whether Islam favoured capitalism or socialism. It recurred in the 1970s and 1980s in discussions of the place of women, in analysis of the proper role of the clergy in an Islamic society, in the debate on Islamic teaching on tolerance after the Rushdie affair, and so forth. Opponents of Islamist movements tend to reproduce this essentialist assumption in discussing such questions as whether Islamic societies can ever be democratic, or whether there is some special link between the 'Islamic mind' and terrorism.

The reality is that no such essential Islam exists: as one Iranian thinker put it, Islam is a sea in which it is possible to catch almost any fish one wants. It is, like all the great religions, a reserve of values, symbols and ideas from which it is possible to derive a contemporary politics and social code: the answer as to why this or that interpretation was put upon Islam resides, therefore, not in the religion and its texts but in the contemporary needs of those articulating an Islamic politics. These needs are evident and secular enough: the desire to challenge or retain state power; the need to mobilize dominated, usually urban, populations for political action; the articulation of a nationalist ideology against foreign domination and those within the society associated with it; the 'need' to control women; the carrying out of social and political reforms designed to strengthen the state in the post-revolutionary period.

Finally, let us now turn to the criteria we might employ for judging the 'success' of Islamist movements. Once 'Islam' and 'Islamism' are disaggregated, the movements that proclaim their adherence to Islam can be seen both within their own specific contexts and as part of a loose, variegated and uncoordinated international arena. It may in this way become easier to arrive at a yardstick for assessing their impact and achievements. The criterion often raised after the Iranian revolution was whether or not there would be a repetition of what happened in Iran: on this criterion, the Iranian revolution has not spread and fundamentalism has been contained. But this criterion is in two major respects an inadequate one. First, it adopts too small a timescale. Revolutionaries themselves, whether Islamic or other, are impatient and expect other peoples to imitate them immediately: in this sense they become disappointed just as quickly as their opponents become relieved. But in historical perspective it would seem that the timescale for assessing the international impact of revolution is not a few years but several decades: the impact of the French revolution was felt throughout the nineteenth century; it was in the late 1940s, thirty years after 1917, that the USSR enjoyed its greatest external expansion; it took Castro twenty years to secure a revolutionary ally on the Latin American mainland, in Nicaragua. In the case of the Iranian revolution, however, there is a further reason to regard the criterion of state power as inadequate: the impact of the Islamic upheaval in the region and beyond has been substantial even though no other state has become an Islamic republic. It is only necessary to see the rise in Islamist political consciousness in a range of countries to see how far the Iranian model has influenced political behaviour, or to recognize the increased interest amongst young people in Islamic clothing, Islamic literature, mosque attendance, and so forth. It is commonly asserted that Iran lost its following in the Arab world after it became embroiled in the war with Iraq in 1980: but while that war was often presented by Arab states as just another example of Persian expansionism and Shi'ite heterodoxy, a general identification with the Iranian revolution was evident in many countries, and, in some, such as Lebanon, took organized form. Whether or not Islamist forces of the Iranian variety do come to power in the following years or decades, the impact of the revolution and of the broader trend with which it is associated is undeniable.

As was noted earlier, each of the three forms of Islamist interaction with politics has evident relevance to the contemporary international situation, and to the Mediterranean in particular. Thus the movements in Algeria, Tunisia, Egypt, Israel, Lebanon and Turkey are all variants of the first category, that of populist revolts from below against the state: indeed 'Islam' has become the dominant idiom in which such resistance is expressed. Within this category there are also major differences – some are led by clerics, others by lay personnel; some are Sunni, others Shi'ite. The use of 'Islam' by established regimes to promote their own legitimacy is also widespread: thus in their attempt to pre-empt Islamist revolt from below, Egyptian rulers Nasser, Sadat and Mubarak have all presented themselves in Islamic garb. In a more militant form, Qaddafi has also done the same thing: yet Qaddafi's espousal of the Islamic cause can be seen as much as a radical extension of the Nasserist Arab nationalist use of Islam as something involving a clear primacy for Islam. His territorial claims are Arab nationalist – on a par with the Iraqi claim on part of Iran, the Syrian on part of Turkey, the belief that Eritrea and the Canary Islands are 'Arab', or occasional evocations of *malta arabiyya*. Qaddafi has clashed with the clerical and Islamist opposition within his own country, and is widely believed to be responsible for the death of the Lebanese Shi'ite leader, Musa Sadr, in 1978. In recent years he has taken to stressing the primary role of the Arabs within Islam and has attacked non-Arab Islamic forces, such as the Jama'at-i Islami of Pakistan and the *tabligh* movement prevalent amongst Muslims of Western Europe. The role of Islam in confessional conflicts, the third broad category, is evident on both sides of the Mediterranean – in Egypt and Lebanon, but also in Yugoslavia and in those Western European countries with a larger Islamic population.

The analysis that follows will focus on two of the most prominent cases of Islamist revival, those of Iran and of Tunisia. The one has been the most striking success of Islamism, with consequences that still remain to be worked through. The second represents the rise of an Islamist movement in a North African context that was, Qaddafi aside, considered until the early 1980s to be relatively immune to the appeals of political Islam.

*Islamism in power: the record of the Khomeini decade*

The death of Ayatollah Khomeini on 3 June 1989 brought to an end the first decade of the Islamic Republic of Iran and provides one point from which to assess the character and consequences of Iran's revolution. The consolidation of the regime after 1979 and its continuation after Khomeini's death provide much material for analysis of what Islamism means in practice as far as political and social control are concerned. It also illustrates the greatest failing of these movements which is their lack of an economic programme.

There is not space here to review the revolution itself and the analytic questions it raised: suffice to say that the Iranian revolution involved a mass revolution from below against an authoritarian modernizing state, and that its success was made possible by the political leadership it received from Khomeini and his associated clerics. This provided not just the organizational framework but also the ideology with which the mobilization became possible. Central to this ideology were three tenets, oft repeated in Khomeini's speeches and sermons.[12] The first was the supposedly 'traditional' and 'fundamental' belief – a novel interpretation of Islamic doctrine – according to which it was possible to have an Islamic state in the contemporary world, even in the absence (the *gheiba* or occultation) of the Prophet's successor, the Imam. Khomeini argued that this could be implemented through the role of the 'jurisconsult', or *faqih*, the position held by Khomeini during his lifetime. The second core ideological element was the division of the world into two categories, the oppressed or *mostazafin* and the oppressors or *mostakbarin*, two Quranic terms turned to modern, populist, usage, as has already been mentioned. Khomeini appealed to the poorer excluded elements of society in the name of a revolutionary ideal. Third there was the appropriation in Islamic terms of what was in essence a third world nationalist appeal: against the twin Satans, of East and West, against the world-devouring (*jahan-khor*) forces that had long oppressed Iran. Khomeini's appeal to Muslims was not so much the offensive, aggressive one of converting the world to Islam, the earlier meaning of *jihad*, but rather that of defending the Islamic world against occupation and corruption from outside. *Jihad* in this context acquired an inward-looking, defensive character, but one that served to divide the world clearly into the camp of the struggling oppressed third-world peoples and their enemies, the non-Islamic powers. Many aspects of the revolution were peculiar to Iran, not least the specific organizational and ideological autonomy of the clergy from state control, a feature not present in Sunni societies. But the impact of the revolution, carried out in the name of Islam and under the leadership of the clergy, had enormous impact across the Muslim world.

Khomeini's achievement was considerable – in making the revolution, in remaining in power, and not least, in ensuring a smooth transition after his death. Two factors were important here. One was that his regime had been run by a group of clergy that had been his students years before and who constituted a loose but effective revolutionary cadre around him. It was these people who maintained sufficient unity after 3 June 1989 to ensure that Rafsanjani, already the most influential government personality after Khomeini, was able to assume power and be elected to the new chief executive position of president. The other factor, evident in the popular response to Khomeini's death, was the immense authority which the revolution and the Ayatollah in particular retained within the population, despite all the difficulties of the post-revolutionary period. The revolution and eight-year war with Iraq had brought immense privations to Iran, and sections of the population had been alienated by repression. But there can be no doubt that ten years after Khomeini came to power, the Islamic Republic enjoyed considerable legitimacy within Iran: it was this support that made it more possible for Khomeini's associates to organize a smooth transition.

Khomeini's last years were, however, marked by great difficulties: to a considerable extent these followed from uncertainty within the ideology of the revolution itself. The first uncertainty was that of the role of the state in the new post-revolutionary situation, and the relationship between government and Islam itself. In the early period of the Islamic Republic, greatest emphasis was laid on the question of how Islamic thinking could influence the policy of the state: thus the new constitution was newly written to include the concept of the *velayat-i-faqih*, the vice-regency of the jurisconsult; economic policy was altered to preclude the taking or granting of interest-bearing loans; education was transformed to reflect Islamic thinking, as was the law; women were forced to wear Islamic clothing. However, this Islamization of the state went together with another debate on the degree to which the precepts of Islam could act as a constraint upon the actions of government. This was an argument put forward in the first instance by opponents of the Khomeini regime, who argued for an Islamic limitation of the new republican regime; but it soon came to be prevalent within the state itself, in arguments on such issues as government control of trade and finance and intervention in the economy in the name of planning. Those within the government who adopted a more conservative attitude to economic policy, opposing state intervention, used this Islamic argument to block reform measures.

It was in this context that Khomeini, in January 1988, made one of his most important political pronouncements in the form of a letter to the then president, Khamene'i. Khamene'i had apparently argued that the government could exercise power only within the bounds of divine statutes. But Khomeini disagreed, stating that government was 'a supreme vice-regency bestowed by God upon the Holy Prophet and that it is among the most important of divine laws and has priority over all peripheral divine orders'. He itemized a set of issues on which, if his view was not valid, the government would not be able to take action:[13]

> Conscription, compulsory despatch to the fronts, prevention of the entry or exodus of any commodity, the ban on hoarding except in two or three cases, customs duty, taxes, prevention of profiteering, price-fixing, prevention of the distribution of narcotics, ban on addiction of any kind except in the case of alcoholic drinks, the carrying of all kinds of weapons.

Khomeini continued:

> I should state that the government which is part of the absolute vice-regency of the Prophet of God is one of the primary injunctions of Islam and has priority over all other secondary injunctions, even prayers, fasting, and *hajj*. The ruler is authorized to demolish a mosque or a house which is in the path of a road and to compensate the owner for his house. The ruler can close down mosques if needs be, or can even demolish a mosque which is a source of harm . . . The government is empowered to unilaterally revoke any *Shari'a* (Islamic law) agreements which it has concluded with the people when those agreements are contrary to the interest of the country or to Islam. It can also prevent any devotional or non-devotional affair if it is opposed to the interests of Islam and for as long as it is so.

This explicit statement was not just a legitimation of what already existed in Iran, namely a clerical dictatorship. The concept of the 'absolute vice-regency' (*velayat-i mutlaq*) was a major new formulation of Islamist politics in the context where an Islamic state had already been created. Yet like all legitimations, such as the dictatorship of the proletariat, it contained its contradiction: for the legitimation of the state and of the *faqih* lay in its fidelity to Islamic perceptions, and yet this authority, derived from Islam, was now being used to justify overriding whatever Islam enjoined. The key to this new legitimation was given by the concept, invoked in the quotation above, of *maslahat* or 'interest' of the Muslim people: it was in the name of this interest, which the *faqih* alone could identify, that the specific injunctions of Islam could be overridden. Conservative opposition had been based in the Council of Guardians, a clerical body designed to see whether parliamentary decisions contradicted Islamic precepts: Khomeini broke this deadlock by creating a new committee for the 'Discernment of the Interest of the Islamic Order' (*Tashkhis-i Maslahat-i Nizam-i Islami*) which now had overall power. Never were the underlying political priorities of Islamism clearer: the tactical concern of Khomeini was to use the concept of 'interest' and of the absolute authority of the jurisconsult to override conservative opposition within the regime; the overall goal was to invert Islamic authority so as to remove any Islamic restrictions, particularly with regard to property, from the actions of the state.

A similar political determination could be seen in the manner in which Khomeini handled another difficult area of state policy, namely the export of revolution. In common with all revolutions, that of Iran presented itself as a model for other peoples and sought to promote this process elsewhere. The term 'export of revolution'*(sudur-i inqilab)* was commonly used by Iranian officials: it included the conventional means of exporting political radicalism – arms, financial support, training, international congresses, propaganda and radio programmes. Islamic tradition also provided specific elements to this process: thus at the ideological level, Khomeini could claim that the Islamic peoples were all one and that in Islam there were no frontiers. In organizational terms, the already established links between different religious communities across the Muslim world provided a network for building revolutionary links. Until the clashes of 1987, when around 400 Iranians were killed, the *hajj*, the annual pilgrimage to Mecca, acted as a means for propagating Iran's revolutionary ideas.[14]

The most important component of this policy was the attempt to export Islamic revolution to Iraq: Iran had called for this before the Iraqi invasion of September 1980 and this became Khomeini's stated rationale for continuing the war after July 1982 when the Iraqis were driven out of Iranian territory. In the end, of course, it failed: the Iraqi population did not rise up and the regime did not collapse. In August 1988, Iran was forced to accept a cease-fire. In his speech calling for a cease-fire, Khomeini stated that for him this was worse than drinking poison: but political and strategic necessity forced him to do it. This enormous setback in the promotion of revolution abroad did not, however, lead to an acceptance that promotion of Islamic radicalism abroad was impossible. Iran continued to play a role in arming and guiding Shi'ite guerillas in Lebanon and Afghanistan, and in the bitter aftermath of the war it maintained a steady criticism of Saudi Arabia whose corrupt rulers it saw as enemies of Islam.

The proclamation of Iran's continued role as leader of the oppressed across the world was important not just for external reasons, promoting the image and prestige of Iran, but also internally, as a means of sustaining the morale of the population and preventing 'liberalism', or the possibility of the emergence of a spirit of compromise or accommodation with the outside world. After the August 1988 cease-fire, Khomeini felt there was a danger that the Iranian revolution would falter and that it would lose its revolutionary orientation. It was in this context that he reasserted his view that Iran should remain independent of international economic forces, even at the cost of austerity.[15] But he also used an issue that gave him the opportunity to provoke a major crisis with the non-Islamic world and at the same time to present Iran as the leader of the Islamic cause, namely the Salman Rushdie affair. Iran's position on this, calling for the death of the author of *The Satanic Verses*, was a means for Khomeini to meet both of his main policy goals – mobilization at home, confrontation internationally.

Both of these policies reflected the political thinking of Khomeini, and the way in which priorities of power and maintenance of state control determined his use of Islamic concepts and interpretation of 'tradition'. The measure of Khomeini's achievement should not be understated: the regime has survived for two decades and after Khomeini's death saw a quick and smooth transition to the successor leadership. It retains considerable support from its own population, has permitted a greater degree of political pluralism than any other modern revolution, and its impact upon Muslims the world over continues.

*Islamism in the central Mediterranean: the case of Tunisia*

Tunisia is historically the most open and Mediterranean of the Arab countries, an improbable site for a 'fundamentalist' upsurge: but the Islamic and Arab worlds have produced enough surprises in recent years for it to be most uncertain what the future holds, not least because it is in urban areas like greater Tunis that Islamic challenges have grown the most. During the 1950s and 1960s the initiative in Tunisia was held by secular parties, loyal to some variant of socialism. Since the 1970s there has been a persistent challenge from the Islamist opposition, and it was this threat to the regime which in part accounted for the coup of 7 November 1987 in which Habib Bourguiba, leader of the country since 1956, was deposed. In a break with the autocratic practices of Bourguiba's reign, greater freedom of expression was allowed, and elections for the presidency and for parliament were held in April 1989. Yet this opening of Tunisia, designed to reduce polarization and reintegrate the Islamist forces into political life, soon ran into difficulty. By the end of 1989 it was clear that the regime was not prepared to make serious concessions to the opposition and in 1990, taking advantage of the Kuwait crisis to strike a nationalist pose, the regime cracked down heavily on its challengers.[16]

These changes left open the question that divided Tunisia before and after the coup of 7 November 1987. The new president Ben Ali had ended the rule of President Habib Bourguiba because the latter's regime was increasingly associated with brutality and corruption. Earlier challenged by the socialist and secular opposition, Bourguiba had in his later years faced opposition from the Islamic forces, the Islamic Tendency Movement (MTI). They had led nation-wide protests in 1984 against price rises, and Bourguiba had staged show trials of their leaders in 1986. It was widely believed that had Ben Ali not stated his coup on 7 November radical Islamist elements in the armed forces would have tried to do so themselves.

In the months after Bourguiba's departure Tunisia lived through an ambiguous honeymoon. Bourguiba himself was under a form of house arrest in his native town of Monastir. Squares named after his birthday, 3 August 1903, were now called after 7 November 1987. Some of his statues were pulled down. But streets were still named after him, and his grand mausoleum and mosque remained well tended in Monastir. Ben Ali, who had served as minister of the interior and prime minister under Bourguiba, presented himself as the man of 'renewal' and called for political pluralism and respect for human rights. He opened a dialogue with the opposition forces, socialist and Islamic. An amnesty released hundreds of political prisoners and allowed thousands to return home. The press was much freer. But the state over which Ben Ali presided was still that inherited from the French and shaped by Bourguiba: government policy was, in effect, 'Bourguibism without Bourguiba'.

During the election period of 1989, the uncertainty of Tunisia, caught between a secular state and a religious opposition, was graphically evident at the entrance to the walled old city, the *medina* of Kairouan, the holy city of North African Islam. There stood a vast portrait of Tunisian President Ben Ali, installed for the elections: the president gazed out confidently over this, the centre of traditional religious opposition to the state, while the hoarding proclaimed him to be 'Protector of the Sanctuary and of Religion'. In the *medina* itself the walls were covered with the electoral programmes of the competing parties: red for the ruling Democratic Constitutional Rally (RCD), mauve for the opposition 'independents', the rubric under which the Islamic forces whose party had not been legalized were running in the elections. But the main candidate of the RCD was himself a cleric: Sheikh Abdulrahman Khlif, famous throughout Tunisia for leading a protest in the 1960s against the filming of *The Thief of Baghdad* at the Kairouan shrine.

As the example of Kairouan shows, the regime had gone some way to presenting itself in Islamic garb, much as in Egypt Sadat and Mubarak sought to appropriate some Islamic legitimacy. Posters of Ben Ali during the election campaign showed him in the white robes of the *hajji*: soon after 7 November 1987 he had gone on the *'umrah,* the individual pilgrimage to Mecca. Election posters for the ruling party showed a set of hands with the slogan 'The Hand of God is with the Assembly'. Government speeches now began with an invocation of God and ended with quotes from the Quran. Religious programmes were broadcast on television, something previously forbidden under Bourguiba.

Nowhere was this shift more evident than in the attitude to the Muslim month of fasting, Ramadan. Bourguiba, intent on modernizing the country, had ordered restaurants to stay open and told people to eat: 'Il faut manger,' he had declared. On one occasion he had even taken the symbolic step of drinking a glass of orange juice during a public rally held during Ramadan. Yet even at the height of the secularizing drive, in the 1960s, there had been widespread observance of fasting. During the Ramadan of 1989, which began in early April, observance was over 90 per cent. In an excess of zeal, brought on in part because there has been no religious education in Tunisia under Bourguiba, many believers that year fasted even when Islamic codes advised they should not – pregnant women, children under the age of puberty, people such as diabetics or kidney patients who should eat or take medicines regularly. In 1989 the press published widely on the significance and rituals of Ramadan.

In the parliamentary elections on 2 April, the government list triumphed in Kairouan, as it did everywhere else in Tunisia. There was not a single opposition candidate in the 141-seat assembly. The most delicate issue facing the regime, therefore, remained that of the Islamic opposition. In the elections the Islamist 'independents' won around 17 per cent of the vote, displacing the secular left who won around 3 per cent as the main opposition. Given that around 1.2 million of those of voting age were not registered, and given the almost complete control which the ruling party has in the rural areas, it can be assumed that the Islamist strength was considerably greater than that 17 per cent: in the Tunis area, the figure was reportedly around 30 per cent. Until the latter part of 1989, the Islamists themselves played their cards carefully. They seemed intent on maintaining their dialogue with the regime in the hope that their party would be legalized.

Rachid Ghannoushi, the leader of the Islamic Tendency which had gone to the polls under the designation of the 'independents' laid greatest stress on those issues that he saw as challenging the Bourguibist legacy: the need to lessen the power of the state and to make the economy more egalitarian and independent. In an interview immediately after the elections, Ghannoushi declared:

> Our social objective is to contribute to laying the cultural and social bases of a civil society which assumes its most important functions and which the state serves and which constitutes the only source of legitimacy. There is no place for dominating society in the name of any legitimacy – neither historic, religious, proletarian, nor pseudo-democratic. Bourguiba put forward the slogan of the state's prestige, but its real content was the monopoly of the party and of the capitalist interests within which power in the country was located, as was the monopoly which Bourguiba exercised over this state. The time has come to raise the slogan of the prestige of society, of the citizen, and of the power which serves both.[17]

Proclamations stressed the need for Tunisia to return to its 'Islamic and Arab traditions': but it was not spelt out what these were. Ghannoushi demanded that the day of rest be moved from Sunday to Friday, but he was cautious on the question of women: while many Islamists called for the repeal or revision of the Personal Statute introduced by Bourguiba in 1956, Ghannoushi claimed this would not be necessary. He made much of Ben Ali's electoral use of Islam, arguing that this showed the state rejected European ideas of secularism. There was a world of difference between the calculations of a Ghannoushi and those of more traditional leaders like Sheikh Mohamad

Lakhoua from Tunis, who was reported to have called for the return of polygamy and of slavery.

During and after the elections, the Islamists therefore requested that their Party of the Renaissance, *Hizb al-Nahda,* be legalized, but after a long period of uncertainty this was finally refused in June 1989. The truce that had lasted for some time between government and opposition began to break down. The Islamists denounced government authoritarianism, and Ben Ali in a major speech on 27 June warned against a proliferation of parties and the dangers of instability. By late 1989 the honeymoon was over: Ben Ali denounced those who mixed religion with politics and refused permission for the Islamists to form a legal party, allowing them only to publish a newspaper, *Al-Fajr* (Dawn). For their part, the Islamists began to denounce the 'secular left' in more violent terms and mobilized students in support of an Islamization of the curriculum. Spokesmen for *al-Nahda* also went further than hitherto in their calls for an Islamization of society: their demands now included the compulsory veiling of women, the basing of all law on *shari'a,* the allocation of constitutional and legal authority to the *ulema,* and the gradual ending of tourism. If part of the explanation for this radicalization of the political scene was simply the ending of caution on both sides following November 1987, another was the increasingly polarized situation in neighbouring Algeria, where the FIS was taking a more aggressive stand against the FLN and what it saw as alien and secular social practices. By the end of the year there was, therefore, no longer any hope of compromise. The Gulf war provided the opportunity for a government crackdown, leading in 1991 to the arrest of large numbers of army personnel accused of complicity in a MTI coup attempt.[18] While the regime resorted to repression, it was helped both by international support and by the improvement in the economic situation which it had been able to engineer.

The hope of the French-educated secular elite who run Tunisia was that, with a combination of concessions and firmness, the opposition threat would recede. After November 1987, hopes were indeed high that Ben Ali could resolve the country's economic problems – high unemployment and regional imbalances. He improved Tunisia's relations with its neighbours, Algeria and Libya, and his standing in the West was high: President Mitterrand visited Tunis in June 1989 and there was firm, if discreet, American backing – Ben Ali was known to have worked closely with the CIA during his earlier career. Yet despite all the initial respect for dialogue on both sides, it did not take long for a more antagonistic relationship to develop. The post-Bourguibist regime remained as committed to a monopoly of power and to its secular programme as did *le combattant suprème* himself. On their side, the Islamists were at first biding their time, presenting a moderate face and consolidating their support, in the hope of an opening in the future.

The broader implications of this uncertainty in Tunisia are evident enough. Tunisia has long been regarded as one of the West's more sympathetic interlocutors in the Arab world and, together with Morocco, is regarded as exerting a stabilizing influence on its neighbours, Algeria and Libya. Western military and economic aid to Tunisia serves evident strategic purposes. The Tunisian government itself is keen to maintain these links, and also to strengthen its ties to the EU. But the rise of the Islamist movements during the 1980s raised other possibilities which the transition to Ben Ali did only a limited amount to assuage. On the one hand, the Islamist forces in Tunisia attracted the support of a variety of external forces – Libya, Saudi Arabia and Iran. Much of this support may take a uniquely rhetorical form, but it was certainly the case that these states, rivals amongst each other within the Islamic world, wanted to encourage a change of orientation in Tunisia. Little wonder then that, in private, Tunisian leaders were bitterly critical of the Saudi role in promoting Islamism up to 1990. Tunisia had, thereby become the site of conflicts within the Arab and Islamic worlds as a whole, illustrating as much divisions within 'Islam' as any confrontation with the West.

### The revolt against the modernizing state

In the context of Islamism itself the Tunisian movement has certain characteristics that enable it to be compared and distinguished from those in other societies. First, it represents a revolt against the secular modernizing state. As with other movements, including that of Iran, it has been the product of a growing opposition between state and society, reflecting the loss of mobilizing power and legitimacy of the modernizing state. In the 1950s and 1960s the Bourguibist regime had considerable success in generating support from the population, through its nationalist policies, its social interventions, and its organization of much of the population into the Neo-Destour Party and its mass affiliates. Gradually during the 1970s, the strength of the ruling party began to be eroded with the onset of rapid social change in the form of urbanization and expanding access to education, in particular. With

Bourguiba's growing authoritarianism and the corruption of the ruling party, this alienation of the population increased.

What the Tunisian Islamist movement of the late 1980s therefore represented, as did the Iranian upsurge of a decade earlier, was the crisis of the post-independence regime. Broadly speaking, in the first decades after independence the initiative was held by parties and regimes that espoused a 'modernizing' programme: strengthening the state, spreading modern and secular values, seeking to transform their countries in order to bring them closer to some model or ideal of what a modern society should be. The reforms of Bourguiba, like those of Atatürk in Turkey, the Shahs in Iran and Nasser in Egypt, fell into that category. So too, in a different context and with a distinctive ideology, did those of post-revolutionary communist and other third-world revolutionary regimes.

The record of these regimes was, however, contradictory. On the one hand, there was much that was not changed or transformed, despite official appearances. Religious beliefs, pre-nationalist loyalties, family and clan ties persisted. The drive by such modernizing states to intervene also served to antagonize social groups who felt their interests, values and status threatened. Equally important, however, the very success of these regimes acted against them: for it was on the basis of changes which these modernizing regimes introduced that much of the opposition arose. One such change was education: in Iran as much as in Tunisia support for the Islamist movements draws on educated young people, and often ones with a scientific technical qualification. Another was urbanization: this brought large numbers of people into cities, an environment where they were more easily organized and mobilized by opposition forces and where the tensions and problems of social change, including corruption and government inefficiency, were more evident.

Equally important is the manner in which these Islamist currents have challenged and to a large extent displaced the more traditional leaders of opposition, the parties of the secular left. This reflects several factors: in Iran, Turkey, Egypt, Tunisia and Algeria the opposition of the immediate post-independence period tended to take a left form, with communist and radical socialist forces playing a significant role. Their main criticism of the government was that it was not going far enough in its social reforms, but they also tended to criticize the modernizing regimes for their foreign policies, especially, as was the case with Iran, Turkey, and Tunisia, for their links to the West. Left parties therefore sought to present themselves as radical social critics and as bearers of nationalist legitimacy. What has happened in the 1970s and 1980s is that these left-wing forces were displaced by the Islamist ones. Left parties have been marginalized – as is evident in Iran, Egypt, and Tunisia – and have often adopted a defensive ideological posture vis-à-vis Islamism. They now claim to respect Islamic values and seek compromise with the Islamists which the latter, often confident of their greater appeal, may not want to reciprocate.[19]

This displacement has come about through several mechanisms. First, the left parties with their own secular and modernizing ideologies came to be associated with the culture and ideology of the ruling parties. They were seen more and more as just another representative of that state-centred and alien modernization that the Islamists rejected. Secondly, the social groups amongst whom the left had been based were often the secular intelligentsia and parts of the working class. Few had any following amongst the peasantry or the urban poor who were not in modern industrial employment. In the new social conditions this has meant the development of other social bases for opposition, ones to whom the left was unable to appeal. Equally important, however, has been the success of the Islamists in acting as an organized and ideologically coherent opposition, that is to say, in rivalling the traditional left opposition in its own terms. Much as Islamist movements use traditional forms of religious organization – mosques, the madrese or religious school, sufi and other underground religious sects – they have also developed modern techniques and forms of organization normally associated with secular parties: welfare programmes, including educational and health centres, cassettes and videos of sermons and speeches by opposition leaders, nation-wide political organizations, and fund-raising mechanisms. One of the greatest surprises of the Iranian revolution was the extent to which the apparently unworldly Islamist forces were able to bring millions of people onto the streets and run what was, by any standards, a very successful nation-wide opposition political campaign.

This success in the field of organization is matched by a success in the field of ideology. Here much emphasis has been placed, by Islamists and their rivals alike, on their appeal to 'traditional' values. They are represented as speaking for a set of values that are more in accord with the traditions of the country and hence with its people. There is no doubt that this image corresponds in some measure to the truth. That the decades of secular leaders and dirigiste states talking to their peoples in the language of modernization and development did not resonate with the world-view of these peoples was often not understood. Their ideological impact turned out to have been far less than appeared to be the case at the time. This is as true of the relevant Islamic countries as it is of the USSR and other communist states. 'Traditional' values did survive, with greater hold on the populations than the new state-down, modernizing programmes. But this apparently straightforward articulation of tradition also conceals 'contemporary' choices. On the one hand, there is a choice as to which parts of tradition to articulate – the more democratic or the more authoritarian parts, those relating to collective or individual values, not to mention varying views on the place of women, slaves, foreigners and so forth, within the Islamic society. The Islamists of Iran and Tunisia have made choices as to which parts of their tradition to emphasize, and that choice is given not by the weight of tradition itself, but by modern, secular and political concerns. Khomeini's views on the power of the state to override the *shari'a* are a clear example of this, as are Ghannoushi's calculated views of women's role in society.

There is a second important element of the ideological success of the Islamists, namely their appropriation of the values and claims of the left. There is no need to believe that Khomeini actually read any Marxist writings or that any other Islamists have done so to see the influence of Marxist and radical ideas of the 1950s and 1960s on these third-world thinkers. Anti-imperialism, dependency, cultural nationalism, hostility to monopolies, solidarity of the oppressed peoples of the world – all these standard themes of the earlier nationalisms of the third world recur in the statements of these Islamic leaders. The economic programme pursued by Iran in the 1980s reflects many of the ideas on 'de-linking' and self-sufficiency propagated by dependency theorists such as Samir Amin, André Gunder Frank and Franz Fanon.

Two central ideas are populism and nationalism: the assertion of a common popular interest against the oppressors, and not least against the intrusive authoritarian state and, at the same time, an assertion of national legitimacy against external enemies.[20] The existence of an external enemy that is rejected on both national and religious grounds, namely Israel, has of course fuelled this Islamist appropriation of nationalism, leading the left in Egypt, for example, to vie with the Islamist right in anti-Israeli, and often chauvinist, criticisms of the Camp David accords. For all the differences, the analogy with fascism is evident: just as 'national socialism' took over some of the ideas of its left-wing competitor and provided a rival, equally well-organized and ideologically more successful force than the communist and socialist parties, so the Islamists have both challenged and appropriated the ideologies of the more traditional opposition parties. The ideological success of Islamist movements *vis-à-vis* the left has therefore involved a dual process, of ideological and political displacement combined with appropriation of the latter's ideas and appeal.

### Conclusion: Islamism and the future

In the immediate aftermath of the Iranian revolution it was believed by many that the Islamic world would be swept by mass revolts. This did not occur, and in August 1988 the Iranian regime faced its greatest setback by accepting the cease-fire with Iraq. However, the causes of Islamist militancy are deeper and more enduring than the particular influence of Iran, and in this sense there is every likelihood that movements of this kind and states more or less influenced by Islamism will continue to articulate such ideas and policies for a long time to come. The incidence of populist Islamism in Tunisia and Algeria is indication enough of the long-run appeal of such ideas. So too is the recurrent tendency of ethnic and communal movements involving Muslim interaction with non-Muslims to take an Islamist form (as in Western Europe, the Caucasus, Lebanon and Egypt). It would seem to be likely that those living on the frontiers of the Islamic and non-Islamic worlds, where these run within rather than along state boundaries, will face many difficulties in the years ahead, and as much on the non-Christian (Hindu, Confucian) frontiers as on the Christian.

Much external discussion has focussed on how the Islamist upsurge constitutes a 'threat' or challenge to other states, particularly the West. The issues of oil and terrorism are particularly prominent here. Analysis of the last ten years suggests however that these international consequences are overstated. The oil market was remarkably little affected by the Iran-Iraq war and all states need to sell their oil. Terrorism is an issue but, compared to other global problems, a subaltern one and not one confined to the Middle East. Indeed, for all the rhetoric and occasional spectacular act involved it could be argued that the Islamic states are if anything weakened by these new ideologies, since they create internal tension and conflict that lessens their ability to play an effective international role.[21] The greatest challenge presented by Islamism is, therefore, directed not to the non-Islamic world, but to the Muslim peoples themselves: the ability to find and implement a viable economic development strategy, the creation of co-existence and tolerance between different ethnic and confessional groups, the promotion of democracy and political tolerance. These are all goals which the heightened militancy of Islamism makes it more difficult for these states to attain.

PART III

Reportages

### CHAPTER 8

# Tehran 1979: The Revolution Turns to Repression

It does not take one long to sense the ferocious right-wing Islamist fervour that grips much of Iran today. In the airport arrival hall, in front of the (unattended) health controls, hangs a poster on which the dove of peace is being ripped open by a hammer and sickle. Underneath runs the simple message: 'The Mirage'. Along the walls on the way into Tehran the slogans 'Death to Communism' and 'Death to the Fedayin' can be seen, and amid the plethora of renamed streets none is called after any left-winger who gave his or her life in the 25 years struggle against the Shah. Huge placards show an Iranian revolutionary breaking through shackles imposed by both the Russian and US flags. The walls of the massive Soviet embassy compound in the centre of the city are daubed with hostile slogans.

The second night I was in Iran I attended the first major public rally held by the Tudeh, or Communist Party, in the 30 years since it was banned by the Shah. A crowd of around 50,000 people had gathered to hear Ehsan Tabari, the party's leading theoretician and the grandson of an Ayatollah, who was now a candidate in the coming elections for a Council of Experts to discuss the constitution. Most of the crowd appeared to be students, but there was more than a sprinkling of older people, gnarled representatives of another age. As several hundred stewards with linked arms guarded the perimeter of the meeting, groups of right-wing youths, named 'Phalangists' by their opponents, roamed around chanting, 'Death to the Tudeh and the Fedayi Social Parasites', and repeating the most frequent rightist slogan heard in Iran: 'There is no Party but the Party of God, no Leader but the Spirit of God', the latter being a reference to Khomeini. Thwarted in their main aim of disrupting the meeting, these Islamic militants turned on a hapless Iranian press photographer and, after chasing him across the campus grounds, smashed his equipment and pummelled him to the ground, amid chants of 'God is Great'.

This hysteria is not confined to Muslim activists on the street, but can be found at the centre of the Islamic government from which it receives strong encouragement. Three of Khomeini's top advisers whom I interviewed – Foreign Minister Yazdi, Radio and TV Director Ghotbzadeh, and Economics Adviser Bani-Sadr – all blamed the left for Iran's present troubles and claimed that it had played no role in the revolution that overthrew the Shah. A similar view is held by Hijjat al-Islam Nuri, one of the key organizers of last year's anti-Shah demonstrations in Tehran.

For weeks, offices and bookshops belonging to left-wing organizations in the provinces have been attacked. On Friday, 10 August, for example, crowds coming out of the mosque in the Azerbaijani town of Urumieh burnt down the Fedayin bookstore. This was followed by attacks on left-wing offices and bookstalls in Tehran on the following Monday. The new press law, which makes criticism of the Ayatollahs illegal and enforces wide-ranging censorship of domestic and foreign reporting, is another blow to those who criticize the policy of the Islamic government.

In Tehran last Tuesday when I arrived at the offices of the opposition newspaper, *Ayandegan,* I was told by the armed men at both entrances that no-one was at work that day. At first I thought they might be protecting the paper from right-wing opponents who forced the paper to close for a few days in May. But soon it became clear that the guards touting Israeli Uzi machine guns and US R-3 rifles were themselves part of the new assault on Tehran's most critical daily. 'These people are renegades,' the guards said, using a term (*munafiqin*) originally used by the prophet Muhammad to refer to hypocritical supporters of Islam. 'They are printing criticisms of Imam Khomeini and getting money from Israel.' The teenage vigilantes, who said they were acting on the orders of the Dadsetani (Public Prosecutor's) Committee, itself an instrument of the main Revolutionary Council, insisted they were enforcing the new Iranian press law which forbids criticisms of the country's religious leaders.

All this time other guards were holding the editorial staff of *Ayandegan* captive in the paper's offices, where they were being questioned by the Committee's representatives. Although they were allowed to go home, later in the day twelve of them were arrested and accused of working for a foreign power. Two days later a sit-in by the paper's printing workers was broken up by armed Committee men; five of the workers had to go to hospital. At least four other papers were also closed.

Any doubts about the regime's intentions were dispelled when, earlier this week, I interviewed Foreign Minister Ibrahim Yazdi and radio and TV director Sadegh Ghotbzadeh, Khomeini's two main spokesmen in Paris and now two of the most powerful men in the regime. Both fulminated against *Ayandegan* which they claimed had gone beyond 'criticism' to produce 'provocations'. Using documents going back to the sixties, they insisted there had been US and Israeli involvement in the establishment of the paper. I was far from convinced. Perhaps there had been some inaccurate reporting but the main bone of contention – the *Ayandegan* coverage of divisions in the leadership – is one on which Prime Minister Bazargan has often spoken publicly. As I pointed out to Dr Yazdi, the logic which tars today's *Ayandegan* with the associations of a decade ago could, with as little justification, be applied to himself: he was for many years an employee of the US Veterans Association.

The real motivation for the attack on *Ayandegan* lies in the paper's exposure of the political and economic problems Iran faces. It spoke out against the ballot-rigging and religious interference in the elections for the Council of Experts that will decide on the constitution, and it has highlighted the grievances of the non-Persian minorities such as the Kurds and the Arabs. With a circulation of over 100,000, it had become the main mouthpiece of the opposition. In a context where an almost Manichean perception of US and Israeli influence exists, people quickly believe accusations of foreign interference. As I left the Friday prayers at Tehran University last week, at which Ayatollah Taleqani had spoken, the crowds around me were shouting 'Death to *Ayandegan*, the Paper of the Foreigners.' Judging from conversations I had, most people believe the paper had been working for the Israelis, just because the radio and some religious leaders said so. It is not easy for an overwhelmingly illiterate population to gauge such an accusation for itself.

The left-of-centre National Democratic Front responded by organizing a march on Sunday in support of *Ayandegan*. As I watched from a side-street, several hundred Muslims armed with stones and clubs, tried to break up the demonstration, shouting, 'Death to Communism.' Later I found myself amongst a crowd of these *hizbullahis* ('party of God people') who assured me that 'the communists' had killed ten people in front of the university gates. Next day the *Jumhuri-yi Islami* (the Islamic Republic) claimed that *Ayandegan* supporters had attacked women dressed in Muslim headscarves. It also claimed that Israeli and BBC broadcasts criticizing the limitations of press freedom were proof of the foreign interests behind *Ayandegan*.

Monday was the day of the *hizbullahis*. From early morning crowds of youths chanting, 'God is Great' roared around the University. The headquarters of the Fedayin guerrillas, amongst the bravest of the Shah's opponents, were sacked. One woman, whose eldest son had been a Fedayi killed fighting the Shah, said that as she saw the guerrillas' literature being thrown from windows and burnt in the street she felt she had sacrificed her son in vain. Later that day tens of thousands of *hizbullahi*s were bussed into central Tehran, among them squads of black-cloaked women who marched ten-abreast chanting, 'Death to Communism'. Ironically neither the Fedayin, nor the Tudeh Party, whose building was also attacked, had officially supported the protest march in support of *Ayandegan*, but this policy had not saved them from the rightists' wrath. The Bazargan government is now apparently trying to calm the situation, but the closure of *Ayandegan* and the new press law indicate that the government is moving against its opponents, nonetheless, and in the provinces attacks on opposition papers and offices have been underway for weeks.

The attack on the left by leading government officials often takes the form of a rather crude scape-goating. Bani-Sadr told me that the left was to blame for the standstill in industry. Both he and Ghotbzadeh blamed the unrest among Turks, Arabs and Turcomans on leftist interference, avoiding the question of whether the demands of these people were legitimate or not. Their defence of current policy towards the Kurds sounded like Ethiopian officials legitimating their repressive policies in Eritrea on the grounds that the regional opposition forces were also 'agents' of foreign powers.

In a tragic irony, many of those who were in the forefront of the struggle against the Shah are now once again on the receiving end of government repression and right-wing violence. Muhammad Reza Sa'adati, a member of the Mujahidin of the People guerrillas, who spent years in jail under the Shah, has now been arrested on charges of being a 'Soviet spy' and has the dubious distinction of being the first of the new political prisoners known to have undergone torture. Slogans calling for his execution have been written on walls in Tehran. Over a dozen members of the Socialist Workers Party, arrested weeks ago in the southern town of Ahvaz, still await trial, as does the poet, Nasim Khaksar, who earlier spent eight years in the Shah's prisons. Hushang Izabeglu, a lawyer, had spent three years in jail, had been tortured by hanging on a cross – 'like Spartacus and his poor friends,' as he put it to me – and had then had both his legs broken by SAVAK agents after his release. He was recently kidnapped by unknown assailants and taken up into the hills north of Tehran where he was badly burnt on his back and chest.

Mosadeq's grandson, lawyer Hedayat Matin-Daftari, who was flogged and thrown over the side of a mountain in 1967, and imprisoned by the Shah last year, had to flee last week into hiding in order to escape arrest after the national Democratic Front, of which he is one of the leaders, organized the demonstration to protest the closure of opposition papers. A few days later I had lunched with him and had found him, despite the evident tension in the country, to be quietly optimistic. He sensed, as other opposition members did, that the *akhunds* or religious leaders, were overreaching themselves by interfering in so many areas of public life and by their apparent inability to run the country. Many people felt that despite the current government onslaught the left, allied with the movement for regional autonomy, could in the longer-run establish a democratic system. One Azerbaijani poet I met went so far as to argue the daring thesis that events in Iran would mean 'the end of Islam', as popular revulsion against the *akhunds* led to a backlash in the months ahead.

Some signs of such resistance can be seen on the streets of northern and central Tehran. Music banned on the state radio is available in cassette form, and even though this is the month of Ramadan when all-day fasting is obligatory stalls selling soft drinks are open. People are smoking and playing music in public, and hosts proudly produced the odd bottle of whisky or champagne. In the oilfield, so I was told by a reliable source, the government is taking no chances with the oil workers who demonstrated their power so effectively last year: there the workers' canteen remains open all day, Ramadan or not.

Yet the power of the Islamic right must not be underestimated. Its appeal is not just an ideological one, since its strength rests on a set of institutions that retain great power at the neighbourhood level. Hajjat al-Islam Nuri, for example, explained how he could call on thousands of people all over Tehran who had been students at his lectures over the past few years. The new anti-left tone of Khomeini's regime is transmitted not just over the radio but in the Friday sessions at the mosque and through local Islamic associations.

The position of women illustrates the uncertain status of the new Islamic regime. Khomeini's claim before his return to Iran that Islam guarantees the equality of men and women was always untrue, given the theory and the practice of all Islamic societies. But the attempt to impose Muslim clothing, whether the cloak-like *chador* or the scarf-like *hijab*, was successfully resisted by the women's demonstrations of last March. Since that time, there has been no marked increase in the wearing of Muslim clothing by women in the centre and north of Tehran, and many women even in government offices remain without it. However, Khomeini may well try to enforce the *hijab* in the future: he is reported to have told a women poet who visited him that he would do so after the Islamic constitution becomes law. In the meantime other factors are eating away at women's position. Although there are still women announcers on the radio, all solo women singers have been taken off the media – and Ghotbzadeh tried to tell me this was because they had all been connected with the Imperial Court. Women's sports have been virtually stopped, and the few women judges serving in the courts have been reallocated to other positions. A young male judge told me, with evident disgust, that once Muslim law is imposed in the courts the Islamic prescription that one man's testimony as a witness must be considered equal to that of two women will come into force. One woman was elected to the 73-person Council of Experts now discussing the draft constitution, but she was a nominee of Khomeini's: her election poster was a tragi-comic one, showing two eyes and a nose emerging from behind a black *chador*.

Probably the gravest attack on women's position has come in the realm of employment where, as in other countries, discrimination is justified on grounds of economic constraint. Additionally, the organized feminist tide that was so successful in March has not continued. Most left groups seem to regard the question of women as a secondary one, but while I saw no women at the Fedayin headquarters wearing headscarves, the Mujahidin told me that all women who join their organization must wear one.

One change the government will find hard to put through is the segregation of schools, since only 15 per cent of primary school teachers are men and an almost reverse situation operates in secondary education. But the everyday pressures on women continue and it is easy for the demagogues of the right to talk of women's emancipation as part of some 'alien' imposition on Iran. Even the late Dr Ali Shariati, supposedly the theorist of a new enlightened Islam, argues in his *Ommat va Imamat* that women's liberation is a plot by the Western monopolies to boost their exports to the third world. Here again, the power of Islamic reaction over women must not be underestimated. One has only to see the phalanxes of chanting black-cloaked women on right-wing demonstrations to realise that Khomeini and his people can mobilize large numbers of women for their cause, much as fascist movements in Europe did in the 1930s.

The position of the urban working class is, as yet, uncertain. Many factories are idle or running at a reduced level of output, and the masses of migrant workers who flocked to the cities to work in construction have been dispersed by the standstill in this sector, evident in the lines of unmoving cranes along the Tehran skyline. In the factories some of the workers' committees set up during the last months of the struggle against the Shah have continued to operate. But it seems that many of these have been taken over by the *akhunds* or by the Revolutionary Committees and no substantial organizations linking different factories have yet emerged to form the basis of a new trades union structure. The Islamic forces have been quick to see the need to pre-empt any threat from this source. While he fulminates against the left, Khomeini appeals to the workers in the name of Islam. A widely distributed poster depicts an industrial worker holding an Islamic banner beneath a quotation from the Quran promising a speedy victory.

The rhetoric of the regime places great emphasis on what it is doing for the 'oppressed' *(mustazafin)*. A classic populist concept, it is designed to appeal to the working class without thereby scaring off the other class allies of the Islamic movement. Yet it would seem that despite the immense sums of money available from oil, the new regime has not brought tangible benefits to these people. Loans for housing of up to £12,000 (300,000 Tomans) are available but only to those who can make a deposit of one tenth this amount. The economics correspondent of one pro-Islamic paper told me that apart from providing electricity of under 100 Kilowatts free of charge nothing had been done to benefit the poor in the six months since Khomeini came to power. Meanwhile inflation runs at over 30 per cent. The standard themes of Islamist theorists are those familiar to right-wing populist, and indeed, fascist movements elsewhere. Bani-Sadr's 'unitary economics', *iqtisad-i touhidi*, a farrago of Islamic and socialist ideas, is little more than confusionist rhetoric, laced with some religious allusions, and has so far led to no concrete programme that could begin to solve Iran's economic problems. When I met him, Bani-Sadr laid great emphasis upon how Iran remained a dependent country in which imperialism still played a major role, but neither what he told me, nor what he had previously written, led me to believe that he has a coherent grasp of the Iranian economy. Earlier, he told me that the spirituality of Khomeini had an important consolatory role to play given the serious material privations to which the people would be exposed.

The oft-heard slogan 'There is no Right nor Left in Islam' and Khomeini's appeals for Islamic unity are the conventional fare of overtly fascist regimes, coupled as they are with attacks on all opponents as being 'enemies of Islam' and with a facile attribution of links with imperialism to all who question his views. Although he hardly ever mentions Iran, much of Khomeini's Islamic rhetoric is nationalistic: his favourite ploy is to attack the left for being Western-influenced and alien to Iran's traditions. His denunciation of the intelligentsia, especially writers and lawyers, and his attacks on the press indicate a willingness to stifle all critical discussion on the grounds that they are part of an 'imperialist conspiracy'. Yet so devalued have such accusations become that more than one Iranian I met was able to argue at great length how Khomeini himself had been installed by the CIA . . .

It is as yet hard to evaluate the forces opposed to Khomeini, but they certainly go beyond the organized parties of the left. While Ayatollah Taleqani seems to have fallen into line behind Khomeini's rightist crusade, Ayatollah Sharriat-Madari, who called on his followers to boycott the recent elections, remains a powerful force, especially in his native Azerbaijan and among the estimated 1.5 million Azerbaijanis who live in Tehran. The other non-Persian nationalities are also resistant to the centralizing tendencies of the Islamic government, and the Kurds in particular are well-armed and should be able to resist the central government for a long time. While they stress that they do not want to secede from Iran, the Kurds do want some form of substantial regional autonomy. The draft constitution offering only some ill-defined local councils which bear no relation to the nationalities themselves is clearly inadequate to their demands.

The left itself, based in Tehran but with substantial provincial support, comprises a number of competing groups. The National Democratic Front, which broke away from the National Front in March, comprises a number of liberal and socialist groups. Although not a party, and formally nearer the centre that other left organizations, it has so far been the most consistently critical of the Khomeini government. Not only did the NDF call for a boycott of both the referendum on the Islamic Republic and the Council of Experts elections, but it took the initiative in organizing the protests against censorship that sparked the recent clashes.

The two main former guerrilla groups, the Fedayin and the Mojahidin, enjoy substantial support among young people and could probably mount some kind of armed resistance to a right-wing onslaught. But their leadership, drawn from people who have spent much of their adult life in jail, is inexperienced and they have been indecisive in their attitude to Khomeini's regime, trying to conserve their militant following while not breaking completely with the government. Like the Peronist guerrillas who emerged into the open after the fall of the Argentinian military dictatorship in 1973, they have found it difficult to turn their undoubted prestige as militant fighters against the old regime into a durable political movement. At the Fedayin headquarters, a former SAVAK building, I met militants emerging from clandestinity and returning from abroad.

The oldest and wiliest of the left groups is the Tudeh, in effect the Communist Party. Founded in 1941 their leadership is much older than that of other groups, and they evidently have a substantial organization. They have chosen to back Khomeini without major reservation at this time: 'We consider him on balance progressive, and since we cannot lead, we have to choose,' was how Ehsan Tabari, the party's leading theoretician, explained it to me. They remain in the most traditional sense a pro-Soviet party, something that must do them immense harm in the current Iranian situation where anti-Russian feeling runs high. It is unlikely that their concessions to Khomeini will in the end spare them from the force of the rightist onslaught: their paper is among those closed this week. Indeed, the authorities have just sealed the offices of the party.

The core of Khomeini's support lies in the poorer, southern districts of Tehran and in the cities running southwards from there along the edge of the great desert that forms the core of Iran – Qom, Isfahan, Kashan, Yazd, Shiraz. The second main holy city after Qom, Mashhad, may also favour him. Resistance to his concept of an Islamic Republic in the rest of the country is still fragmented. But with the economy in a major recession, and unrest in the regions, the initiative is slipping from the government's hands. It is in these circumstances that the state of the army and other repressive units becomes of major importance. Most estimates I heard indicate that about half of the pre-revolutionary army, say upwards of 150,000 men, remains in existence and there certainly seemed to be plenty of soldiers in the barracks I saw in Tehran and in the mountains to the north. The air force is still flying missions, although Foreign Minister Yazdi categorically denied the reports put out by opposition papers that some dozens of US technicians had been brought back to the country. The army and air force have, however, lost most of their top commanders, and it will certainly take time to rebuild the esprit de corps and the command structure previously reliant on the Shah which were shattered in the revolutionary period.

An extremely ominous development is the growth of irregular military units, recruiting young unemployed men to carry out vigilante duties. Security Chief and Deputy Premier Mostafa Chamran is said to command a force called the Regiment of Youth, and a group named the Black Shirts has been growing in south Tehran. The Jamshidabad barracks in Tehran are the centre of another semi-official force called the Army of Guards, and then there are both the Guards of the Islamic Revolution, organized by the government, and the Committee Guards, under individual mollahs and district chiefs. Ill-trained and divided as these units may be, and incapable of facing seriously armed foes like the Kurds, they are nonetheless a formidable force for urban repression and can be sure of further expansion in a time of high unemployment. In late July up to 60,000 of such irregulars paraded through the streets of Tehran. In a clampdown on the left it would be to these elements, as much as to the regular army, that Khomeini would be likely to turn. Equally sinister is the rise of a new secret police organization called SAVAME, *sazman-i ittila'at va amniyat-i millat*, SAVAK with just one word altered ('country' has been changed to 'nation'). According to one man who recently came out of Evin jail, the imprisoned members of the former counter-espionage section of SAVAK were summoned to the central office there some weeks ago and asked to start working again, for SAVAME. Some of the indictments against left-wingers now in jail are based on old SAVAK files.

Amid the clamour and confusion of contemporary Iran, it has become obvious, more quickly than was generally expected, just how incapable Khomeini and his associates are of running Iran and how quickly they are falling back, turbaned *akhund*s and Western-educated ministers alike, on demagogy about 'foreign plots' and repression. Unwilling to guarantee basic democratic rights to the press, the opposition or the nationalities, or to implement a serious programme of social change, they are dragging the country towards a bloodbath the outcome of which no one can predict. Khomeini may believe that God is Great, but it certainly seems to be the Devil who is working overtime in Iran today.

*Postscript:. London 1984: An encounter with Muhammad.*
*I left Tehran in the middle of August, as the crackdown on the left gathered pace.*
*Within a few weeks the offensive against the Kurds in Western Iran had intensified. On 5 November the Bazargan government fell, amidst the crisis surrounding the seizure of the American embassy personnel. The following September Iran was invaded by Iraq, and an eight-year war in which hundreds of thousands of Iranians died followed. In June and July 1981 the Mujahidin launched an urban uprising which was quickly crushed. In 1983 the leadership of*

the Tudeh Party was imprisoned and the party banned. Khomeini was to retain power till his death in June 1989.

Of the people I interviewed in that summer of 1989 Ibrahim Yazdi was removed as foreign minister in the crisis of November 1979, and has remained in Iran, subject to restrictions and harassment as a leader of the semi-legal MLI. Abol-Hasan Bani-Sadr was the official candidate in the presidential elections of January 1980 but came into conflict with Khomeini: he fled Iran, in the company of Mujahidin leader Masud Rajavi, in July 1981. Sadegh Ghotbzadeh was arrested in April 1982, convicted of participation in a pro-American plot, and executed. Ehsan Tabari was imprisoned along with other Tudeh leaders in 1983: like most of the other Tudeh leaders he later made a confession of his political errors and was exhibited on television in propaganda discussions. He was to die in prison. Hedayat Matin-Daftari was forced into exile in France. Manuchehr Kalantari, a Fedayin member with whom I had worked for several years in Britain and who accompanied me on my visit to the Fedayin headquarters, was shot by government forces in 1982, while trying to flee the country. In 1984 I was visited in London by a former member of the Iranian left, now supportive of the regime.

> We don't give a damn for the United Nations. We don't give a damn for Western public opinion. We don't give a damn for that bloody organisation, Amnesty International. We don't give a damn what anyone in the world thinks.... We have made an Islamic Revolution and we are going to stick to it, even if it means a third world war. We're not worried. If we have to blow up the whole of America, we'll do it. And if we discover how to kill thousands and thousands of people by releasing bacteria from four hundred boxes in different parts of the US and if this is the only way we can defend ourselves in some future confrontation with the States, then we'll do that. We want none of the damn democracy of the West, or the so-called freedoms of the East. We represent the third way.

Muhammad had never been one for understatement. In the old days I had known him as a laggard member of the Iranian opposition in Western Europe. A womanizer, drunkard and an intermittently engaging raconteur, he had epitomized the secular intelligentsia of Iran in exile. He hated the akhunds and the clergy, and he looked back to the nationalist leadership of Dr Mosadeq's premiership of the early 1950s.

Then came the revolution. The jokes about Khomeini increased. And then he went back, and disappeared. Some said his socialist path had put him at odds with the regime. Then there was rumour that he had succumbed to secret police pressure and became an informer for SAVAK. Perhaps the files had now been opened. Then it emerged that he had become an ardent supporter of the Khomeini regime, a born-again Muslim. Could it be true?

*I have never changed my point of view. I have always been for the oppressed, the* mostazafin, *which is a far more precise term than proletariat. We have made a* mostazafin *revolution in Iran. The people are really free, and for the first time since the period of Mosadeq, Iran has a popular government.*

Muhammad is keen to tell us of the need to reject Western values and Western culture. Gone are the socialist books from his bookshelf. Now he announces that he has discovered the wonderful writings of Ayatollah Motahhari. He has read all 60 volumes of his works. I suggested this was all obscurantist rubbish. No, he told me, it was all derived from the Quran.

*There are no human rights violations in our country. Of course, you cannot go against what the Quran says. If it lays down 80 lashes, you cannot just give 79. And I'm sure that when Mr Lajevardi, the head of Evin prison in Tehran, orders an execution he sincerely believes he is doing it for God. Maybe some local groups mistreat prisoners without authorization. But no torture is allowed by the government.*

*And the reports from abroad?*

*That's the work of our enemies. We know them. The Baha'is, the Zionists, the Mujahidin and the rest. They're using the tricks we used to have when we were in the opposition against the Shah, like the pregnant woman story. They say that pregnant women have been shot in Iran. That's something I always used to say whenever you wanted to get attention for some story about prison conditions under the Shah, you'd throw in something about a pregnant woman being shot. I did it all the time.*

Muhammad has no sympathy for those who have died fighting against Khomeini. 'They've killed twice as many of our people as we have of theirs,' he says. Over 7,000 Khomeinists have been assassinated by the opposition. 'We have killed only about 3,500 of them. My son,' he tells me, 'has to sleep with his rifle by *his bed. He guards the local mosque. Three of his teenage friends have already been shot by the opposition.'*

*The war with Iraq is a particular source of pride.*

*We have one million people at the front, half the army of China. They will go on fighting till the whole Ba'thist regime in Iraq is overthrown. The removal of Saddam Hussein will not be enough . . . We are pausing now, because to press on would involve terrible loss of life. But there will be no peace, no compromise. The whole world has taken note of us. We are a small nation of 40 million people. But we have our one million people at the front, many of them teenagers. . . We have a new word in Persian, an 'RPG-zand' – an RPG rocket thrower. The Iraqi tanks know to fear them: they may kill sixteen of them, but the seventeenth person will get to the rocket and blow it up. You must understand the culture of martyrdom in our country.*

*The Kurds too, so it seems, have had their just deserts. 'All those stupid KDP and Komeleh people you used to write about have all been cleared out now,' he said with pride. The regime will last because it is popular. 'You know,' he assured, 'Rosa Luxemburg would have had an orgasm if she could have come to Iran now and seen the wonderful democracy we have created there'.*

*He sat there pleading with me to believe him, in his Islamic revolutionary khaki and wearing a shining Islamic Republican badge. We talked of a mutual friend, a socialist opponent of the Shah who was killed by Khomeini's forces after the revolution. 'He made a terrible mistake,' Muhammad mused. 'I tried to warn him. I offered help. If he had come to me, and told me where he had hidden 200 rifles it would have been all right. But I never heard from him, even though I gave him my telephone number. The next thing I heard from his family he was dead. They imagined that I could do something to locate his body. But I couldn't.'*

### CHAPTER 9

# Saudi Arabia 1997: A Family Business in Trouble

It does not take one long when travelling to Saudi Arabia to realise that one is entering a domain of sanctioned religiosity. At Jeddah airport, the customs officer searching for alcohol and other prohibited imports enquires when the arriving passenger is going to convert to Islam: prefiguring the claim of a lecturer who told me that he taught traffic regulations by reference to the words of God, the customs official notices I can read Arabic and tells me that the answers to all the world's problems are to be found in the Quran. 'Next time you come through, you should have converted,' he cheerfully opines.

Nonetheless, on the occasion of the National Festival for Culture and Heritage, universally known as 'al-Jinadiria' after the suburb of Riyadh that houses an annual handicrafts exhibition, a certain ecumenical spirit seems on offer. The Jinadiria is one of the few occasions when Saudis can express themselves more freely in public: a fare of camel-racing in the day and metaphysics at night throws a curious light on the society and its concerns. A favourite royal visitor from Britain, referred to in Arabic as the Emir of Wales, lectures on the shared values of Islam and Christianity. Perhaps more is read into this than is warranted: in the Gulf the position of crown prince is usually associated with political office – prime minister in Kuwait, deputy prime minister in the Saudi Kingdom. His enthusiastic participation in the *arda*, or Saudi tribal dance, backed by a cast of over two hundred from a beduin operetta, and cheered by the all-male crowd who burst onto the stage, seems to delight his royal hosts.

Officialdom seems less well pleased with Helmut Schafer, the German foreign office minister, whose speech to the Jinadiria criticizing the denial of human rights in Europe *and* the Islamic world is only selectively reported in the press. The Emir of Wales is introduced as coming from *shaqiq* Britain – a term implying close family links normally reserved for Arab states. Germany is merely *sadiq* – friendly, but not too much so.

This is not a country where it is easy to come by reliable information.

There are no firm statistics on the most important economic indicators, oil output or revenue. Few independent observers believe the official population statistics of around 15 million. No-one seems to know how many Saudi princes there are, each entitled to a *khususia* or allowance of hundreds of thousands of dollars, and to perks including free air travel. Much depends on the atmosphere and in this, the year 1417 by the Islamic calendar, the rulers and owners of the Kingdom of Saudi Arabia give the sense of having some short-term reasons for feeling a little more at ease.[1]

The price of oil (which costs domestic consumers 50p a gallon) has risen by 35 percent, adding an estimated $9 billion to an income of around $42 billion. In the tense context of the Gulf, the two main sources of unease, Iraq and Iran, both appear temporarily to be in defensive mood. Within the country, the wave of opposition known as the *salafiin*, the conservative and in some ways fundamentalist critics of the regime, have been less in evidence, as repression, exile and money take their toll.

But in other respects unease continues. On Riyadh's 'Thirty Street', so called because of its width in metres, a thoroughfare better known as a place where men can thrust their visiting cards through the windows of passing women in cars, the empty site where a bomb went off in November 1995 destroying a US-Saudi military training centre still stand empty. A later bomb, in Dhahran, killing 17 Americans and wounding over 300 remains unexplained. There are rumours that those involved in the first, for which four men were executed after a secret trial, were associated with the *mutawwa'in*, the Islamic vigilantes attached to the Ministry of the Interior who tour the city in brown jeeps, harassing inadequately covered women and those who do not observe the hours of prayer. Investigations on the second bomb remain even more obscure: there have been many arrests in areas suspected of fundamentalist influence, Sunni and Shia, above all in the al-Thuqba district of Jubail, known for *salafi* influence. But some Saudis suggest that there is a high-up connection, possibly some prince or military commander, whose disclosure would embarrass the regime.

It is not such bombs that pose, however, the biggest problems for the Saudi state. These reside in longer-term problems for which no easy or rapid solutions appear available. The first is paralysis at the top: in Riyadh there is more than a hint of late-Brezhnevite Moscow, of an Islamic tribal variant of 'stagnation'. The three key people in the country are King Fahd, Crown Prince Abdullah Commander of the National Guard, and Sultan, the minister of defense. The king is 74, in poor health, and has assumed power again after a temporary regency by Abdullah. The other leading princes, all sons of the founder of the regime, Abd al-Aziz ibn Saud, who died in 1953, defer to him: there is much talk of 'paralysis' at the top, as major policy issues, not least economic change and the crab-like pace of constitutional reform, remain unsettled. Abdullah is believed to be more sympathetic to Arab nationalism, and to want a stronger control on princely corruption.

The second problem is jobs: whatever the precise population figures, Saudi Arabia is becoming a more 'normal' country. Over the past decade per capita income has fallen by up to two thirds, to around $6,000 a year, and more and more young people are looking for employment: attempts to Saudianize the economy meet with resistance not just from foreign but from Saudi employers. Graduates of the Islamic universities set up by King Feisal, who ruled from 1962 to 1975, in an attempt channel Islamist sentiment, are particularly unemployable. This discontent over jobs and money is accentuated by something never far below the surface in the kingdom, namely regional differences: in the more cosmopolitan, Western region, the Hijaz, there is resentment by Hijazis of the beduin tribesmen who overran them in the 1920s and take a disproportionate part of the oil revenue; prominent Hijazis, close to the top of the regime, will openly scorn the claim that their country is not ready for a more democratic system. 'We had newspapers and elections, before the Saudis conquered us,' one told me. In the eastern Shia regions, site of the oil fields, a partial relaxation in the early 1990s has now gone into reverse and the teachers at the Islamic universities openly denounce the Shia as un-Islamic.

The third problem is the state's reliance on the USA. Saddam's invasion came as a big shock to Saudi Arabia, showing that there were real threats to the country, and also exposing the hollowness of the warrior ethos upon which the Saudi ruling family had hitherto based its legitimacy. Attempts by concerned princes to promote the record of their troops in the conflict do not seem to have convinced anybody. Yet, in what others might see as inconsistency, many Saudis resent the US military presence in the country, phrasing this in terms of non-Muslim troops despoiling sacred territory – a fatuous argument for opponents of the Saudi regime to make, since it is only the Saudi state that claims the sacredness of the whole territory, even beyond Mecca and Medina. Resentment against the USA is particularly strong at a time when Washington, through blocking Security Council condemnation of Netanyahu's policies, is seen as being too partial to Israel. The regime is, however, caught: it has moved US forces out of the cities, after the bomb blasts, but they are very much not out of mind.

There is a growing nationalism in Saudi Arabia against the West, as well as against other money-requesting Arabs, but it is a nationalism laced with views of international conspiracy. There is a vogue for books on *istishraq*, 'orientalism', understood as the study of the Arab world seen as part of an imperialist plot. In the opulent bookshops the section on 'orientalism' is next to that on espionage and Western or Zionist conspiracies. Many Saudis believe that the articles in the *Wall Street Journal* and other US papers over the past two years questioning Saudi financial reserves are officially inspired.

Saudi Arabia is a country obsessed with control, most obviously political: no parties or independent publications are allowed. The most striking building in Riyadh, visible on the arterial King Fahd flyover, is the Ministry of the Interior, an inverted pyramid, which claimed the lives of 63 Korean workers when being built with wooden scaffolding. Yet this very obsession, as in other strict Muslim countries like Iran or in communist states, only rebounds. Whisky (for years imported in a weekly flight from Manchester by a now deceased elder brother of the king) abounds at closed social gatherings, even if some at least of the imbibers break off for prayer. While hi-fi shops are illegal, as supposedly violating Islamic precepts, videos, cassettes and journals of all kinds circulate underground. Conversation switches easily from the exalted to the most direct of anatomical issues – Saudi males of an older generation seem especially interested in the facilities offered in London for reinvigorating their genitals: jokes about transplants abound.

This growing social unease on the part of males is mirrored in two striking respects. One is the growing pressure from women: women are almost entirely absent from the public space in Saudi Arabia, fleetingly glimpsed in black cloaks at shopping malls, or being driven by male drivers and relatives around town. At universities women students have to follow lectures over video linkups and conduct tutorials by telephone. Yet levels of education amongst Saudi women are high, in many cases higher than amongst males: 65 percent of the graduates from Riyadh University last year were believed to be women. Certain sections of economic activity, notably banks, have divisions that are entirely female-staffed. There is a large network of social organizations, under the umbrella of 'charity', in which women are active. Many Saudi women have travelled abroad, and have access to media images and information from abroad on a daily basis. Now that neighbouring Qatar has lifted its ban, Saudi Arabia is now the only country in the world that does not allow women to drive. Literature on gender relations abounds, from assertions of the orthodox Islamic position to studies of women and discourse, replete with quotes from Julia Kristeva, Marilyn French and Laura Mulvey.

Another area of tension is in regard to the law. Officially Saudi Arabia is governed by *shari'a*, or, more precisely, the Hanbali version of legal commentary upon the holy texts. As such it does not need lawyers, and none are indeed trained. Religious judges, or *qadi*, are produced by the Islamic universities and training institutes. The lack of Saudi specialists in law, accountancy and management remains dire. Yet, in response to economic pressure, a code of commercial law, based on the Geneva convention, has been taken over wholesale: to avoid offending the orthodox, it does not fall under the aegis of the Ministry of Justice but is administered by a committee under the Central Bank.

The conflicts involved in this obsessive and increasingly threatened control are visible. One of the subtler forms of media control is evident from the grades of representation of the human form. The ban on portrayals of living images, often associated with the Quran, is in fact a later accretion, borrowed from Judaism and Christianity and without Quranic authority. But in Saudi Arabia and, in an even more extreme form, in Afghanistan it has become part of public morality. Thus on the advertising billboards around Riyadh no human faces are visible: an advertisement for car seat belts shows a headless midriff, one for a four-wheel drive shows a male, his head covered in a headdress. In government offices, however, or on postage stamps portraits of the Saudi kings and princes are everywhere. Gradations of revelation operate in the press: in the Arabic-language Saudi press printed in the kingdom no photographs of females are allowed on the front pages, and only those of pre-adolescent girls inside; in the English-language press women, suitably covered, are printed; in the Saudi-funded Arabic press printed outside, but freely available in the kingdom, unveiled, adult, women abound. On television sitcoms and soap operas with unveiled women are broadcast – but they are licit because their storylines take place in domestic settings and no males are filmed as present.

Another striking index of these undercurrents is to be found in literature: perhaps the greatest surprise for the visitor to Saudi Arabia is the scale of the bookshops. The pre-Islamic poetry of Arabia is the original source of Arabic, and traditional Saudi literature took the form of poetry. No official gathering seems complete without the delivery, in staccato beduin tones, of words in praise of the ruling family and their great works. Poetry remains an important source of inspiration: the work of the exiled Hasan al-Qurashi mixes lyrical and political themes. But poetry is now matched by the novel and the short story. The exiled Abd al-Rahman Munif, in his novel, *Pillars of Sand*, portrays the corruption of dynastic rule in a thinly disguised Saudi Arabia. Ghazi Algosaibi, although a former minister and now ambassador to London, has seen two of his novels, *Apartment of Freedom* and *The Madhouse*, banned in the country: they provide a fascinating insight into the world of the nationalist intelligentsia, the former set in Cairo of the 1950s, exploring radical nationalist politics and sexual experience, the latter following the trail of an Arab who goes to America, falls in love with a woman who is Jewish, and ends up in a Lebanese mental asylum. One book by Algosaibi advocating secularism was denounced by the religious establishment for 'apostasy'.[2]

There is now a body of short stories which focus on Saudi women's experience of a stifling society, and the conflicts which they face. These encompass the themes of alcoholism, coercive arranged marriages, male privilege in all its forms, and the denial of individual freedom by family, society and state alike.[3]

Caught by these social pressures and by such dramatic developments as the Gulf war of 1991, the Saudi regime has tried to accommodate change without ceding its privileges. Thus a consultative assembly, and a set of provincial assemblies, were set up in 1993. The regime has also tried to refashion its ideology: although in the past presented as an alliance of the tribal elite – the Al Saud, and its religious counterpart, the Al Shaikh – there is now almost no mention in official statements or in the naming of public buildings of the religious origins of the regime in the eighteenth century revivalism of Abd al-Wahhab. Although some of his descendants, the Al Shaikh, retain positions of influence (as ministers and ambassadors) this is more by virtue of their personal qualities than by descent. Saudi Arabia has sought to give itself a new, more conventional national identity: thus in 1986 the king took the title of 'Servant of the Two Holy Places,' that is, Mecca and Medina.

As demonstrated by the Jinadiria, the state now promotes a sense of national heritage including, to a limited extent, recognition of the architecture and artefacts of pre-Islamic times. The problem with attempts to reclaim this archeological heritage is that over-zealous Wahhabis, who come across statues and paintings by chance, too easily proceed to hack out the faces in accordance with their beliefs. Concern about conservative religious response is believed to explain the long delay in opening a planned national archeological museum in Riyadh, as it has similarly blocked the opening of a lavish cultural centre completed some years ago.

But there are clear limits to this process. Neither the king nor any possible successor look as if they are really able to tackle the abuse of financial and other power by the princes of the royal family: US embassy officials resignedly talk of the $14 billion or so of revenue, about a third of the total, that is 'off budget', or unaccounted for. Stories abound of the commissions, (*nisbat*), allocated tanker cargoes and arbitrary land seizures obtained by princes. One has cornered the market in courier services, another in a branch of car sales, others declare themselves owners of a piece of land where construction is about to begin. As social and economic pressures mount, this issue of unaccounted funds will become pressing: it has already become the number one bone of contention in neighbouring Kuwait where parliament can ask, without much success, for an account of state finances.

At the same time, any process of liberalization will have to encounter two-fold opposition: resistance comes both from the *malaki*, the royal elite at the top, and from the *ahli*, the popular constituency below. '70 percent of the people in this country are not living in the twentieth century,' one exasperated long-term Arab resident commented to me. Those who have attended the almost weekly carnivals associated with public executions in the centre of Riyadh report no lack of public enthusiasm for them elsewhere. Opposition to increased freedom for women comes as much from males threatened by more competent and less controllable women as it does from the princes at the top.

In this world of uncertainty, rumour, amazing oligarchic wealth and ostentation, it is easy to foresee dramatic futures. There are certainly those, ranging from the militant *salafiin* within, to Saddam, or some in the Iranian regime without, who would like to see such a turn of events. An estimated 15,000 Saudis went, with official and US blessing, to fight in Afghanistan: now they form a discontented and experienced nucleus, represented in extreme form by Ossama bin Ladin, member of a wealthy family who is threatening terrorist actions from a hideout near Jalalabad. It is less than two decades since a group of armed tribesmen seized and held for two weeks the holy mosque in Mecca.

Yet there could also be another path, one in which the power and greed of the princely caste is gradually but firmly brought under control, and a greater degree of cooperation between the princes and the rest of society, male and female, promoted. There are certainly assets on which to build – enormous wealth in the ground, an increasingly educated society, a substantial public service sector, and an at least significant, if not large, liberal middle class. The Saudi family business cannot go on for ever, and if it does not change it will court ruin. It could, however, as others have done, become a public company, shedding some of its pietistic pretensions and royal privileges. That might well be the best outcome both for the inhabitants of this curious state itself and for the rest of the world that, for better or worse, will continue to rely on its oil for many a decade to come.

### CHAPTER 10

# Turkey 1998: Secularism in Question

There is no better way to grasp the conflicts of interest and identity definition that rend this fascinating country than to observe the fate of its most outstanding shrines. Ankara, the Anatolian town which has served as the capital since Atatürk moved it from Istanbul in 1923 was, until recently, dominated by one building: the Anıtkabir, the tomb of Atatürk himself, a neoclassical columned structure shorn of all religious or Middle Eastern associations. The visitor approaches through an entrance flanked by heroic statues symbolizing liberation and the emancipation of women, and along a solemn avenue. It is here that all official foreign visitors pay their respects: on the day I visited it, there was a wreath from the Democratic Turkish League of Kosovo. On the steps up to the main hall are the words *Hakimiyet Milletindir*, 'Sovereignty to the People,' at once an appropriation of the message of the French revolution and a rejection of the claims of Sultan and religious authority alike.

This is the shrine to the Atatürkist legacy which is today still the ideology of the state. It is a legacy based on an individual who remains to a degree almost unknown anywhere else in the modern world. Atatürk's portrait, bust, lapel buttons, postcards are seen throughout the country. Museums display his clothes, his cigarette cases, the text of his famous six-day speech, the *Büyük Nutuk* and, in more questionable vein, photographs of cloud formations and shadows that appear to represent his profile or eyes. He is the *murşhit*, the guide, the *ebedi çef*, the immortal leader, the *halaskar gazi*, the saviour warrior. The state promotes this reverence, as do those notably educated women who fear the Islamist advance. Many respect him for his decisiveness, in breaking with both the religious and imperial pasts. 'If he was alive we would have built a metro in Istanbul long ago' one intellectual remarked to me. 'Why can't they grow up and take decisions themselves,' remarked another. All is not, however, as it appears: there are also those opposed to Atatürk's legacy who mask their subversion in an exaggerated cult.

The challenge to this legacy has been long in the brewing, and comes from several directions. One now stands as an alternative focus in Ankara itself: the Islamist municipal authorities have erected the Kocatepe mosque which rises in the city centre, floodlit at night in challenge to the shrine. Yet the Kocatepe is, to Western eyes, an incongruous symbol: beneath it is a parking lot and a shopping mall. This is not the end of Islamist aspirations: in Istanbul there was for a while discussion about building a comparable mosque in the city centre, in Taksim Square, and some militants also demonstrated regularly in favour of the reconversion of Aya Sofya, long a museum, into a place of Muslim worship. For many Turks this rise in the public demonstration of Islamist power is, like the Kocatepe mosque, an insult: in 1997 hundreds of thousands of people marched through Ankara protesting against *irtica*, reaction, in rejection of the claims of the Islamists to redefine Turkish society. They protested at what the Islamists had done in power, be it as mayors of Istanbul and Ankara, or in their period in office, in coalition with the Doğru Yol (True Path) party of Tansu Çiller.

A very different clash of symbols and programmes can be observed at the holiest shrine of Istanbul, the Eyüp mosque, named after Ayyoub al-Ansari, one of the associates of the Prophet Muhammad, who died during the siege of Constantinople in 674-8. If the main appeal of the Islamists is to a religious heritage, to a just society (*adıl düzen*) and defence of Turkish morals *(akhlak)* against foreign influences and tourists, one of their other resorts has been to appropriate the Ottoman past. The Atatürkists, too, appropriate some of the Ottoman past, but dislike the dilution of Turkish identity associated with such institutions as the Janissaries, recruits from the Christian regions of Europe, and later decadent and opportunistically pan-Islamic rulers such as Abdulhamit (1876-1909).

The Ottoman legacy is, therefore, available to the Islamists as part of the past they can deploy, and ransack. A beautiful collection of shrines on the upper reaches of the Golden Horn, Eyüp was immortalized for Western literature in the writings of the French novelist, Pierre Loti. It was to the Eyüp that the Ottoman Sultans came to be crowned as *padisah*, or king of kings. It has remained a symbol of both the Islamic and Ottoman pasts: alms are still distributed to the needy, couples come to have their marriages blessed, and to seek a cure for their problems. The neighbourhood is dominated by Islamists, much like neighbouring Fatih, site of the mosque build by Sultan Mehmet, the conqueror of the city in 1453 who rode his horse into Aya Sofya and repeatedly had it kick over the vessels on the altar. In Eyüp and Fatih bearded men and covered women dominate the streets. But this Islamist atmosphere mingles with the revival and instrumental use of the Ottoman past: thus a cafe just outside the Eyüp is called the *Hünkar*, a word for sultan. On the Friday morning before Kurban Bayramı, the feast of the sacrifice, sheep and calves were being brought in for symbolic slaughter. The streets were enlivened by a *mehter* band, a group of musicians dressed in Ottoman military uniforms and chain mail, playing martial music to the rhythm of two steps forward, one backward: some Turks take the *mehter* step to be symbolic of modern Turkey as a whole. In their attempt to promote this appropriation of the Ottoman past, Islamist publishing houses produce books on the great victories of the Ottoman military commanders and idealize the Tulip Age, the first three decades of the eighteenth century.

The contrast with Iran is striking. In Iran empire and monarch were associated with the modernizing, secular state: hence to be Islamist is to be republican. In Turkey that state, under Atatürk, sought to reject the Ottoman past – its institutions, its empire, its clothes, its script – and hence Islamism is monarchical. Like other European imperial states the empire has very much come home: waves of immigrations from the Balkans, the Caucasus and Central Asia have settled here, now joined by communities of the 'suitcase trade', from the former Soviet republics. In a symbolic gesture, the body of Enver Pasha, a Young Turk leader who died fighting the Bolsheviks in Central Asia, has been brought back to Istanbul and buried with his associates in Independence Park.

It is not, however, only the Islamists who pose a challenge to the Atatürkist legacy. Since 1984 the southern-eastern part of the country has been gripped by a war between the Turkish army and the guerrillas of the PKK, the Kurdish Workers' Party. Many thousands have died, over three thousand villages have been destroyed, and hundreds of thousands have been made refugees. The war is estimated to cost $7 billion a year, roughly equal to the net cost to London of its role in Northern Ireland. The PKK itself is a descendant of the militarized far left of the 1960s and 1970s. When it began its armed struggle in 1984 it is doubtful if it had widespread support: but the response of the Turkish state, and the lack of a legitimate space for Kurdish political demands, have led to the growth of PKK support far beyond its initial base. This broader Kurdish support, combined with the impasse of the guerrilla resistance itself, has had a moderating influence, in that the PKK no longer demands independence.

The Turkish state, however, has given little ground and refuses to recognize as minorities any communities other than those stipulated in the 1923 Treaty of Lausanne. The constitution includes a clause, itself denoted as unchangeable, on the indivisibility of Turkey and on the monopoly of the Turkish language – this precludes not just secession, but what most would regard as any meaningful regional autonomy. Several parties seen as representing a Kurdish interest have been harassed and suppressed: state policy has, in this way, promoted the hegemony of the PKK over Kurdish intellectual and political life. There has been some movement in the 1990s: Kurdish is now permitted in public places, and the derogatory phrase for Kurds, *dağ Türkler*, (mountain Turks) is no longer used. Both President Demirel and his predecessor President Özal have recognized the existence of a Kurdish community, the press reports openly on the issue, through not on the progress of the war. One newspaper columnist wrote an article under the title 'Atakurd' – a play on *ata*, meaning father of – and speculating on how Turks would feel if things had turned out the other way round. There are many in public life, including the Turkish employers' federation TÜSIAD, who have called for a political solution. A report by the Migration Commission of the parliament blamed the security forces, and in particular the 'Special Teams' held responsible for particular persecution of the Kurds, for mass emigration from the south-east: the report called, for the first time in Turkey's history, for official recognition of a Kurdish identity.

The problem goes back, however, to the military: they are, in most if not all significant respects, still the effective rulers of Turkey. On the Kurdish question, as on other issue such as Cyprus, they hold the key. While the range of public discussion and awareness of the Kurdish issue has expanded very substantially in recent years, few people I spoke to saw any prospect of a significant move in the near future. Turkish nationalism in its more extreme form has adopted some questionable claims but, predictably, repression from above is matched by some alternative simplification from below: the *Turkish Daily News* of 3 April 1998 printed an interview with the head of a Kurdish cultural foundation who argued that, since the Turks had no word of their own for 'thank you', using either a French (*mersi*) or Arabic (*teşekkür*) word, they were 'a rude people who were unable to express appreciation'.

The Atatürkist legacy has also come under attack from another modernizing current known, at least by its enemies, as the 'second republic-ans'. They accept much of what Atatürk did but argue that the time has come to move on, to fulfill that integration of Turkey into Europe which the *Gazi* began and to liberalize towards the left and towards Kurds, as much as towards women who wish to wear the headscarf, to end the brutality that still marks the activities of the Turkish police, and above all to get the military out of politics. Much of Turkish life is overshadowed by the security organizations – the army and the MİT, the political police – in a way that civilian politicians do not control, and with underhand links to the mafia. Turkey's most prominent writer, Yaşar Kemal, himself a Kurd, argues that the number one problem facing the country is human rights. Some have also argued for a more open, critical account of the massacre of Armenians in World War I. This critique of the authoritarian, outmoded conception of Turkish identity and interests is articulated by human rights groups: the disruption by the Istanbul police chief of a meeting between the European Union representative in Turkey and a group of NGOs the latter had invited to his office is cited as typical of the archaic attitudes of the security forces. In their own rendering of the Ottoman legacy, some secular left intellectuals contrast its diversity and cultural cosmopolitanism with the centralism that has pervaded Turkish reformers from the mid-nineteenth century onwards. Not for nothing was the military regime that came to power in 1908 called the Committee of Union and Progress.

No-one should have any doubt as to the fact that the military are in charge, and the military would not want it any other way: television news on the night of 27 March 1998 led with film of the monthly meeting of the National Security Council, where civilian politicians meet, (that is to say, are given their instructions by) the top military personnel. The body language of assertion on one side and embarrassed attentiveness on the other told it all: the politicians were instructed to clamp down further on the Islamists or face the consequences, which would be another military coup. For Atatürkists, on the other hand, the 'second republicans' are a group of dreamers, a product of an Istanbul elite that has never reconciled itself to the power of Ankara. The miserable showing (under 1 percent) of one party that embodied its programme, that of Cem Boyner, in the elections of 1995, is taken as showing how little real following they have. More seriously, the Atatürkists charge that the 'second republicans' are a fifth column, promising disin-tegration of the country, the unchallenged advance of the Islamists and a descent into chaos. Like others in the region the Atatürkist elite has drawn its own lessons from the collapse of the USSR: they do not intend to make the same mistake.

Much hinges, inevitably, on an assessment of the Islamist forces themselves, and of the challenge they pose. Some parties are openly secularist and support the ban on headscarves. The litany of Islamist provocations is many: their former leader, Erbakan, a man with a long record of support for nationalist causes (he advocated the occupation of the whole of Cyprus in 1974) and, a rare thing in Turkey, an exponent of anti-semitic views, has said that they will come to power by the ballot or by force. Some mayors have refused to shake hands with women, some have sought to enforce a ban on male doctors treating women, some have forced women employees to choose between wearing the scarf and standing in the street all day counting cars. The leaders have been careful to keep within the law: Fethullah Gülen, the leader of one group that claims to be inspired by the model of Pakistan, has argued that 95 per cent of Islam's programme is not political. But this has not done them much good: Erbakan has been banned from political life for five years, and his Refah (Welfare) party, a coalition that he successfully held together, was closed down and reconstituted itself as the Fazilet (Virtue) party, while his successors fell to squabbling over his inheritance. A strong candidate to succeed him was the mayor of Istanbul, Recep Tayyip Erdoğan: but he ran into difficulties after reading the lines of a poem at a public meeting in 1997 which went 'The minarets are bayonets, the domes helmets, the mosques our barracks, the believers our soldiers.' He was prosecuted as a result. Fethullah's apparent moderation, on the other hand, has won him few friends: there are open allegations that his project of a 'safe' Islamism is inspired by foreign powers – America, or, failing that, Germany. One secularist intellectual who visited the television station controlled by Fethullah was struck by what he found: a building peopled only by men. Fethullah is, he insisted, surrounded by a lot of dangerous looking bearded young men. My own encounter with the correspondent of his paper, *Zaman*, was not reassuring: he asked me for my views on Pakistan, and when I told him about the political chaos, ethnic conflict and narcotics trading, he put down his pencil. The interview had ended.

It is, for outsiders as much as for Turks, hard to get a handle on the Islamist current in this formally secular country. In the elections of 1995 Refah won 21 percent of the votes in the national elections and control of many cities. Parallel to Islamist parties, there has been a revival of unofficial Muslim organizations, notably the *tarikat*s or sects banned by Atatürk, a sort of pluralised freemasonry that now pervades business and political life. There is also a thriving Islamist business sector: posters on the road in from Istanbul airport advertize the Ihlas Finance Group and the Albaraka Bank (*ihlas* is an Islamic term for devotion, *baraka* for blessing); travel companies sport names like Hilal (Crescent); there are Islamist fashion houses, and perfume shops in the name of Furkan (literally 'the Divider' that is between truth and falsity), a name for the Quran. The signs of a growing public pietism are evident – in cafes where the food, music and even chairs have been changed to conform to a more traditional model. All of this, however, has its limits: alcohol is freely available, the press has a wide range of comment and bodily display, there is none of the public prostration at prayer time that is commonplace in Egypt or Saudi Arabia.

There are, however, other problems with any evaluation of this Islamist challenge. The first difficulty is with the official conception of secularism. This, one of Atatürk's six 'revolutionary principles', is taken off the shelf of enlightenment values as it were, from the French revolution: hence the Turkish work is *laiklik*. What it means in reality is not atheism, or the exclusion of religion from public life, but state control and appropriation of religion. Through the Directorate of Religious Affairs the state pays the salaries and thereby controls the Friday speeches of 180,000 clergy. It is now attempting not to close, but to bring under state control, another 10,000 or so unauthorized mosques. For all its repudiation of the Arabic and Muslim past the very language of Atatürkism is replete with Islamic symbolism: thus the Turkish flag displays the Islamic crescent, the word used for Atatürk on everyone school playground bust is *murşhit*, ('guide') a term of Islamic resonance. The national liberation struggle that defeated the Greeks, French and British in the early 1920s is called the *Milli Mücadele* (National Struggle), both *milli* and *mucadele* being originally words with religious connotations. Secularism is conceived of not, as in most other countries, as a matter of degree and as a cognate of tolerance, but rather as opposition to all that the secular and authoritarian elite despise. Small wonder then that the opposition to this Atatürkist experiment has been growing over the decades: the roots lie in the opposition of small towns, traditional elites, to the state in the 1940s. Twice, in 1960 and 1971, the military intervened to arrest the process. But in 1980, faced with a militant left, the military to some degree endorsed Islamism: like the Israelis with Hamas, and the FLN with the FIS, the response was to promote Islamism, hopefully controlled, to diminish the left.

For their part the Islamists offer a mishmash of ideas, articulated with a mixture of quotes from the Quran and the Prophet, and ideas taken from late twentieth-century discourse of opposition. In book fairs and book shops the Islamists offer a wide range of texts – studies on the holy texts, replete with studies such as ones on 'hypocrites in Islam' and on the devil, teach- yourself manuals, accounts of the Ottoman period, studies of Western corruption via globalization and the media, and translations from a selection of Western literature: predictable entries such as Tolstoy's *Hajji Murat*, and Walter Scott's *Saladin,* together with works deemed to have an appropriate, and appropriable, moral message, including *Crime and Punishment, Don Quixote, Faust* and *Coriolanus.* Those themes in contemporary Western thinking that suite the challenge to the Turkish state are also happily recruited: much is made of the Ottoman practice of multiculturalism, now linked to the recently imported idea of *farklılık* (difference), while a bestseller in Islamist bookshops has been Paul Feyerabend's *Against Method.* Concepts have a way of being turned to strange uses: thus the term 'enlightenment' has been appropriated by, respectively, the Kemalist left and far left in its Turkish form, *aydınlık*, while in its Islamic form, *tenvir*, it has become a watchword of the Islamists. This leaves the original concept with the enlightened but authoritarian state.

The question that secularists in Turkey repeatedly pose is both clear and unanswerable: 'Will the Turkish Islamists take Turkey down the road of Iran, Algeria, Afghanistan?' The arguments against are obvious enough: so far, the Islamists have not resorted to mass violence; Turkey is a very different kind of society; the leaders of the main Islamist faction have made some reasonable, conciliatory noises. None of this cuts much ice with secularists. First of all, it was thought that such countries as Iran or Lebanon, or for that matter Algeria, were immune to such mass authoritarian religious movements: but they were not. Secondly, the issue of violence is not so clear: there has been no resort by Islamism to urban guerrilla warfare in Turkey, that place being reserved for the unreligious, militantly Marxist-Leninist PKK. But secularist writers have been the target of murder – among them Turan Dursun, Çetin Emeç and Uğur Mumcu, all accused of criticizing Islamists and, most spectacularly, in the case in Sivas in 1993 when 37 participants in an Alevi festival attended by the late Aziz Nesin, defender of Salman Rushdie, were burnt to death by an Islamist mob and the survivors beaten by the local, Islamist-controlled, fire brigade who came to their rescue. Whether it was the Islamists, or elements in the security forces who killed the writers remains, however, unclear. As one generally critical Turkish intellectual put it to me: 'These people have not engaged in mass killings, not yet'.

Perhaps the most vulnerable group of all in Turkey are those from the Islamic minority sect, the Alevis, comprising up to 20 percent of the total Turkish population: as virtually everywhere else in the Muslim world, such minorities, faced with a potentially dominant Islamist majority, are themselves secularist (the Baluch and Pathans in Pakistan, the Kurds in Iran, and the Kabyles in Algeria all provide comparable examples). Some of the worst Islamist violence, mediated through the hands of the Istanbul police, has been against Alevi Kurds, regarded by Islamists as not proper Muslims. Much use is also made of the word *takiye*: in Islam, particularly in Shi'ite Islam, this means dissimulation in the face of tyrannical government, in other words concealment of political goals (and one's faith). Erbakan, Fethullah and the others are therefore charged with *takiye*, and not to be trusted. The largest problem, however, lies not in the realm of intention. For what is evident from reading and listening to the Turkish Islamists, as with their confreres in other countries, may not be that they are dissimulating, but that they may well believe everything they say: one prominent spokesman, the brother of the late President Özal, assured an endless late night TV discussion, which I had the dubious satisfaction of participating in, that since Islam was a religion of love, everything would be solved when a government true to its ideals came to power. The Islamists get a large Kurdish vote – more than the semi-legal Kurdish parties: but this may be more a form of protest than of identification with the Islamist programme. When asked about the Kurdish issue the standard reply is that since all Turkish nationals are Muslims there is no problem. What their record in office, at local and national, level has shown is that while on particular symbolic issues, such as veiling, they have a view of a retrograde kind, on the broader challenges facing the country they do not have coherent policies. Their economic policy is the very secular, early modernist one of industrialization in small towns. It all turns out to be the same confused and mediocre mess, much indulged by kindly Western searchers for authenticity, and attractive to a mass of recently arrived rural migrants, but of scant relevance to the problems of Turkey today. In such a context of intellectual vacuity and national crisis, the Islamists could easily lapse into violence, whatever benign words their spokesmen currently offer.

These debates on Turkish politics and identity are inevitably exacerbated by changes in the global environment. Turkey belongs to three worlds – to Europe, which has since Atatürk been the official point of reference, to the

Middle East with which, despite Atatürk, Turkey has developed commercial and political ties since the 1970s, and to the newly emergent world of Turkic states and communities stretching, in the words of President Demirel, 'from the Pamirs to the Adriatic': this compromises the Uighur in Chinese Sinjiang, the Central Asian states (Turkmenistan, Uzbekistan, Kirghiztan, Kazakhstan), the northern mainly Uzbek region of Afghanistan, Azerbaijan in the Transcaucasus, the numerous peoples of the northern Caucasus, and, in the Balkans, Bosnia, Albania and Kosovo. Whether Turkey is or is not part of Europe is, as it is also in the case of Russia, an empty argument: it has been so for five hundred years. But the attempt to become part of the European Union has foundered, and is unlikely to succeed in the foreseeable future: while Turkey enjoys trading access, fears of migration, human rights violations, the domination of the military, the very financial burden Turkish membership would impose, all add up to an enduring holding operation on political union. After the Luxemburg summit of December 1997, where Turkey was excluded from the list of next applicants, then Prime Minister Mesut Yılmaz broke off contacts with the EU. Many in Turkey oppose this, seeing in the European link an important bastion against Islamist advance: the military criticized Yılmaz for his critical stance on Europe. The Middle Eastern connection has also been a mixed blessing: trade has declined since the Iraqi invasion of Kuwait in 1990, and there are fears of fundamentalist influence from the Arab states, especially Libya and Saudi Arabia.

In the last three years Turkey has consolidated its military relationship with Israel: this made sense in Ankara, given the fear of Syrian-backed Kurdish guerrilla operations, but has led to a growing antagonism in relations with the Arab world. The Turks themselves do not seem too worried: they put the blame on the Arabs. They also seem to get on well with Israelis: 'It is one country where we are treated as equals,' remarked an academic observer. As for the Turkic world, it has turned out to be a dubious opening: Turkish small businessmen and building contractors are active in Central Asia, and there is enormous interest for reasons of economic security and of prestige in the construction of oil and gas pipelines from the Caspian region through Turkey. But six inefficient, very corrupt and authoritarian former Soviet republics, with bad communications and infrastructure, are not a global option. Most of Turkish trade is with Europe, most of its investment goes into Russia and the Ukraine, rather than into the Turkic countries. The politics and funding of pipelines is itself very complex and there is, as yet, little certainty about how this energy will be shipped to the outside world.

Inevitably, the internal debate on identity and the external debate on orientation become intertwined. For the secularists the argument is clear: Turkey must be incorporated into Europe not so much because it is already ready to be but because this is the only way to consolidate democracy and human rights inside the country. For pan-Turkish nationalists it was Atatürk's abandonment of the Turkic world that led to the country's isolation: they want to see a more militant line on Chechenya, Bosnia, Sinjiang and Azerbaijan, as well as Cyprus. One of the more unusual additions to the public monuments of Istanbul is a shrine, just off the Hippodrome, to the 'martyrs of East Turkestan', that is, the Chinese north-West. In April 1998 the manageress of a Chinese restaurant in Istanbul was assassinated by East Turkestani militants. For the Islamists the option is the Middle East: they are not sure which one, of course, and Erbakan's experiences as premier, when he went to Libya professing Muslim solidarity and got a public scolding from Qaddafi on Turkish chauvinism, did not reinforce this aspiration. Erbakan, however, was undeterred: after his party was closed, he embarked on his 27th *hajj* or pilgrimage to Mecca.

Iran remains an uneasy neighbour: despite talk of historic enmity the two countries have lived on good terms for most of nearly six centuries. In the Topkapı palace there are gifts exchanged with Nadir Shah of Iran in the 1740s, in the Atatürk Mausoleum Museum, similar exchanges with Reza Shah in the 1930s. But there is also distrust. An Ottoman saying goes, 'If you learn Persian, you lose half of your faith', a reference to the hedonistic influence of Hafez, Sa'adi and Omar Khayyam. Since 1979 Turkish secularists have feared the influence of the Iranian revolution: this has been confirmed by the refusal of Iranian officials to lay wreathes at Atatürk's tomb, preferring instead to visit Konya, the town of the Sufi saint, Jalal al-Din Rumi. Turkish envoys to Tehran have declined to visit the tomb of Imam Khomeini. The Iranian ambassador was expelled after taking part in a 'Jerusalem Day' organized by a Refah mayor near Ankara where the Iranian envoy made an anti-secularist speech.

None of these issues allows of an easy or rapid solution. The military elite and their civilian allies who run Turkey continue to maintain an unbending, brittle resistance to anything that smacks of weakness: authoritarian stubbornness at the top is matched by police and army brutality towards political dissent at the bottom. Yet much is changing. The press and 26 television channels are in large measure free and there is a vibrant intellectual and cultural life. Non-governmental organizations operate in a way unimaginable in Iran or the Arab world. It is possible to debate in public many issues that, even a decade ago, were taboo. This is a country with immense human as well as natural resources: its elite reflects a degree of astounding social mobility, something inherited from the Ottoman times. Its top universities produce graduates of world quality: the questioning after a series of seminars I gave in Istanbul and Ankara was at a higher level, and less given to irrelevant point-scoring, than in any other country I have visited.

At the same time the challenges faced by the semi-democratic institutions of Turkey are not imagined: in addition to the authoritarian immobilism of the military elite, there is hyperinflation in the economy, a retrograde, devious and fecklessly vacuous Islamism at the mass level, a Kurdish opposition that replicates the worst of the authoritarian Marxist past, but which has now, in the face of state intransigence, come to hegemonize Kurdish politics in the country. The programme which Atatürk drew up in the 1920s was in many ways relevant then and remains so to this day: whether it can be altered and developed to meet the challenges of the contemporary world, and to conform to a definition of European modernity that has itself altered much in the ensuing seven decades, is a question that will for many years to come preoccupy the versatile people of Turkey. It will equally be of no little relevance to all three of the international communities – Europe, the Middle East and Central Asia – to which Turkey belongs.

### CHAPTER 11

# The *Millet* of Manchester: Arab Merchants and the Cotton Trade

Behind the desk of Mr Emile Abu-Fadil, for many years Lebanese Honorary Consul in Manchester, hung the copy of a painting whose outlines are known to many generations of English school children. '*Phoenicians bartering with ancient Britons*' by Frederick Lord Leighton dates from 1894-5[1] and portrays two groups confronting each other: on the left are wild men and women – savages almost, clad in animal skins – while on the right are a group of darker figures, upright and noble, draped in fine robes, with pointed beards and skullcaps. The scene is Cornwall in south-west England, some time before the advent of the Romans and the birth of Christ: the barbarians on the left are natives of Britain, the nobles on the right are Phoenician traders, merchants who ventured out from Tyre and Sidon in what is now Lebanon and who sailed to Britain, via the Straits of Gibraltar and the north Atlantic, to exchange their goods for Cornish tin.

The degree of continuity between today's Lebanon and ancient Phoenicia is, of course, a subject of controversy: the state of Lebanon as we now know it is a very recent and fragile creation, having been forged out of the wreckage of the Ottoman empire at the end of World War I. Most of those Arab merchants from the Ottoman empire who came to Britain in the nineteenth century would have called themselves Syrian (*suri*) before calling themselves either Arab or Lebanese, since the word Syria covered what is now Lebanon until the latter was delineated. But the majority came from what is now Lebanon, from the same region as the traders two thousand years ago. At the same time the motivation of these commercial links two millennia later, was the reverse of that which had operated in the earlier period: what attracted Arab merchants to England in modern times was not the raw materials available but the manufactured and in, particular, cotton goods produced in Lancashire which made of Manchester the free trade capital of the nineteenth century.

*Manchester and international trade*

The Lancashire cotton industry sold its goods to the world through Manchester and from the 1830s onwards, as political and economic conditions permitted, the merchants of that city developed an increasing interest in the Middle East: in the markets of the Ottoman empire, in the possible transit through the region to India and China beyond, and in the expansion of cotton growing in the more fertile areas. The commercial pressures exerted on the Ottoman empire by Britain opened the door to textile goods, amongst other items, and from the 1860s the opening of the Suez Canal plus the growth of cotton output in Egypt, the latter to replace US output lost in the civil war, contributed to placing the region in a major commercial relation with industrial England. A historian of the textile trade has described this connection:

> The export of plain cotton goods to the Levant had been greatly stimulated as a result of the Anglo-Turkish Commercial Treaty signed at Balta-Liman in 1838; and by the middle of the century the Sultan's dominions were taking more Manchester piece goods than all the European countries put together. The transport facilities for this expanding trade were at first very inadequate, and caused much delay; while severe losses through pilfering were experienced when goods and mails were sent overland, e.g. through France or Austria.[2]

This trade expanded for half a century after the 1838 Treaty but it then began to decline and the domination of the Middle Eastern market by British goods was ended by World War I. In the areas they now controlled the French gave preference to their own products, while in the Middle East and West Africa, as elsewhere, the new might of Japanese goods drove British competition away. The interwar period also saw the end of free trade on an international scale and with it the decline of Manchester within the world economy.

*Table 1: Exports of cotton piece goods to Eastern countries*
*(Million yards)*

|  | 1865 | 1880 | 1913 |
|---|---|---|---|
| Turkey | 229 | 383 | 360 |
| Persia | - | 15 | 40 |
| China | 113 | 448 | 716 |
| Dutch East Indies | 39 | 77 | 304 |
| Japan | - | 61 | 50 |
| Philippines | 31 | 51 | 17 |
| Siam | - | - | 42 |
| Indo-China | - | - | 2 |
| Total | 412 | 1,035 | 1,531 |
| % Total Exporters | 20.6 | 23.0 | 22.1 |

Source: A. Redford and B. Clapp, *Manchester Merchants and Foreign Trade*, vol. 2, (Manchester, 1934), chapter VII. Note: 'Turkey' includes Arab areas then under Ottoman rule.

While British merchants organized in the Manchester Chamber of Commerce were dominant in this trade, the importance of Manchester attracted a colony of foreign traders to the city where they established trading houses for the export of cotton goods back to their own countries of origin and to third countries in which they had trading connections.[3] According to Fadlo Hourani, a Lebanese trader and Honorary Lebanese Consul from 1946 to 1960, there were four such foreign trading houses in 1798 and around four hundred by the 1870s.[4] Most of these were from other European countries – Germans, Danes, Dutch, Swedes, Greeks. The German community was especially well established, coming from Britain's main industrial rival, and at its peak numbered around one hundred and fifty businesses. A Martin Luther Church was established in Park Road, Stratford, and the names of at least two prominent families have remained famous in connection with activities engaged in whilst their members were resident in Manchester: the Hallé family gave its name to the orchestra which it patronized, whilst the junior partner in the firm of Ermen and Engels was to use his observations of Manchester in the 1840s as the basis for a classic study of urban conditions in industrial society.[5] The growing commercial links between Manchester and the Middle East naturally led to the growth of a foreign community from that area itself, and towards the end of the nineteenth century up to one hundred and fifty Middle Eastern merchant houses had been established. While these included Greek and Armenian houses (all 'Levantines' in the old usage) a substantial number, several dozen, were Arab trading houses. The Arabs included 'Syrians' in the old sense of the word, from what is now Lebanon and Syria, and a smaller distinct group of merchants from Fes in Morocco. Both communities preserved their language, customs, religion and in some cases dress, and they lasted as identifiable entities into the interwar period. Yet whilst they retained their family links with the Arab world their commercial links went far beyond as they exported Lancashire cotton goods not only to their countries of origin, but also to Arab merchants who had themselves emigrated; the merchants from Fes exported to their associates in other countries surrounding the Mediterranean, the Lebanese and Syrians to fellow traders in the Americas and West Africa, as well as to the Middle East. Manchester therefore became a link between different sections of the Arab commercial emigration and the Middle East, the economic centre of a triangle of trade and kinship that stretched across five continents in the era of free trade.

*The Fasi community*

Trade had been the main activity of the city of Fes since the seventeenth century, and a sizeable émigré merchant community had spread around the Mediterranean by the late nineteenth century to handle this business. There were in 1898 up to 1,500 Fasis in Cairo, as well as smaller communities in Gibraltar, Naples, Geneva and Marseilles. Trade with England had been carried via Gibraltar for a long time and the Fasi merchants exported a few goods to England – beeswax, dates for Christmas and canary-grass (alpiste), an ingredient in the making of whisky. In 1895 a clash in the countryside prevented the merchants from getting the dates to Britain in time for Christmas and they lost money accordingly.[6]

At some point in the nineteenth century, as English cotton goods entered Morocco via Gibraltar and Tangier, Fasi merchants began to settle in Manchester as they already had in other cities. The precise date is unclear, one source giving the first Fasi arrivals as the 1830s.[7] Whatever the truth, there were in the last decade of the nineteenth century over a dozen

Moroccan families in Manchester, and the community reached at its height about thirty families or one hundred and fifty persons. Nearly all were from Fes, although one was a Fasi who had earlier traded in Cairo and another family came from the Moroccan port of Mogador.

From one work of local history published in 1905 we have an impressionistic view of how a local merchant saw this community:[8]

Early in the sixties as you passed along the business streets of the City, you would suddenly come in sight of some white turbaned individual, whose gay Eastern dress appeared in such strong contrast to the sombre hues of the attire of all those about him. At first the sight of one of these men in Moorish garb was a very uncommon occurrence, and people would stand and smile as one of them passed along. But now they have ceased to be a wonder, and so they go to and fro and do their business in their usual quiet way, and make their purchases at the shops without more than perhaps a casual glance from the passers by.

Apparently, the British traders who dealt with the Moroccans took time to adjust to their more open business methods:

If you had any communication to make to any of their number you were often obliged to make it in the presence and hearing of the entire conclave; and as a result there was no disposition to keep their transactions secret from each other, and at times they would consult amongst themselves before the one in treaty with you would make up his mind as to placing an order. At times this was somewhat embarrassing to the seller, but their manner of doing business was pleasant and easy enough when you had once been admitted to their general friendship.

Hayes mentions a number of controversies involving Moroccans who disappeared without settling their debts, but also records that a number of them had to return home on the orders of the sultan to act as tax-collectors. In order to lessen the pressure on them from the ruler, they would try to get themselves appointed as agents for British firms, and so be entitled to protection from the relevant English consul.[9] It was known in Fes that these Manchester Moroccans had a special building, known as 'the office', from which their business was carried out, and this is confirmed by an interesting article from the local press which provides a vivid account of the community.

Although the informant is not named, he was probably a Mr Jones, an Englishman who spoke Moroccan Arabic and who worked for them as an adviser from offices in Market Street. This report bears an evocative title summarizing the main features by which the community was known: 'Special Wives Bought in Slave Market; Wore Red Fez; Always had Umbrellas; Never in Court'.[10] It read as follows:

A Manchester merchant who had close connections with the Colony for over forty years . . . gave some interesting details of the Moroccans, who conducted all their business and foreign correspondence from their homes, in Arabic.

'This community was well known in the locality by the wearing of the red Fez, with which was worn a huge overcoat which covered the native dress and invariably also was carried an umbrella', he said,

The womenfolk – mostly black women, some of whom had been previously purchased in the slave market, married and brought to England, as it was considered 'infra dig' to bring one of the real white wives to England – in a short time mastered the language, much quicker than their lords and masters. Having borne a large family, many of the children born in Manchester enjoy British nationality, and although returned to their native city of Fez, other generations born in Morocco claim by right British nationality, of which they are very proud and value its privileges, although they may never probably see the country, which through accident of birth they claim, and which will be enjoyed for generations to come. The British Consul at Fez has records of these numerous British subjects. These privileges are unfortunately lost to the female sex when they marry.

The habits of this Moroccan Colony in Manchester were not unusual, except that one of the gentlemen undertook to see that the meat was provided in accordance with the Mohammedan rights. A butcher in Rusholme had the monopoly of supplying Welsh lamb, having in his yard a small abattoir, and each morning this gentleman proceeded with the killing of the required number of sheep. This same gentleman also led them to prayer every Friday, the service of which was held in a house in Parkfield Street. Their offices in the city were mostly in the building known as Chepstow House, at 32 Oxford Street, and many readers will no doubt remember the following names: Canoon, Elhadjwy, Madhani Tazi, Lazarak, Guesus, Benab-delsh, Benchocron, Benquiran and Boeyed.

These Moroccans enjoyed a name second to none for honest and good citizenship. One of its members, well remembered for his perfect speaking of English, was looked upon as their chief adviser, and was the means of settling many differences which arose in business. When any merchant had recourse to legal advice, there was an old-established firm in King Street (Messrs. Atkinson, Saunders & Co) who can be termed to have been the official solicitors for the Moroccan merchants, and the late Mr. Seville, a partner of the firm, always managed to keep the Moroccan merchants out of court. Despite the enormous business they did in the city, it is not within memory that they ever had recourse to the Assizes.

I remember many times the kind hospitality which I enjoyed. Luncheon consisted of many highly spiced dishes, followed by Oriental sweets and a quantity of fruit. Green tea served with mint helped to digest the unusually heavy meal. Of course, food was only served to the men, the womenfolk having their meals separately; and what appeared most odd was that the dishes that went back were those intended for the womenfolk.

While it would seem that the majority of the Fasi merchants were Muslims, a number were Sephardic Jews and visited the Sha'are Sedek synagogue for Sephardim at Old Landsdowne Rd, West Didsbury, in South Manchester. For their part the Muslims, as mentioned, were careful to respect the prescriptions of their religion. They used to purchase kosher meat from a Jewish butcher before they had their own, and in this connection are believed to have contacted the Islamic reformer, Muhammad Abduh, in order to get from him a declaration of religious propriety, a *fetwa*, concerning the eating of meat killed by non-Muslims. What Abduh said is not know but there seems little doubt that the Muslim religion was strictly enforced in the Manchester Moroccan community.

We have one vivid account of this period from within the Moroccan community, in the form of the autobiography of the Moroccan writer, Abd al-Majid Bin Jilloun, *Fi al-Tufula* (In Childhood).[11] His family moved from Casablanca to Manchester soon after he was born in 1910 and he lived there for eight years before returning to North Africa. The book is an account of childhood in a large house with a garden in Manchester, presumably

Didsbury, and of his family's commercial and social interaction with British society. There are trips to Blackpool, encounters with Father Christmas (*Sheikh al-Milad*, literally 'the old man of the birth', a less common Arabic rendering than the conventional *Baba No'il*), and bad memories of being humiliated and beaten at school, an experience which by Bin Jilloun's account was to leave him timid for the rest of his life. Bin Jilloun writes that when he returned to Morocco he was at first perceived as a 'Christian' because of his clothes and long hair.

The community's presence ended dramatically in the interwar period, when the competition from Japanese goods made it impossible to export Lancashire textiles to Morocco. In 1936 the community returned to Morocco and, it seems, adopted Moroccan citizenship when that country became independent twenty years later. As the local paper put it: 'Apart from the considerable material loss to the city, Manchester has lost a body of good citizens who, while retaining all their oriental customs and attributes, built up for themselves a reputation second to none for honest dealing and clean living.'[12] A few members of the community did remain behind. Some of the Abulafia family for example remained in Britain.[13] The family of Bin Sikri, who anglicized their name to Sicree, became solicitors in Manchester. However, as already suggested, the majority who returned to Morocco in the 1930s or even before were probably re-absorbed into that country's population. Abd al-Majid Bin Jilloun reported that in Morocco, Manchester, pronounced *manitshistir*, retained a mythic association, while some of the goods brought from Britain, machine-made carpets and teapots from Sheffield, were especially valued.

### The Syrians and Lebanese

More substantial was the community of merchants from Syria and Lebanon. As with the Moroccans it is not absolutely clear when the first merchants came, but the main body was certainly formed after the 1860s. According to one source, the first of these merchants was a Catholic trader from Aleppo named Kebaba and the existence of some community would seem to be attested by the fact there was an Ottoman consul in Manchester from the 1850s, a merchant named Idlibi.[14] The first merchant from what is now Lebanon proper was Abdullah Tarad, who came to Manchester in 1862 and established a trading company anglicized as 'Abdullah Trade'; after him the dozens of other Lebanese followed.[15]

The history of Lebanese emigration in general relates to the troubled economic and political condition of that country which drove so many of its young to work abroad. As one writer has put it: 'Probably only the Irish rival the Lebanese is exporting themselves.'[16] The classic work by Elie Safa on the subject gives a number of causes, beginning with the overcrowded condition of Lebanese agriculture, and including the restrictions on trade especially by Christians under the Ottoman empire, and the decay of the economy in that area in the last part of the nineteenth century.[17] The consequence is that the great majority of Lebanese emigrants proper (that is, people from what is now Lebanon) were Christians. A survey carried out in 1932 gave the Christian proportion as 83 per cent, of which 48 per cent were Maronites and another 22 per cent Greek Orthodox. According to statistics compiled in the late 1950s, no less than 1,214,500 Lebanese emigrants could be counted, of which the major communities were as follows:

*Table 2: Lebanese emigrant communities 1960*

| USA | 400,000 |
|---|---|
| Brazil | 350,000 |
| Argentina | 200,000 |
| Mexico | 40,000 |
| Canada | 20,000 |
| Venezuela | 15,000 |
| Uruguay | 15,000 |
| Cuba | 12,000 |
| Australia | 25,000 |
| Africa | 70,000 |

Source: Elie Safa, *L'émigration libanaise* (Beirut, 1960)

Of the 1.2 million total, only around 3,000 are estimated by Safa to have come to Europe, and of these the majority settled in France. The Manchester community was, at its height around World War I, in the region of three hundred and fifty people.[18] In nearly all cases the Lebanese and Syrian emigrants were of peasant origin but, unlike peasant emigrants from other countries (Ireland, Italy, Yemen), they were nearly all able to rise up the social scale and become merchants; thus in many countries of the world, particularly ones with rapid social mobility through immigration, the Lebanese/Syrians were quickly established in prominent positions within the commercial centres.[19]

Very few of those who came to Britain were Muslims, the majority being either Christians or Jews. In the case of the Christians it was not Maronite Christianity but Protestantism that formed the dominant belief, because England was associated with Protestantism and in Lebanon those who espoused Protestantism tended to adhere to sympathy for Britain as well. We have a revealing account of this pro-English sentiment among Lebanese Protestants from Edward Atiyah who sets it within the overall context of Lebanon at that time. Atiyah writes: 'The Muslim population leaned towards Turkey; the Roman Catholics and Maronites developed strong French sympathies; the Greek Orthodox identified themselves with Russia; and the Protestants drank tea in the afternoon and were called "Ingliz".'[20] Atiyah came from a family with long ties to England: his paternal grandfather had been converted to Protestantism and had written books on the conversion of Muslims to Christianity, even travelling to Edinburgh to discuss their translation into English with the orientalist, Sir William Muir; his maternal grandfather had taught British missionaries for forty years, and both his father and his mother knew English.[21]

Stressing the way in which each religious group in Lebanon identified with an outside country Atiyah emphasized how he and other Protestants idealized Britain: 'In this contra-national atmosphere it was my lot to adopt England – not the soil of England, for I did not see that till I was nineteen years old – but everything else, the spirit and prestige of England: her kings and heroes, armies fleets and victories; her history and literature and all the things that were lacking in my own national background.'[22] So great was his identification with England that, he says, 'My first nationalist ambition was that Syria would come under British rule'; and on his arrival in Oxford as an undergraduate he delivered his maiden speech on the theme that the Eastern races should develop along Western not Eastern lines. Atiyah later revised his views in the light of British policy in Palestine, and became the secretary of the Arab Office in London after 1945; he was to die of a heart attack while addressing the Oxford Union in 1964 and trying to make himself heard above sustained pro-Israeli barracking.[23] Atiya's vivid autobiography provides a clear insight into the mixture of religious and political feeling that underlay the link between Lebanese Protestants and England and which was reflected in the affiliations of the merchant community in Manchester. That many of the children were called George, Albert or Victoria was also, in a small way, a reflection of this loyalty.

The oriental Jews who came to Manchester, although generically referred to as 'Sephardim', included both Sephardim in the proper sense of the term – descendants of Jews expelled from Spain and Portugal in the sixteenth century – and what were known as 'Babilim', Jews such as the Baghdadis, who were from communities which had been permanently established in the Arab world for millenia, since the time of the captivity. In Manchester they formed part of both the Middle Eastern and the much larger, and mainly Ashekenazi, Jewish communities.[24] Most of the Arabic-speaking Jewish community in Manchester were Sephardim, came mainly from Aleppo in what is now Syria and settled along with most other Sephardim in north Manchester, in contrast to the Ashkenazim who were to be found in both north and south of the city. It appears that in general the Jews assimilated much less to Manchester society than the Protestants did. If anything their assimilation was impeded by the fact that they felt acutely the difference between themselves and the Ashkenazi Jews. Even within the Sephardic Arab community, which included Jews from Aleppo, as well as about 14 families from Baghdad and a few Moroccan Jews, the distinctions were preserved. As the late Haim Nahmad put it to me: 'We Halabis [that is, people from Aleppo] did not mix with the Baghdadis and the Maghrebis.'[25]

When the great influx of Eastern European Ashkenazi Jews came to Manchester in the late nineteenth and early twentieth century the barriers were even greater. The Eastern Europeans pronounced Hebrew in a different way and spoke Yiddish, a language meaningless to the Arab Jews; the Sephardim included in their liturgy poems by the Andalusian Hebrew poets which the Ashkenazi did not. The latter referred to the Ashkenazis' Yiddish tongue as a jargon, and to the Eastern Europeans themselves as *ishlakhtiya*, apparently an Arabized conflation of the Yiddish words *schlach*, meaning 'a disorderly or messy person', and *schlecht*, meaning 'terrible'.[26] The Sephardim discouraged intermarriage between the Jewish communities and tried to keep the newcomers out of their synagogue. One Ashkenazi man was however admitted because he had an Andalusian name – Laredo: his family must therefore, it was felt, have been Arab at some time in the past. These social tensions were soon reflected in religious organization: two years after the founding of the Spanish and Portugese synagogue, in Cheetham Hill Road in north Manchester in 1872, the Aleppo Jews were expelled as heretics or

Karaatites, and established the separate Arab synagogue at Old Landsdowne Road in south Manchester.

By contrast the Arab Jews did maintain closer contact with other non-Jewish immigrants from the Middle East. Arabic was the common tongue of those immigrants, and in the Didsbury area of Manchester it was common to hear Arabic being spoken in the streets by people out walking on a Saturday or Sunday afternoon even after the Second World War. The older immigrants spoke an Arabic strongly infused with Turkish words: they said *tembel* instead of *kaslan* for 'lazy' or 'stupid', and *doğri* for 'straight'. The second generation members tended to have English as their first language, but many could understand Arabic even if they could not speak it, and the Arabic-speaking immigrants organized Arabic language classes to which Jews, Christians and Muslims all went. For some time it was the Sephardic Rabbi, Rabbi Mendoza, who gave the Arabic classes, and one second generation Aleppan Jewish immigrant, Mr Haim Nahmad, was to become the author of a standard work on written Arabic:[27] he was taught Arabic by his father, and kept an Arabic diary thereafter. In other countries of the Jewish diaspora, the Aleppo Jews have the reputation of being the ones who have continued to speak Arabic the longest, Arabic remaining the spoken language amongst Halabi communities in the New York area to this day.

A portrait of the broader Sephardic community in Manchester at the time is to be found in the memoirs of the Bulgarian writer Elias Canetti, who lived as a boy in Manchester from 1911 to 1913.[28] Although Canetti's family did not have any special ties to the Middle Eastern community, they formed part of the broader Sephardic immigration in the West Didsbury and Withington districts and, in the case of his mother's family, members of whom had moved to Manchester a few years earlier, exported cotton goods to the Balkans. Among the family friends remembered by Canetti was one from the Middle East:

The most mysterious one for me, when he first appeared, was Mr. Innie. He was darker than the others, and people said he was an Arab, by which they meant an Arabic Jew, he had only just recently come from Bagdad. I had *The Arabian Nights* in my head, and when I heard 'Bagdad', I expected Caliph Haroun in disguise. But the disguise went too far, Mr. Innie had gigantic shoes. I didn't like that, and I asked him why he had such big shoes. 'Because I have such big feet,' he said, 'would you like to see them?' I believed he was really about to take the shoes off, and I was scared.[29]

All the Arab immigrants were, whatever their degree of assimilation, conscious of the differences within their community and of the even greater one between their community and the outside. They established themselves in Didsbury very much in the style of their appropriate English counterparts, with large houses and gardens. They attended their places of worship, and on the appropriate days they visited each other – at Christmas, Eid, Tabernacle Day and so on. Social visiting after meals was also quite common: the men would drink coffee, play *ta'uli* (backgammon) and listen to records of Arabic music. By contrast, social mixing among first- generation immigrants and English families was less common. As Albert Hourani, son of Fadlo Hourani, put it to me: 'It was like a *millet*. Except that the English were the Muslims. They didn't visit us, and we didn't visit them. And you had to be careful because they could turn nasty at any moment.'[30] Food reflected both cultures – *kibbe* and *mujaddara* on Saturday, English roast and apple pie or milk pudding on Sunday.[31] Fadlo Hourani himself tried to send his three sons to the local preparatory school in Didsbury, but the school would not take 'foreigners' so he set up a school himself to which other Arabs, as well as some Ashkenazi Jews and English families, sent their children.

*'The Dodges of Levant and Syrian Traders': press reports in the 1890s*

Albert Hourani's observation about the environment that could, at any moment, turn nasty was never more evident than in the response of some local papers to a set of bankruptcies that occurred in 1892, involving a number of firms trading with the Ottoman empire and Egypt. There may or may not have been deliberate malpractice involved, but it is worth recalling that there had been a major stock market crash in 1891, and that one of the charges against the merchants was precisely that they had invested on the stock exchange money that should have been paid back to suppliers. How far the sentiments expressed in these reports were held by the Manchester population at the time is impossible to say, but it would appear legitimate to suppose that the very fact of their being voiced and letters to the press published attested to the confidence of the writers. One letter to the *Manchester City News* was published with the headline, 'The Dodges of Levant and Syrian Shippers'.[32] While the main brunt of these articles was directed at Jewish traders from the Middle East, and were therefore indicative of a general license for anti-Semitism, these Arab Jewish traders were also made to stand for all the suspicions which were directed at those originating in the Levant and the East. Of particular interest is the term of abuse used to apply to these bankrupted traders, 'Levanters', a word that seems to have disappeared from English usage in the meantime: the *Oxford English Dictionary* gives two distinct etymologies and meanings for this term. One is derived from the general term for the geographical area Levant, the other from the Spanish word *levantar*, to dismantle or break up a camp, and hence to run away. In the first sense, and apart from meaning a ship that trades with the Levant, as well as a wind, Levanter was a pejorative term for Levantine ('The Levant and the Levanters . . . are usually in need of cash'); in the second, originating in the seventeenth century, it meant 'one who absconds, especially after losing bets'. The late nineteenth-century usage of the Manchester press seems to have run the two together to produce a composite, dual term of abuse for someone suspected of financial misbehaviour.

The tone of this reporting was set in an article in the *Manchester City News* in early 1892 commenting on the recent incidence of bankruptcies:

> Some classes of Manchester traders have been hardly hit recently. There have been quite a number of failures of small shippers connected with the Cairo and Syrian trade, and a number of grey-cloth agents, job sellers, calico-printers, and bankers find themselves creditors with slight hope of any decent dividend. Most of those who have failed – and there seems to have been something like a ring of them – are a peculiar nondescript race, mostly descended from Jews expelled from Spain or Italy some two or three centuries ago. They now swarm over the various islands of the Mediterranean Sea, North Africa, Syria, and Egypt, and in course of time have got the bulk of the trading into their hands. They are a prolific race, and the business is generally managed by brothers on this side and brothers or cousins on the other. The consequence is that, when failures do occur, the assets are all on the other side – Cairo, Syria, or elsewhere – and in the very same hands so far as the debtors are considered. Very little remains to be done by English creditors but accept the meagre composition which these gentry can generally get 'a friend' to find . . .
>
> It is one of the peculiarities of Manchester trade that, be an Englishman ever so hard-working and honest, it takes a lifetime to gain even a

moderate credit, but let a foreigner of any race or clime come here and take an office, furnish it with a stool, inkstand, and blotting-pad, and paint on the door-cheek an unpronounceable name, and he is immediately given credit left and right and his miserable business keenly competed for.[33]

Similar views, including disparagement of the merchants' office furnishings, were expressed in a letter by 'A Keen Observer' to the same paper printed a few weeks later under the headline 'Reckless Credit to Foreigners in Manchester':

Amongst the many causes of bad and unprofitable trade in cotton goods there is one that I should like to call attention to, as being in my estimation and that of many gentlemen with whom I have come in contact, which is working ruin amongst Englishmen generally, and sapping the very foundations of all British home, family, and social prosperity and well-being. I refer to the idiotic and far reaching ruinous custom of manufacturers giving credit to foreigners, such as Armenians, Greeks, Arabs, Moors, German, and other mongrel Jews, Turk, and other itinerant tribes, to an extent that it is simply astounding when compared with the credit which they will give to solvent English traders . . .

What chance is there for an Englishman to get a faire return for his outlay and exertions whilst this state of things continues? An Armenian, a Jew, an Arab, or any other unconscionable foreigner, arriving in Manchester with about 1100 at his command, takes a dog-hole of an office, furnishes it with an ink-pot and an almanac, a brass plate on the door, and then he is a full-blown, highly respectable British shipper.[34]

When, later in 1892 and in 1893, some of the bankruptcy cases came to court, involving the firms of Bigio and Sciama, further details and hostile comment emerged. At the hearings on the firm of Bigio Brothers, held in August 1892, the details of the firm's history emerged: Saul Bigio had founded his firm in Manchester in 1862, his brother Joseph had joined him in 1865, and had then founded branches in Alexandria and then moved it to Beirut. Another brother had opened a branch in Aleppo and a third had opened one in Cairo.[35] The Sciama family had originally had their trading house in Aleppo but had later transferred their business to Cairo.[36] An article in *The Times*, from its Alexandria correspondent, reported that a group of nine firms were involved in a scheme to defraud Manchester merchants by shipping goods to related firms in the region, accumulating debts and then declaring themselves insolvent.[37]

These reports of commercial malpractice, and the court hearings themselves, were given especially hostile commentary in a weekly magazine, *Spy*, which appears to have specialized in anti-Semitic and xenophobic coverage, cartoons and gossip. Thus an article in May 1892:

> The character of these Levant Jews and Beyrouters was perfectly well known to anyone who knew anything about the print trade. Some printers were cautioned, but preferred to take their miserable orders against the judgement of their Manchester salesman, and have deservedly been 'let in'. I have only known three men in the Beyrout or Cairo trade whose word I would trust for a shilling.

The tone of *Spy* was one of innuendo: while its main focus was anti-Semitic, it included abusive coverage of 'Levanters' in general and even one disparaging reference to the Cheetham Park district of the city as 'the Manchester Lebanon'.[38] When in one issue the firm of Tasso was linked to the Jewish traders, and a correspondent wrote in to point out that the Tassos were Christians, *Spy* was not deflected:

> Moise Besso says Tasso is a Christian. I am obliged most regretfully to admit that he is, and also a naturalised Englishman. Tasso Brothers 'did' the Manchester banks to the tune of some 140,000 on false bills of lading and bous bills, and some calico printers and cloth agents to the tune of 120,000. But I may inform these creditors that Tasso Brothers have returned to their ancestral home amid the Syrian Highlands, some miles away from Beyrout, and are enjoying the best of health. I shall offer a few more observations on Levanters next week.[39]

The authors of these articles did not, however, have it all their own way. Correspondents wrote in to the local press to praise the contribution of the foreign merchants to the economy, and *Spy* itself was the subject of a libel suit by one trader, A. Besso, for allegations of financial misbehaviour it had printed. When the case came to court, in March 1893, *Spy* admitted its error and paid damages, and the judge spoke out strongly against the paper: 'It seemed to belong to a class of disreputable literature that always made his blood boil.'[40]

*Trade and the homeland*

Whilst in the first years the majority of the exports by Arab merchants in Manchester went to the Middle East, this changed as the nineteenth century wore on, by which time Manchester Arabs were exporting an increasing amount of their goods to other Lebanese-Syrian emigrants, in West Africa and in South America. The West African connection was especially important since, although the Lebanese there were numerically not as large – numbering a few thousand in each country – their position as traders was very strong given the previously low level of international commerce in that region.

The figure of the Arab trader in West Africa is well known to students of British literature, exemplified as it is in the person of the Syrian merchant in Graham Greene's *The Heart of the Matter*, and certain direct ties between the West African and Manchester communities certainly exist. One account of the West African community mentions a Saul Raccah, a Jewish merchant from Tripoli in Libya with a Lebanese wife whose brother was resident in Manchester in 1914 and who was instructed by the brother to establish a trading centre in Nigeria.[41] Aziz Kahale, a merchant whose grandfather came to Manchester in the 1870s and who was a trader for fifty years, confirmed to me in 1975 that a substantial part of his trade had been with West Africa. In a speech by the Lord Mayor of Manchester during a visit to Lebanon in 1962 to celebrate the hundredth anniversary of the arrival in Britain of Abdullah Tarad, believed to be the first Lebanese emigrant trader, he praised the Lebanese merchants for having 'opened the doors of West Africa' to British goods.[42] It was said by members of the Hourani family that they had invented the national dress of at least one former British colony in West Africa in order to secure a market for their cotton goods.

Yet despite this trade with Africa and the Americas the Arab merchants did not lose contact with their homeland, and most sent money back to their families and villages. As Mr Emile Abu-Fadil, a merchant in Manchester since the 1920s and Honorary Lebanese Consul since 1960, put it to me, 'None of us came here to make money in this country.' They were and remained Arab traders who never lost their links to their international markets or to their homeland. Mr Fadlo Hourani, for example, returned to his home village of Marjayun no less than twenty-four times in the course of his lifetime, and helped to finance a number of projects in his village: a cemetery improvement, a water provision scheme, electricity and a secondary school. The observatory in the American University of Beirut was also donated by a Manchester family. Many Arab merchants would go back to their country in order to acquire wives, and the links were such that some of the second generation children either returned to the Middle East or moved on from Britain to Arab communities in the Americas. Commerce and kin together maintained the links. One anecdote has it that, after 1918, the Dweik family from Aleppo were given the contract by the British government to design a headdress for the newly formed Arab Legion and that this is the origin of the red Palestinian *kaffiyah*, distinguished by colour from the blue garment worn by ordinary people at the time.

In political terms the evolution of the community reflected developments at home. It has been said of the Arabs in West Africa that, 'The *jaliyah* (community) is emotionally more involved with political events at 'home' than with these on the ground in West Africa'[43] and this was certainly also true to a considerable extent in Manchester. In the middle of the nineteenth century none would have considered themselves 'Arabs' or 'Lebanese', but as 'Syrians'. And as long as the Ottoman empire remained in control of their country, these Christian merchants were favourable to the idea of another colonial power, namely Britain, taking over in the area.[44] These aspirations were to find dramatic expression, and subsequent disappointment, in the World War that broke out in 1914.

### Didsbury and the Arab revolt: the Syrian Manchester Association

The idea of British suzerainty has been mentioned already in the context of Edward Atiyah's biography, and it was one that acquired practical relevance in World War I when the Manchester community for the first and only time in its history formed a communal organization, the Syrian Manchester Association (SMA). During the war the sons of some of the Arab merchants also joined the British army and as the British involvement in the Arab revolt increased two dozen or so of them were drafted as officers and interpreters onto Lawrence's staff. This active participation in the campaigns against the Ottomans further fuelled feeling in the community about the link between the British campaign in the Middle East and the freeing of their homeland from Ottoman rule.

The Syrian Manchester Association was in the first place organized as the Manchester Syrian Relief Committee, to provide assistance to those at home affected by the war, but from the middle of 1918 onwards it became more broadly involved in the mobilization of Syrian support against the Ottoman empire and in favour of a solution favourable to Syrian national aspirations in the post-war settlement. The official responsible for Middle East affairs, Sir Mark Sykes, records in an account of a visit to Manchester in June 1918 that the total Syrian community was around 350: most were Christians, but around 20 of the 120-odd members of the SMA were Muslims, and around 90 of the community as a whole were Jews from Aleppo and Baghdad. The main leaders of the SMA were Kahle, Jebara and Hourani. Sykes brought with him two officers from Syria itself, one of whom, Lt. Hosheymi, recited a nationalist poem to the gathering of SMA members:

> When he had finished there were many in tears, and Mr. Jebara, whose wife is English, and who is a typical Manchester man of some 30 years standing said to me, with the tears running down his cheeks: 'Sir Mark that young devil, has brought all my childhood back to me. I had forgotten my country and my people, I thought I was an Englishman only but I find I am a Syrian as well.'[45]

A list of twenty-nine of those supporting the SMA's campaign during the war is attached to Sykes' report: as he himself points out, the Jewish members of the community also backed the SMA's work at that time. A month later Fadlo Hourani, Secretary of the SMA, transmitted a memorandum to Sir Mark Sykes on Syrian support for the allied war effort:

> The members of this Association, composed entirely of Christians and Muslims, are unanimously of opinion that the time has now come when Syrians living abroad should make a determined effort to help the Allies in freeing their Country from the blasting rule of the Turks, and are resolved to spare no effort in bringing about this desired end.

The memorandum goes on to advise the British government to mobilize the support of Syrians who have emigrated to the Americas behind their war policy by building its policy on two propositions:

> A. To make a declaration which finds an echo in every Syrian heart viz:- that Syrians have had more than enough of the rule of the Turks, and are determined, God helping them, to bring this rule to an end . . .

B. to raise the cry 'Syria for the Syrians, under the protection of the Allies'. We believe that such a policy if supported by a clear declaration from Great Britain, France and the United States, promising autonomy for Syria under their joint protection and supervision, will act like magic on all Syrians, and will kindle their patriotism as nothing else will do, especially if it was made know that Recruits will be officered by their Countrymen under the High Command of the Allies.

Hourani reported that the SMA had already raised the sum of £5,000 to help send a mission to the Syrian communities in America to promote this policy.[46] It is not clear what the immediate British reaction was, but a note by Sykes in early August makes clear that he was not able to enlist French support for such a venture: 'I have submitted this to M. Picot. He does not seem much interested. If the French will not use honest, disinterested, people like these, and prefer their little coteries of Maronites and Parisians they will never make any progress.'[47] At this time hopes were pinned on a common Arab policy, in co-ordination with the British and French, under the leadership of Sharif Hussein of Mecca. In July messages were exchanged between the SMA and Sharif Hussein of Mecca. When Emir Feisal visited London in 1918 at the invitation of the British government four representatives of the Manchester community, including Fadlo Hourani, went to London to meet with him and to discuss further aid to the newly liberated areas: one of the other members of the delegation, Amin Habib al-Kisbani, returned with Feisal to the Middle East and travelled with him on his journey to Damascus.[48] The divergence of Arab aspiration and British policy was, however, already becoming evident and was well illustrated when the prime minister, Lloyd George, visited Manchester in September and received separate addresses from the three main communities concerned with Middle Eastern affairs – Armenians, Syrians and Jews. While the other two pleaded their particular cause, the Syrians congratulated the British government on the defeat of the Ottoman armies and voiced its hopes for the future:

We believe that the victory of the allied cause over the forces of barbarism will assure for our fellow countrymen, the liberty and prosperity which has been hitherto denied them. We await with impatience the hour of final triumph, when an emancipated Syria, Mesopotamia, and Arabia will be able to repay with solid alliance and friendship, the debt of gratitude which they will owe to their deliverers.[49]

A telegram to Allenby, upon the capture of Jerusalem, followed later in September, as did messages to Sharif Hussein from both the SMA and a group of Arab officers based at Grantham. However, a message from the SMA to be sent to Sharif Hussein in early October, discussing possible armistice terms with the Ottomans, was deemed unsuitable for transmission by the British military authorities, on the grounds that it trespassed on the negotiating prerogatives of the Allies.

The final round in the SMA's attempts to inflect British policy in the post-war settlement came with the convening of the Versailles conference in January 1919. In a letter to Foreign Secretary Balfour, four leading members of the SMA – Emile Kahle, chairman, H. Chiha, vice-chairman, N. Doki, treasurer, and F. Hourani, secretary – made a plea for a single, independent Arab state in the area. The letter begins with a definition of the geographical area encompassed by Syria, one that would include today's Syria, Lebanon, Jordan, Palestine/Israel and parts of Iraq:

> For the purposes of these remarks, Syria is the tract bordered North by the Taurus Range, East by the River Euphrates, South East by the confines of Arabia, South by Sinai and the Hijaz, and West by Sinai and the Mediterranean. In our humble opinion the whole of this country inhabited as it is by one people, speaking one language, and having the same customs and traditions, should be under one single administration . . . In reliance on the declaration repeatedly made by the Allied Statesmen and by President Wilson that one of the main objects of the War was to give small nationalities the right of self determination, we believe that it is the general wish of Syrians both at home and abroad to be granted independence under the guidance of Great Britain, France and the United States of America. With the help of these Powers to whom Syrians owe their liberation and preservation, we believe that the people can be guided to a right and happy future.[50]

The official reply, on behalf of Lord Curzon, gave little away: 'the question will receive the fullest consideration of His Majesty's Government in conjunction with their Allies at the forthcoming Peace Conference.' A hand-written note on the file suggested that the proposal for a larger Syria under tripartite protection might be welcomed as a way of heading off a French demand for sole control of the area. In the end, of course, history was to take a rather different path.

*Dispersal and decline*

The decline of the Moroccan community was, as we have seen, produced by the loss of their home market to Japanese goods and, with few exceptions, they left Manchester abruptly in the mid-1930s. The Lebanese-Syrian community declined for essentially similar reasons, but in a less clear-cut manner. After World War I there was in fact a small addition of around twenty Syrian families from Aleppo, but from then onwards the community began to drift apart: on the one hand the commercial prospects were less, and on the other, the second generation, anglicized in a way their parents could not be, moved out of trade and out of the community to become absorbed into British life.

There are three general patterns discernible in the second generation. One group decided that, with the decline in Manchester trade, they should move to more prosperous areas and they emigrated once again, to other areas where Syrian and Lebanese traders were active. The majority seem to have gone to the USA, where there is a community of over one million Arabs from the Syrian-Lebanese area, and a few went to West Africa. Another group of second generation Manchester Arabs returned to the Middle East: of the six children of Fadlo Hourani, four married spouses from the Middle East and two returned to live there, without breaking their ties to England. Very few of the Jewish families had members who went to Israel, but with the rising tide of anti-Zionism in the Arab world it was obviously improbable that any of them should return to their original countries.[51] Finally, a substantial portion of the Lebanese community remained in England, either as traders or in other walks of life.

In 1975 there were reckoned to be between twenty-five and thirty families of Arab descent still living in the Manchester area, and a few remained in the commerce sector. Some second generation Manchester Arabs acquired a reputation in other areas. The late Albert Hourani (1915–1993) was for three decades one of Britain's leading experts on the Arab world. Fred Majdalany (1913–1967) was a well-known correspondent, most famous for his account of the siege of Monte Cassino in 1944.[52] Although not directly from the Manchester community there were other people of Lebanese descent with prominent positions in British life: Michael Atiya, one of the two sons of Edward, became a prominent mathematician and later Master of Trinity College, Cambridge and President of the Royal Society, whilst Sir Peter Medawar, the outstanding scientist, was the son of a Lebanese merchant,

Nicholas Medawar, who had originally emigrated to Brazil and then later married an English wife, Edith Dowling.

The fate of the Manchester Arabs is closely paralleled by that of another 'Levantine' immigrant community, the Armenians. The Armenians were, as already noted, along with the Syrians and the Zionists, one of the three Manchester communities who petitioned the British government over Middle East policy at the end of World War I. Here too a combination of commercial decline and second generation dispersal has reduced what was once a closely knit entity. Some Armenian merchants still work from Manchester – the city was once known to have the best Armenian restaurant in the country – and one descendant of the Kouyoumdjian family became, under the name Michael Arlen, a well-known novelist. But in both cases the original forces leading to the creation of the community have long since ceased to operate and they have been too small in numbers to retain a visible identity once these conditions altered. To return to Albert Hourani's idiom of the English *millet*, one can say that the barriers have now come down and the confined minority has been absorbed into the wider 'English Muslim' world beyond.

*The body of the material in the above article is based on research conducted in the mid-1970s on behalf of the Arab League into Arab communities in Britain. The remaining part of this investigation, on the Yemeni community, has been published as* Arabs in Exile, Yemeni Migrants in Urban Britain, *(London, 1992).*

*I would like to repeat here my thanks to the Arab League office in London, and in particular to Muhammad Wahbi and Lakhdar Brahimi for their support in this work. I am also most grateful to a number of people with knowledge of the Manchester community and its context who have helped me at various stages of the research: in particular to the three members of the Manchester community, the late Emile Abu-Fadil, the late Albert Hourani and the late Haim Nahmad, for the very informative interviews they gave me in 1975-6, and to Ken Brown, Peter Sluglett, Bill Williams, Ayman al-Uri and Rohit Lekhi for assistance with other aspects of the research.*

# The Middle East at 2000: The Millennial Illusion

An attempt to sum up the state of the Middle East at the onset of the new millennium is hazardous indeed: we should long ago have abandoned any temptation to see the region as a single political or socio-economic whole or to collapse what are perhaps now more than ever contradictory trends. One of the great distortions to have beset the region – one replicated by western stereotyping and regional ideology alike – is that its politics and history can be explained by timeless cultural features, a Middle Eastern essence, rules of the game, or an 'Islamic' mindset.

The millennium, while reflecting one of the many cultural contributions which the Middle East has made to the rest of the world, is of course itself an ethnocentric concept: the incoming year is not 2000 for Arab Muslims, or for Iranians, or for Jews, or for Ethiopians. For them it is 1420, 1379, 5760 and 1992 respectively. Indeed the very dating of the beginning of the Christian era 2000 years ago is a fraud, since the census which compelled Joseph and Mary to leave Nazareth for Bethlehem was held either before or after that year, and most certainly not in the depths of the Palestinian winter. There is a moral here of some contemporary relevance: like so much in today's Middle East and the West that masquerades as God-given, traditional or natural, the dating of Christ's birth to December 0 is a result of retrospective state ideological invention, in this case of Emperor Constantine three centuries later.

Generalization about the region is all the more risky if it is linked to hopes, or anticipations, of a new era. As the new century opens, it may be salutary to recall the several occasions over the past hundred years when a 'new' Middle East was proclaimed: in 1918, when the Ottoman empire collapsed; in 1945, when Britain and France departed in earnest; in 1967, after the Six Day War, when radical movements began to challenge the 'petty-bourgeois' Arab regimes; in 1973, when Egypt forced Israel to negotiate and the Arab states used the oil weapon; in 1979, after the Iranian revolution, when 'Islam' was promised as a new, authentic means of liberation; in 1991, when a combination of the defeat of Iraq and the end of the cold war produced a new diplomatic and, it was hoped, economic climate. Each period of anticipation was followed by one of anti-climax, and often of despair.

## Enduring patterns

The briefest of surveys of the issues dominating the region reveals much that would have been familiar a decade ago, and which is likely to remain. This is so in four significant respects. First, the relationship between the Middle East as a whole and the world economy remains one of weakness and, in large measure, dependency. Oil apart, the region exports no major primary product, and what it does export it exports on terms of structural inequality. Only Israel, Turkey and to a lesser extent Tunisia have significant exports to the OECD states. In terms of food, the region is more and more dependent on imports. There is little capital investment, indeed the region hardly figures in third world discussions of Foreign Direct Investments, up from around $50 billion a decade ago to $250 billion now. On the map of globalization, except as a source of oil and investment funds, the Middle East hardly figures. Meanwhile environmental pressures, in multiple form, are growing: urbanization is producing overcrowded cities; cultivable land is neglected and/or used for other purposes; water reserves are falling; food sufficiency is declining; uncontrolled building scars landscapes and sea shores, and a tidal wave of garbage and plastic bags sweeps over parts of the region.

Secondly, relations between states and the societies they rule remain, in the great majority of cases, dominated by patterns of authoritarianism, complemented by elite theft of on average 30 per cent of state income, and an ideological resort to demagogy of a nationalist and/or religious character. On any indices of democratization or of human rights observance the Middle East ranks, as it has long done, at the bottom of international indicators. Token concessions to multiparty elections, controlled liberalizations of the press, internationally sanctioned privatizations and economic initiatives do not conceal the enduring failure of the majority of Middle East states to meet either the political or economic aspirations of their peoples. Turkey is a partial exception, but the authoritarian military apparatus at its core is now flanked by rival anti-democratic and regressive trends – the Islamism of the Virtue Party on one side and the ultra-nationalism of the National Action

Party on the other. In Iran a partial opening is taking place under Khatami, but remains hostage to the violence and repression of the clerical-security apparatus forged in years of revolution and war. In Israel a functioning democratic system exists for Israeli citizens: yet it has a long way to go to meet the minimal legitimate demands in terms of territory and sovereignty of the Palestinians, and is increasingly threatened by anti-secular and regressive tendencies within Jewish society itself. Elsewhere – in Syria, Iraq, Egypt, Libya, Saudi Arabia and Bahrain – matters remain much as they were a decade ago.

Thirdly, relations between the states of the region themselves remain dominated by suspicion, conflict and latent, when not overt, confrontation. Let us start with the dimension of economic cooperation which other regions of the world – not just Europe and North America, but parts of Latin America and also Southeast Asia – are developing. No one seriously talks, except at moments of lapsed realism, of economic cooperation between Middle East states. Earlier projects such as the Gulf Cooperation Council and the Arab Maghrib Union are stymied. The Arab Cooperation Council collapsed in 1990. Trade, investment, exchanges of know-how and goods between Middle Eastern states are very low. Private capital does not flow across frontiers but out of the region. Where states provide aid, and they do so to a decreasing degree, it is done as always as a function of particular interests and is liable to be directed, turned on and turned off as the donor state sees fit. Far from economic and financial flows being used to lessen political or security tensions, as liberal models might suggest, we see economic factors contributing to greater tensions between states. Turkey and its Arab neighbours to the south, and Egypt and the other Nile riparian states are among the most dramatic recent examples. Trade and investment have most certainly not acted as solvents in relations between Israel and Egypt, or the Arab world more generally.

In military terms, the region is one of the main areas – the Far East being the other – where expenditure and a sense of insecurity, far from decreasing with the end of the cold war, remain as high as ever. Relations between states are dominated by suspicion, a stance reinforced by popular attitudes on all sides in which memories of recent wars remain strong. In the Gulf, Iraq remains contained but resolute and vengeful, Saudi Arabia has embarked upon an arms purchasing boom, and Iran is systematically building up its military potential. Of greatest danger, the nuclear threshold is being crossed: Israel has an estimated 200–300 operational warheads, while others will note the example of the South Asia states which, in an act of supreme self-indulgence and folly, openly tested weapons in May 1998.

Fourthly, in terms of culture, individual freedom of expression and ideology the region remains under the sway of regressive and dictatorial structures. In the literature, popular music, cinema and, not least, political jokes of the region the signs of resistance are clear: here we find chronicles of the dishonesty of rulers, the cruelties of patriarchs, the idiocies of clerics, the ravages of inter-ethnic and social conflict. Anyone who thinks that the aspiration to gender rights, to a decent education or to honest government are some alien Western product has not read or heard this work.

Culture continues to show a vitality and distinctiveness which contrasts with the official surface of paralysis and domination. A press significantly more lively than that of earlier years can be seen in some Arab countries and in Iran. Satellite TV and the internet provide new outlets and sources for those wishing to defy conformity. Yet this cultural vitality contrasts with the protracted agony of official intellectual mediocrity as far as the future development of politics and society is concerned. The educational system is, from top to bottom, riven with control and inhibition. From Khomeini in his attack on Rushdie to Mubarak's attacks on publishing and teaching in Egypt, regimes easily resort to censorship of critical or independent voices in pursuit of cheap demagogic appeals.

In many countries a significant proportion of the intelligentsia has colluded with power and rather than challenge has reproduced official dogma and division: academics, historians, novelists and journalists have all reinforced the myths and paranoia of their rulers. On the one hand, there are regimes and many writers who remain fixed in a diluted national authoritarian mode inherited from the regimes of the cold war epoch. On the other, there are those who espouse a regressive Islamist anti-secularism, sometimes reformist, sometimes violent, which is less and less capable of grappling with the challenges of the modern world or of meeting the needs of their peoples. If one goes into any bookshop, or looks at any street newsagent, one sees row upon row of bearded men whose books, pamphlets and other ramblings provide much of the reading fodder of the young. Into this arena of transfixed stasis has now stepped a third candidate, a neo-liberal regional yuppiedom, mouthing marketing and IT verbiage and seeking to apply gimmicks from Western managerialism to the region.

*The onset of change*

Each of these trends has a dynamic that at once confirms the subjugation of the region to domination, internal and external, and provides opportunities for alternative, more democratic and peaceful futures. Notwithstanding a certain caution about invoking a 'new' Middle East, several trends suggest that even as older tendencies endure there are newer developments that may have their impact.

First, the people are changing, quite literally. At the top leaders who have dominated the region since the 1960s are leaving the scene. The faces are perhaps more vicious and determined that their predecessors, but perhaps not. At the bottom, the population is exploding, with the result that the majority are under the age of 25 and have little memory of the formative events before 1990. Therein lies, of course, both an opportunity and a danger: if they are not provided with decent economic and political conditions, and if they are taught by rulers and by demagogic oppositions to view the world in paranoid and confrontational terms, and to use history as an instrument for perpetuating hatred, they could easily lend support to chauvinist currents. If, on the other hand, the economic, intellectual and political challenges are met, then there is a possibility of moving beyond the politics of past decades.

Movement is also evident in the realm of ethnic identity and conflict. The successive waves of the post-1945 epoch – secular radical nationalism and Islamism – are both facing a challenge. So too are established definitions of identity in either idiom. The great fallacy perpetuated by the orthodox, whether nationalist or religious, is that identity can be defined and then frozen: to insist on this is to ignore the fact that all the constituents of identity – language, music, religion, dress, political community – change constantly in response to forces both internal and external. The Middle East is no exception.

In Iran twenty years of the Islamic Republic have led to a widespread debate on Iran's political and cultural future. A hundred voices are being heard. There is no certainty, and diminishing authority. In the oil-producing states of the Peninsula a new generation, connected to the internet and to international youth culture, no longer accepts the stifling pieties of Wahhabi and related orthodoxy. In Turkey, a cultural shift, challenging Kemalism, reinventing Ottomanism and, of considerable political significance, accepting the existence of a Kurdish identity, has developed since the early 1990s. In Israel a debate on Israeli identity and its relation to Jewish identity, on

Zionist history, on coexistence with Palestine has underpinned a political evolution.

The international context in which the Middle East is located has also changed. The end of the cold war produced two major shifts – the disappearance of the USSR as a significant strategic ally for Middle Eastern states, the emergence of a set of newly independent ex-Soviet republics along the borders of Turkey and Iran, and of an independent Ukraine on the other side of the Black Sea. Russia's two and a half centuries of contiguity with the Middle East, initiated by Catherine the Great, has ended. The former Soviet republics have provided neither the economic nor the political openings that many in the Middle East had expected: they are in the main isolated, authoritarian and poor. Yet the politics of pipelines on the one hand, and competition for different variants of nationalist and Islamic models on the other, have produced a new geopolitics in which all states – Turkey and Iran most obviously, but also Israel and some Arab states – are involved.

The relation of the Western world to the Middle East has also to some degree changed. To ascribe all the ills of the Middle East to the actions or inactions of Washington is facile: to argue consistently that alternative possibilities are preferable and practicable is not. In some respects, US policy remains fixed where it was a decade ago: there is still disproportionate indulgence of Israel and a willingness to condone authoritarian Arab regimes in the Gulf. The 1990s industry of certifying and election monitoring has been well learnt by Arab regimes. The US has failed to follow the initiatives which European states and Japan have taken with regard to Iran and Libya. On Iraq it has sought to contain any further Iraqi aggression while bolstering the autonomous Kurdish region and waiting for the moment, which no one can predict but many look forward to, when the Ba'thist regime finally cracks. In some respects, however, there has been a shift, and for the better: in contrast to the situation which prevailed for forty years after 1948, the US is now involved in a two-sided negotiation process that contains the possibility of Palestinian statehood. For all the limits of this engagement, and the general and justified criticism of the Oslo agreement, this is a situation far preferable to the climate of blank denial that prevailed in earlier times and is something which, whatever critics from afar may say, is appreciated in Palestine itself. On the largest single ethnic issue in the Middle East, that of the Kurds, there is also movement: the US is defending the Kurdish region of northern Iraq, in spite of the disagreements of the PUK and KDP with each other, and has for the first time called for recognition of the cultural rights of Kurds in Turkey.

## The vagaries of solidarity

Developments in the Middle East over recent decades, and the onset of new trends and uncertainties, pose a challenge not only to those who live in the region, but to those who engage with it from outside. Here too patterns of thought and commitment established in previous decades are open to question. The context of the 1960s and 1970s, in which my own perspective was formed, was one of solidarity with the struggles of peoples in the region and opposition to external intervention. That agenda remains valid: gross inequalities of wealth, power and access to rights – aka imperialism – persist. This agenda has at the same time been enhanced by political and ethical developments in subsequent decades. The struggles include of national groups (Palestinians, Kurds) oppressed by chauvinist regimes and of workers and peasants whose labour sustains these states (remember them), have been joined more recently by those struggling against gender oppression, suppression of press and academic freedom, and denial of ecological security. Recent developments have encompassed a more explicit stress on individual rights, in tandem with those of social groups. History itself and the changing intellectual context in the West has, however, challenged this emancipatory agenda in certain respects. On the one hand, oppression, denial of rights, military intervention are not the prerogative of external states: an anti-imperialism that cannot recognize and denounce forms of dictatorship and aggression indigenous to the region, or which seek, with varying degrees of exaggeration to blame them all on imperialism, is deficient. The Iranian revolution, Ba'thist Iraq, confessional militias in Lebanon, armed guerrilla groups in a range of countries, not to mention the Taliban in Afghanistan, represent as much and often a greater threat to human rights and to the principles in the name of which solidarity is originally formulated as does Western imperialism. Islamist movements from below meet repressive states from above in their conduct. What many people in the region want is not less external involvement, but a greater commitment by the outside world, official and non-governmental, to realizing rights that are now universally proclaimed.

At the same time, in a congruence of relativist renunciation from the region and critiques of 'foundationalist' and Enlightenment thinking in the West, doubt has been cast on the very ethical foundation of solidarity, a belief in universal human rights, and in the possibility of sustaining a solidarity based on them. Critical engagement with the region is now often caught between a denunciation of the West for failing to pursue more actively the democratic and human rights principles it proclaims, and a rejection of the validity of these rights codes and thus of any possibility of external encouragement of them.

This brings the argument back to the critique of Western policy, and of the relation of that critique with the policy process itself. On human rights and democratization, official Washington continues to speak in euphemism and evasion: the issue here is not to see all US involvement as inherently negative, let alone to denounce all international standards of rights as imperialist or ethnocentric, but rather to hold the US and its European allies to the universal principles they proclaim elsewhere. An anti-imperialism of disengagement serves only to reinforce the hold of authoritarian regimes and social practices within the Middle East itself. The challenge of the coming century for those concerned with the critical analysis of the Middle East as much as for those within it is, therefore, a double one: to formulate policies for the democratization and security of the region, while remaining in a resilient and informed manner engaged with the public debate outside.

At the centre of the concept of rights are two moral principles: the right to resist authoritarian and unjust power, and secondly, the moral worth of the individual. Both of these are, of course, inscribed in the value systems of the three great religions which have originated from and still flourish in the Middle East, even as those religions have been, and will continue to be, used to deny such rights. Generalized and in secular form, they can serve as a suitable basis for any prospective analysis of, and solidarity with, the peoples of the region. In this respect, at least, a recuperation of the past at the onset of the new millennium itself may serve a useful emancipatory purpose.

# Notes

*Introduction*

1. *Arabia without Sultans* (Harmondsworth: Penguin, 1974); *Iran: Dictatorship and Development* (Harmondsworth: Penguin, 1978); Fred Halliday and Hamza Alavi (eds.) *State and Ideology in the Middle East and Pakistan* (London: Macmillan, 1978); *Revolution and Foreign Policy. The Case of South Yemen 1967-1987* (Cambridge: Cambridge University Press, 1990); *Arabs in Exile. Yemeni Migrants in Urban Britain* (London: I.B.Tauris, 1992); *Islam and the Myth of Confrontation. Politics and Religion in the Middle East* (London: I.B. Tauris, 1996).

*Chapter 1*

1. Jack Donnelly, *International Human Rights* (Oxford: Westview Press, 1993); David Beetham, (ed.) 'Politics and Human Rights', *Political Studies*, vol. 43, special issue 1995, later issued in book form; Rein Mullerson, *Human Rights Diplomacy* (London: Routledge, 1997).

2. Raymond Plant, *Modern Political Thought* (Oxford: Blackwell, 1991) chapter 9; Chris Brown, *International Relations Theory* (London: Harvester/Wheatsheaf, 1992), chapter 3.

3. Alasdair MacIntyre, *After Virtue* (London: Duckworth, 1984); *Whose Justice? Which Rationality?* (London: Duckworth, 1988).

4. Stuart Hampshire, *Innocence and Experience* (Harmondsworth: Penguin, 1989), p. 78.

5. Michael Walzer, *Thick and Thin. Moral Argument at Home and Abroad* (Indiana: Notre Dame University Press, 1994), pp. 60-61.

6. Samuel Huntington, *The Clash of Civilizations and the Remaking of World Order* (London: Simon and Schuster, 1997), p. 316.

7. The issue of which regimes kill and torture more is not, of course, irrelevant if you are on the ground in one or other country. Thus if you have to chose between being ruled by Saddam Hussein or the Emir of Kuwait you may well find comparison relevant. It is also relevant if violations of rights are related to your ethnic origin. It is irrelevant, however, to the issue of whether or not rights, as defined by internal codes, have been violated by one regime or the other.

8. Fred Halliday, *Islam and the Myth of Confrontation* (London: I.B. Tauris, 1997). See also Anne Mayer, *Islam and Human Rights* (London: Westview, 1991).

9. Former Governor of Hong Kong Chris Patten when asked about the Asian values issue replied: 'I think the Asian values debate is piffle. What are these Asian values? When you hone in on what one or two Asian leaders mean by them, what they actually mean is that anyone who disagrees with me should shut up.'

10. John Rawls, 'The Law of Peoples', in Stephen Shute and Susan Hurley (eds.), *On Human Rights* (New York: Basic Books, 1993), pp. 59, 67.

11. For a critique that in some measure overlaps with this one, see Stanley Hoffman, 'Dreams of a Just World', *New York Review of Books*, 2 November 1995.

12. Charles Beitz, *Political Theory and International Relations* (Princeton: Princeton University Press, 1979); Brian Barry, *A Liberal Theory of Justice* (Oxford: Clarendon Press, 1973), chapter 12.

13. 'The Law of Peoples', p. 43.

14. Ibid, p. 63.

15. Walzer (*Thick and Thin*, chapter 4) uses the term 'tribalism' as an interesting alternative to 'nationalism', not least because unlike the concept 'nation' that of 'tribe' makes no claims as to democratic constitution. Those who live in societies dominated by tribes, e.g. Somalia, or by groups that pride themselves on behaving like them, e.g. Bosnia, might question the deference shown by liberal philosophers towards such institutions and their means of enforcing conformity.

### Chapter 2

1. Anthony Smith, *Theories of Nationalism* (London: Duckworth, second edition 1983), p. 21, gives a list of seven propositions that constitute the core doctrine.

2. Ernest Gellner, *Nations and Nationalism* (Oxford: Basil Blackwell, 1983), p. 1.

3. Isaac Deutscher, 'The Non-Jewish Jew', in *The Non-Jewish Jew and other Essays* (Oxford: Oxford University Press, 1968).

4. Elie Kedourie, *Nationalism* (London: Hutchinson, 1960).

5. Joel Beinin, *Was the Red Flag Flying There? Marxist Politics and the Arab-Israeli Conflict in Egypt and Israel, 1948-1965* (Berkeley and Los Angeles: University of California Press, 1990).

6. Deutscher, 'The Israeli-Arab War, June 1967', in *The Non-Jewish Jew*; Maxime Rodinson, *Israel and the Arabs* (Harmondsworth: Penguin, second edition, 1982).

7. Gellner, *Nations and Nationalism*; Tom Nairn, 'The Modern Janus', in *The Break-Up of Britain, Crisis and Neo-Nationalism* (London: New Left Books, 1977); Benedict Anderson, *Imagined Communities* (London: Verso, second edition, 1991).

8. On the roles of states in defining nationalism, see Fred Halliday and Hamza Alavi (eds.), *State and Ideology in the Middle East and Pakistan* (London: Macmillan, 1988); Amatzia Baram, *Culture, History, and Ideology in the Formation of Modern Iraq (1968-1989)* (London: Routledge, 1991).

9. See, for example, Richard Cottam, *Nationalism in Iran* (Pittsburgh: University of Pittsburg Press, 1964).

10. On Iraqi mobilization of anti-Persian sentiment, see Samir al-Khalil, *The Republic of Fear* (London: Hutchinson/Radius, 1989), p. 17.

11. Anthony Smith, *National Identity* (London: Penguin, 1991).

12. This is, broadly speaking, the argument advanced by Eric Hobsbawm in *Nations and Nationalism since 1780* (Cambridge: Cambridge University Press, 1990); for a

contrary interpretation of the Marxist tradition, see Erica Benner, *Really Existing Nationalisms* (Oxford: Clarendon Press, 1995).

13. *Der Judenstaat* in *Theodor Herzl's Zionistische Schriften*, edited by Leon Kellner, (Berlin-Charlottenburg: Judischer Verlag, 1912), p. 122.

14. Homeland, nation, community.

15. People, nation, Zion, land, redemption.

16. Herzl proposed a white flag with seven gold stars, the white area denoting a new, clean, life, the stars the seven golden hours of the working day (*Der Judenstaat*, p. 123).

17. Israel Gershoni and James Jankowski, *Egypt, Islam and the Arabs: The Search for Egyptian Nationhood, 1900-1930* (New York, 1986), and *Redefining the Egyptian Nation, 1930-1945* (Cambridge: Cambridge University Press, 1995).

18. Ervand Abrahamian, *Khomeinism. Essays on the Islamic Republic* (London: I.B. Tauris, 1993); Sami Zubaida, *Islam, the People and the State* (London: Routledge, 1989).

19. On the shifting emphases on internationalist, nationalist and religious themes in Iranian revolutionary thinking, see Wilfried Buchta, *Die iranische Schia und die islamische Einheit* (Hamburg: Deutsches Orient-Institut, 1997).

20. P.J. Vatikiotis, *The Middle East, from the End of Empire to the End of the Cold War* (London: Routledge, 1997).

21. For a wonderful fictional account of the rise and fall of nationalist sentiment, and of the relation of pan-Arab feeling to other, more specific and local loyalties, see the novel by the Saudi diplomat, Ghazi Algosaibi, *An Apartment Called Freedom* (London: Kegan Paul International, 1996). The novel is set between the rise of Nasserism and the separation of Syria in 1961.

22. Khalid Kishtainy, *Arab Political Humour* (London: Quartet Books).

*Chapter 3*

1. For the North, see J. Leigh Douglas, *The Free Yemeni Movement 1935-1962* (Beirut: American University of Beirut, 1987); Sultan Naji, 'The Genesis of the Call for Yemeni Unity', in B.R. Pridham (ed.) *Contemporary Yemen: Politics and Historical Background* (Beckenham, Kent: Croom Helm, 1984); for the South, T. Bernier, 'Naissance d'un nationalisme arabe à Aden', *L'Afrique et l'Asie*, no. 44, 1958; M.S. al-Habashi, *Aden* (Algiers, 1964); Ahmad Jabir Afif, *Al-Haraka al-Wataniyya fi al-Yaman* (Damascus: Dar al-Fikr, 1982); Joseph Kostiner, *The Struggle for South Yemen* (Beckenham, Kent: Croom Helm, 1984). My own *Arabia without Sultans* (Harmondsworth: Penguin, 1974) provides an early account of the nationalist movement in the South.

2. I am grateful to Anthony Smith for the term 'perennialist', the alternative, in his analysis, to 'modernism', as in the work of Gellner and Anderson. Smith categorizes himself as an 'ethno-symbolist'. For the development of his critique of 'modernism', see *National Identity* (Harmondsworth: Penguin, 1991).

3. See *Millennium, Journal of International Studies*, vol. 14, no. 2, summer 1985, for one survey of debates.

4. In Sami Zubaida (ed.), *Race and Racism* (London: 1978).

5. For standard Yemeni accounts, see Afif Jabir and Said el-Attar, *Le Sous-développement économique et social du Yemen* (Algiers, 1964).

6. Robert Stookey, *Yemen, The Politics of the Yemen Arab Republic* (Boulder: Westview, 1978), chapter 1.

7. 'Abd al-Muhsin Mad'aj al'Mad'aj, *The Yemen in Early Islam, a Political History* (London: Ithaca Press, 1988); Stookey; *Yemen*, chapters 2-5.

8. As in other cases, the attempt to identify a 'historic' territory lends itself to maximalist claims. The Yemeni geographer al-Hamdani born 280/893 gives Yemen land from south of Mecca to well into contemporary Oman.

9. Leigh Douglas, *The Free Yemeni Movement*, pp. 50-68.

10. See al-Habashi, *Aden*, for discussion.

11. Leigh Douglas, *The Free Yemeni Movement*, p. 216.

12. I have gone into this in detail in *Revolution and Foreign Policy, the Case of South Yemen, 1967-1987* (Cambridge: Cambridge University Press, 1990), chapter 4, 'The enigmas of Yemeni 'unity''.

13. On 1994, see Sheila Carapico, 'From Ballot Box to Battlefield: The War of the Two 'Alis', *Middle East Report*, September-October 1994, no. 190; Fred Halliday, 'The Third Inter-Yemeni War', *Asian Affairs*, June 1995.

14. Comparison may be made with a modernizing nationalism in other third world states that avoided colonial rule – Nepal, Afghanistan, Ethiopia.

15. On the role of the Arab Nationalists Movement in Yemen, see Sultan Ahmad 'Umar, *Nazra fi Tatawwur al-Mujtama' al-Yamani* (Beirut: Dar al-Talia, 1970); Joseph Kostiner, *The Struggle for South Yemen* (Beckenham: Croom Helm, 1984); Walid Kazziha, *Revolutionary Transformation in the Arab World* (London: Croom Helm, 1975).

16. See Sultan 'Umar, Kostiner and my *Arabia without Sultans*.

17. One major development in Aden was the building of the BP refinery between 1952 and 1954: this, by far the largest industrial project in the Yemen, was a direct result of BP's need to replace its refinery at Abadan, Iran, nationalized by Mosadeq.

18. Halliday, *Revolution and Foreign Policy*, pp. 105-107.

19. I am grateful to the distinguished Yemeni historian, the late Sultan Naji, for verbal elucidation on this point.

20. Thus in the founding document of the National Liberation Front, the 1965 Charter, the southern area is referred to as both 'South Yemen' and 'the Yemeni south' so that the very name of the organization is rendered alternatively as *al-Djabha al-Kawmiyya li-Tahrir Djunub al-Yaman al-Muhtall* (p. 64) and as *al-Djabha al-Kawymiyya li-Tahrir al-Djunub al-Yamani al-Muhtall* (p. 109): *al-Mithak al-Watani*, text agreed at first congress of the NLF, 22-25 June 1964, Aden, n.d.

21. In the aftermath of the 1994 inter-Yemeni war some people in the South began to reject the term 'Yemeni' and to describe themselves again as 'South Arabian'.

22. The evolution of terminology to denote the area reflected, as much as anything, contingent factors – colonial administrative policy and Arab nationalist influence. Anderson's account of colonial map-making (*Imagined Communities*, chapter 10) can be well applied to the Yemeni, indeed whole Arab, case. *Inter alia* this throws into question any claim that one Arab state is a 'historic' entity (e.g. Iraq) while another is not (e.g. Kuwait).

23. On the Jewish community in Yemen, see the chapters in Joseph Chelhod and others, *L'Arabie du Sud, histoire et civilization*, 3 vols (Paris: Maisonneuve et

Larose, 1984); Nini, Yehuda, *The Jews of Yemen*, 1800–1914 (Reading: Harwood, 1991).

24. In the immediate aftermath of Southern independence, in 1967, some Yemenis did assert this claim, but it was never sustained. A related dispute over the Kuria Muria Islands was also shelved (Halliday, *Revolution and Foreign Policy*, pp. 13, 21).

25. Among the ways in which Hadramaut does not conform is the fact that its inhabitants do not chew the narcotic leaf, *qat*.

26. Paul Dresch, *Tribes, Government and History in Yemen* (Oxford: Oxford University Press, 1989), pp. 389-391.

27. Summary of World Broadcasts, ME/2994/A/9, 7 February 1969.

28. Associates of former President Ali Nasir Muhammad, ousted in an inter-regime clash in 1986, reported in *al-Hayat*, 21 July 1994.

29. See Dresch, *Tribes*, especially Chapter 9, for a discussion of meanings of 'tribe' and shifting 'tribal' identities.

30. In the South, the revolutionary regime in 1967 banned the use of 'tribal' names to denote regions and instead, on the Algerian model of the *wilaya*, divided the country up into six *muhafazat* or governorates. This did not prevent people from continuing to use the 'tribal'/regional names and, in the 1980s, as part of an attempt to reduce the distance between regime and population the anterior names were restored.

31. Robert Burrowes, *The Yemen Arab Republic, The Politics of Development 1962-1986* (Boulder: Westview Press, 1987), chapter 5, 'Political adjustment and socioeconomic development under al-Hamdi: 1974-1976'.

32. *Hizb al-Wahda al-Sha'abiyya al'Yamaniyya*, 'al-Barnamij al-Siyasi', 1979. *Hizb al-Wahda* was the core party around which the larger National Democratic Front set up in 1976 organized. In 1990, following the unification of North and South, it merged with the Yemeni Socialist Party in the South.

33. For one other attempt to do this, in the case of Eritrean nationalism, see Fred Halliday and Maxine Molyneux, *The Ethiopian Revolution* (London: Verso, 1981), chapter 5. Against those (Ethiopians) who denied that an Eritrean 'nation' existed, and those (Eritreans) who claimed one had always existed, we sought to show the particular factors that led to the growth of a mass movement for independence in a region of nine ethnic groups created by Italian colonialism ('Eritrea' being the Greek for 'red').

*Chapter 4*

1. Part II, 'Humane Treatment', in 'Protocol Additional to the Geneva Conventions of 12 August 1949, and Relating to the Protection of Victims of Non-International Armed Conflicts (Protocol II), of 8 June 1977.'

2. Conor Gearty, *The Future of Terrorism* (London: Phoenix, 1997). See also his *Terror* (London: Faber & Faber, 1991) and his edited collection *Terrorism* (Aldershot: Dartmouth, 1996).

3. For one discussion in terms of Western law, see Tony Honoré, 'The Right to Rebel', in Gearty, (ed.), *Terrorism*. Within the Islamic tradition rebellion against those rulers guilty of oppression – *dhulm* or *istibdad* – is legitimate, as it is against those accused of betraying the principles of Islam – *kufr* or *ilhad*. For an eloquent summary of Western political traditions, see Fidel Castro, *History Will Absolve Me*,

a justification of the 1953 attack on the forces of dictator Batista, which ranged across mediaeval and modern Western thought.

4. Alex Schmid, in Alex Schmid and Albert Jongman, *Political Terrorism: A New Guide to Actors, Authors, Concepts, Data Bases, Theories and Literature* (Amsterdam: North-Holland Publishing Company, 1988).

5. I have analyzed US 'anti-terrorist' or preventive and 'counter-terrorist' or retaliatory policies, in Fred Halliday, *Cold War, Third World* (London: Hutchinson Radius, 1989), chapter 3. See also my entry on terrorism in Joel Krieger (ed.), *The Oxford Companion to Politics of the World* (New York: Oxford University Press, second edition, 1999).

6. Trotsky's 1920 text, *Terrorism and Communism*, was a reply to Karl Kautsky's 1919, *Terrorism and Communism: a contribution to the natural history of revolution*. The British translation was *In Defense of Terrorism*. See George Kline, 'The defense of terrorism: Trotsky and his major critics', in Terry Brotherstone and Paul Dukes (eds.), *The Trotsky Reappraisal* (Edinburgh: Edinburgh University Press, 1992).

7. An example of the distortion produced by such a perspective is contained in Edgar O'Balance, *Islamic Terrorism, 1979-95. The Iranian Connection* (London: Macmillan, 1997). O'Balance rightly identifies acts of political violence carried out by pro-Iranian groups – kidnappings in Lebanon, assassinations in Western Europe, bomb attacks in a number of countries. But in casting the net wide in search of a single international logic he includes groups which have no connection with Iran, such as the highly secular PKK in Turkey, and omits those groups that were organized by Iran's opponents – notably the Sunni fundamentalists in Afghanistan, backed by the USA and Pakistan, and the Mujahidin-i Khalq, supported by Iraq. For a scholarly treatment of the issue, see Mehdi Mozafhari, *La violence Shi'ite contemporaine, évolution politique*, Institute of Political Science, Aarbus, 1988.

8. Adrian Guelke, *The Age of Terrorism and the International Political System* (London: I.B. Tauris, 1995), chapter 3, 'The poverty of general explanations'.

9. Here I draw on Walter Laqueur, *The Age of Terrorism* (London: Weidenfeld & Nicolson, 1987) and Guelke, *The Age of Terrorism*.

10. João Quartim, *Dictatorship and Armed Struggle in Brazil* (London: New Left Books, 1971); Jorge Castañeda, *Utopia Unarmed. The Latin American Left after the Cold War* (New York: Alfred Knopf, 1993).

11. For one alarmed, but not necessarily alarmist, account 'The New Terrorism: coming soon to a city near you', *The Economist*, 15 August 1998.

12. 'Fight in the cause of God, those who fight you. But do not transgress limits, for God loves not the aggressors.' For a general discussion, see John Kelsay and James Johnson (eds.), *Just War and Jihad: Historical and Theoretical Perspectives on War and Peace in Western and Islamic Traditions* (New York, 1991).

13. Guelke, *The Age of Terrorism*, p. 17.

14. *Protocols Additional to the Geneva Conventions of 12 August 1949* (International Committee of the Red Cross, Geneva, 1977). Protocol II of 8 June 1977 concerns 'the Protection of Victims of Non-International Armed Conflicts'. The latter are defined in Article 1 (p. 90) as armed conflicts between a state and 'dissident armed forces or other organized armed groups which, under responsible command, exercise such control over a part of its territory as to enable them to carry out

sustained and concerted military operations and to implement this Protocol.' Article 4 (pp. 91-2) lays out the 'fundamental guarantees' concerning humane treatment.

15. The distinction *ad bellum/in bello*, despite its Latinate form, was developed in the League of Nations discussions of the 1920s and 1930s. See Robert Kolb, 'Origins of the twin terms *jus ad bellum/jus in bello*', *International Review of the Red Cross*, no. 320, September/October 1997.

### Chapter 5

1. In its earlier European usages, dating from the sixteenth century, the term 'republican' denoted a state in which power was vested in the people: this could, however, be consistent with monarchical rule, provided such rule was subject to popular, constitutional control. In its more recent usages, however, 'republican' has denoted a system inconsistent with monarchy.

2. 'Down with all the sheikhs and kings, and imams and sultans, and emirs and shahs in the Arabian peninsula and the occupied Arab Gulf.'

3. I apply the term 'monarch' not only to those contemporary Middle Eastern rulers who term themselves 'king', *malik* or *shah*, but also to other dynastic rulers – sultans, emirs, imams and, where they are dynastic rulers, sheikhs.

4. Mehdi Ben Barka, *Option révolutionnaire au Maroc* (Paris: Maspéro, 1964).

5. See Lisa Anderson, 'Absolutism and the Resilience of Monarchy in the Middle East', *Political Science Quarterly*, 106:1, Spring 1991; F. Charillon, 'La monarchie dans le monde arabe', *Revue Internationale de la Politique Comparée*, vol. 3, no. 2, October 1996. For perceptive studies of the Gulf, see Muhammad Rumaihi, *Beyond Oil. Unity and Development in the Gulf* (London: Saqi Books, 1986) and Jill Crystal, *Oil and Politics in the Gulf: Rulers and Merchants in Kuwait and Qatar* (Cambridge: Cambridge University Press, 1990).

6. 'During the Qajar reign monarchs had maintained a close connection with the people. Qajar shahs ruled according to old tribal habits and sat with the people at lunch or in the mosque – since they were after all worshipping the same God. The Pahlavis changed all that. Muhammad Reza Shah, like his father, was handed the crown and therefore lacked the tribal support that would have brought him close to the people. Unlike his father he grew up entirely sheltered and kept a great distance between himself and everyone else. The Shah's introversion , which eventually deteriorated into paranoia and egomania, was the fatal flaw in a man otherwise so conscious of his royal duties.' Manucher Farmanfarmaian, *Blood and Oil* (New York: Random House 1997), pp. 341-2.

7. On the emergence of the doctrine in France, see Albert Soboul, *The French Revolution 1787-1799* (London: New Left Books, 1974), pp. 77ff.

8. The term 'Hashemite' is derived from the name of the clan, the Banu Hashim, to which the Prophet Muhammad and Ali, his cousin and son-in-law, belonged.

9. *al-'amr bi al-ma'ruf wa al-nahy 'an al-munkar* Quran ; Quran 4.59.

10. Bernard Lewis, *The Political Language of Islam* (London: University of Chicago Press, 1988) , pp. 53-6; Ami Ayalon, *Language and Change in the Arab Middle East* (Oxford: Oxford University Press, 1987) pp. 32-42. The relation between kingship and property in the root *mlk* is not, however, specific to Arabic or to Islamic tradition. In the Western European context it is evident in the two meanings of the

word 'domain', both ruled and owned. In Chinese the word for 'country' means 'emperor's property'. Significantly, perhaps, there is no distinction in Arabic between the words for 'monarchy' and 'kingship' – *malakiyya* serving for both. Yet as this discussion of the contemporary Arab world shows only two of the eight monarchs, in Saudi Arabia and Jordan, are from their origins kings.

11. Leigh Douglas, *The Free Yemeni Movement, 1935–1962* (Beirut: American University of Beirut, 1987).

12. The standard Quranic term for an idol is *wathan*, hence the term *wathani* meaning pagan or idolater; *taghut* is, however, another term for idols, often wrongly conflated in its root with the word *taghin*, meaning a 'tyrant'. Khomeini saw his role as 'smasher' of idols. In Persian the word for idol is *bot*, and hence one of Khomeini's official titles was *bot-shekan*, the idol-smasher. Thus beyond being applied to all associated with the Shah's regime, *taghut* was attached to four people in particular: the Shah himself, US President Carter, Abol-Hasan Bani-Sadr, the first president of the Islamic Republic who broke with Khomeini in 1981, and Saddam Hussein. Khomeini considered that he had smashed the first three, but the fourth proved harder to deal with.

13. Aziz al-Azmeh, *Muslim Kingship, Power and the Sacred in Muslim, Christian and Pagan Polities* (London: I.B. Tauris, 1997).

14. Joseph Kostiner, *The Making of Saudi Arabia, 1916-1936. From Chieftaincy to Monarchical State* (Oxford: Oxford University Press, 1993).

15. Susan Meiselas, *Kurdistan In the Shadow of History* (New York: Random House, 1997, pp.64-73).

16. Bernard Lewis, *The Emergence of Modern Turkey* (Oxford: Oxford University Press, 1961), pp. 251-3.

17. P.J. Vatikiotis, 'Royals and Revolutionaries in the Middle East', *Middle East Lectures 2*, (Moshe Dayan Centre, Tel Aviv University, 1997).

18. Ghazi Algosaibi, *An Apartment Called Freedom* (London: Kegan Paul International, 1996).

19. One partial qualification is that of the Arif brothers in Iraq: after the death of President Abd al-Salam Arif in 1966 he was replaced by his brother, Abd al-Rahman, himself ousted by the Ba'th in 1968.

20. Although it did resurface, in what one may also assume was a mistaken testimony to the demonstration effect of the Shah's experiment, as a party in post-1991 Tajikistan.

21. The fate of others who have tried this – Jean-Claude Duvalier in Haiti, Bokassa in the Central African Republic, before that Napoleon – might also serve to discourage.

22. P.J. Vatikiotis writes in *The Middle East from the End of Empire to the End of the Cold War*, (London: Routledge, 1997), pp. 203-5, of literature that appeared in the late 1980s in Egypt setting Farouk in a more favourable light.

23. In Judaism monarchy has a religious association: God is the 'King of Kings', *melekh malkhia ha-mlakhun*. In contemporary Hebrew the term *melekh* is used as a generic term of praise, be it of political leaders or football heroes. I am grateful to Joseph Kostiner for this information.

*Chapter 6*

1. For example, in Ervand Abrahamian's classic study, *Iran Between Two Revolutions* (Princeton: Princeton University Press, 1982) there is no mention of Iraq. Equally, in Hanna Batatu's study of the Iraqi revolution of 1958, *The Old Social Classes and the Revolutionary Movements of Iraq* (Princeton: Princeton University Press, 1978), there is virtually no mention of Iran. These silences are an accurate reflection of events at the time discussed.

2. Samir al-Khalil, *The Monument. Art, Vulgarity and Responsibility in Iraq* (London: André Deutsch, 1991); Amatzia Baram, *Culture, History and Ideology in the formation of Ba'thist Iraq, 1968-89* (London: Macmillan, 1991).

3. 'By drinking the milk of camels, and eating lizards, the Arabs have reached such a state that they aspire to capture the crown of Persia.' The derogatory Iranian expression for peninsula Arabs, *mushkhor* (mouse-eaters) is in similar vein.

4. On this historical background, see Jasim Abdulghani, *Iraq and Iran. The Years of Crisis* (London: Croom Helm, 1984); Keith McLachlan, *The Boundaries of Iran* (London: University College London Press, 1994).

5. For a perceptive discussion of the usages, and suppressed racist connotations, of *shu'ubiyya*, see Samir al-Khalil, *Republic of Fear* (London: Hutchinson/Radius, 1989), pp. 216-20.

6. Saddam was also another one of the 'idols' which the Imam, officially titled *bot-shekan* (idol-smasher) set out to smash.

7. Among many examples, *hich* (nothing) *chare* (remedy), and the half-Persian, half-Arabic *khoshwalad* (good guy).

8. The Kurds qualify for inclusion in the Persian sphere of cultural influence above all by the fact that they celebrate the Persian New Year, *nourouz*, the Zoroastrian festival.

9. Ernest Gellner, *Nations and Nationalism* (Oxford: Basil Blackwell 1983); Benedict Anderson, *Imagined Communities* (London: Verso, 1983).

10. This anti-Arab orientation was no means confined to the official ideologists of the state. From the early nineteenth century onwards Iranian writers identified the source of their country's backwardness with the influence of the Arabs and Islam on their country. Ahmad Kasravi, a twentieth-century theorist of secular nationalism, also sought to locate the backwardness of Iran in the influence upon the Persian peoples of Arab and other, such as Turkish, cultures.

11. Samir al-Khalil, *Republic of Fear*, pp. 152-160. Al-Husri also argued against the possibilities of Muslim unity, counterposing it to a more desirable and attainable Arab unity: in Sylvia Haim (ed.), *Arab Nationalism. An Anthology* (Los Angeles: University of California Press, 1964), pp. 147-154.

12. Shahram Chubin and Sepehr Zabih, *The Foreign Relations of Iran* (London: University of California Press, 1974), chapter IV, 'Iran-Iraq Relations'. Graphic illustration of how much Iraq concerned the Iranian regime can be found in the diaries of the royal adviser, Asadollah Alam, *The Shah and I* (London: I.B. Tauris, 1991). These cover the years 1969-75.

13. Majid Khadduri, *Republican Iraq* (London: Oxford University Press, 1969), pp. 181-5.

14. *Republic of Fear*, p. 17, n. 21. According to Tulfah, Persians are 'animals God created in the shape of humans'.

15. Abdulghani, *Iran and Iraq*, pp. 77-78.

16. Chubin and Zabih, *Foreign Relations of Iran*, chapters V-VII; Fred Halliday, *Iran: Dictatorship and Development* (London: Penguin, 1978), chapter 9.

17. R. K. Ramazani, *Revolutionary Iran. Challenge and Response in the Middle East* (London: Johns Hopkins University Press, 1988) chapter 4. Ramazani argues, persuasively, that it was the fall of the more cautious Bazargan government in November 1979 which precipitated the more militant phase of Iran's policy towards Iraq.

18. 'Never Invade a Revolution' ran the editorial in *The Times* on 1 October 1980, soon after the outbreak of hostilities. For analysis, see references in note 19, and al-Khalil, *Republic of Fear*, 'Conclusion'.

19. The war lasted seven years and eleven months, two months less than the Sino-Japanese war of 1937-45. Among general accounts, see Shahram Chubin and Charles Tripp, *Iran and Iraq at War* (London: I.B. Tauris, 1988); John Bulloch and Harvey Morris, *The Gulf War. Its Origins, History and Consequences* (London: Methuen, 1989).

20. Fred Halliday, 'Iranian Foreign Policy Since 1979: Internationalism and Nationalism in the Islamic Revolution', in Juan Cole and Nikki Keddie (eds.) *Shi'ism and Social Protest* (London: Yale University Press, 1986).

21. On the Iraqi Shi'ite opposition, see Hanna Batatu, 'Shi'a Organizations in Iraq: al-Da'wah al-Islamiyah', in Cole and Keddie (eds.), *Shi'ism and Social Protest*.

22. See Chubin and Tripp, *Foreign Relations of Iran*.

23. See Ramazani, *Revolutionary Iran*, Chapter 3; and 'Iran and the Gulf Arabs', *Middle East Report*, no. 156, vol. 19, no. 1, January-February 1989.

24. Faleh Abd al-Jabbar, 'Why the Uprisings Failed', *Middle East Report*, no. 176, vol. 22, no. 3, May/June 1992, pp. 3-4.

25. Among many analyses, Lawrence Freedman and Efraim Karsh, *The Gulf Conflict 1990-1991*, (London: Faber and Faber, 1992); Amatzia Baram and Barry Rubin, *Iraq's Road to War* (London: Macmillan, 1994); Fred Halliday, 'The Gulf war 1990-1991 and the study of international relations', in *Islam and the Myth of Confrontation*.

26. In itself a debt of $80 billion, roughly half owed to Arab states and half to Western and Soviet institutions, was not catastrophic: Iraq had plenty of oil reserves against which to pledge repayment, and the Arabs had no way of enforcing repayment of their share. But any such arrangements would have involved international agreements and monitoring of Iraqi finances to which Saddam was opposed.

27. Hooshang Amirahmadi, 'Iran and the Persian Gulf Crisis', in Hooshang Amirahmadi and Nader Entessar (eds.) *Iran and the Arab World* (New York: St. Martin's Press, 1993); Said Amir Arjomand, 'A Victory for the Pragmatists: The Islamic Fundamentalist Reaction in Iran', in James Piscatori (ed.) *Islamic Fundamentalisms and the Gulf Crisis* (Chicago: American Academy of Arts and Sciences, 1991).

28. Anthony Cordesman, *Iran and Iraq: The Threat from the Northern Gulf* (Oxford: Westview Press, 1994).

29. Geoffrey Kemp, *Forever Enemies? American Policy and the Islamic Republic of Iran* (Washington: the Carnegie Endowment, 1994); Fred Halliday, 'An Elusive

Normalization: Western Europe and the Iranian Revolution', *The Middle East Journal*, vol. 48, no. 2, Spring 1994.

30. Even if, in a longer-term perspective, such a second Islamic Republic would be most unlikely to enjoy good relations with Iran: one could envisage that, after initial protestations of eternal Islamic fraternity, a revolutionary Islamic Iraq would find itself at odds with Tehran, a Shi'ite China to Tehran's Moscow.

*Chapter 7*

*Note: An earlier version of this chapter was given at the conference on the contemporary Mediterranean held at the University of Malta, in December 1989, and subsequently published in Stanley Fiorini and Victor Mallia-Milanes (eds), Malta: A Case Study in International Cross-Currents (Valetta, 1991).*

1. Clare Hollingsworth, 'Another Despotic Creed Seeks to Infiltrate the West', *International Herald Tribune*, 9 September 1993; ; Samuel Huntington, 'The Clash of Civilizations', *Foreign Affairs*, summer 1993. For analysis of this issue, see James Esposito, *The Islamic Threat, Myth or Reality?* (Oxford: Oxford University Press, 1992); Ghassan Salamé, 'Islam and the West', *Foreign Policy*, no. 90, Spring 1993; Fred Halliday, 'Western Europe and the Middle East: the Myth of the Islamic Challenge', in Beverly Crawford and Peter Schulze (eds.), *European Dilemmas after Maastricht*, (Berkeley, Calif: Centre for German and European Studies, University of California, 1993). I have tried to produce my own, non-essentialist, analysis of hostility to 'Islam' in 'Anti-Muslimism in Contemporary Politics: One Ideology or Several?', in *Islam and the Myth of Confrontation*.

2. Perhaps the most commonly invoked symbol of all for Western intrusion into the Muslim world is that of 'crusader' (*salibi*). It is, however, worthy of note that during the 1991 war between Iraq and the USA over Kuwait the term used in Iraqi propaganda was Hulagu, the Mongol conqueror of Baghdad in 1258. In the Yemeni war of the 1960s the royalists often attacked the Egyptians as 'Pharoahs', leading on some occasions to reports of attacks by 'Pharaonic aircraft' on tribal positions.

3. For an excellent discussion, see Olivier Roy, *L'echec de l'Islam politique*, (Paris: Seuil, 1992); Reinhard Schulze, 'Muslimische Intellektuelle und die Moderne' in Jochen Hippler and André Lueg, *Feinbild Islam*, (Hamburg: Konkret Literatur Verlag, 1993).

4. As Nikki Keddie has pointed out the terms 'fundamentalism', 'Islamism', 'integrism' are used almost interchangeably in current writings on movements that apply Islamic concepts to politics. All have their problems: fundamentalism presupposes a return to first principles but the question of what constitutes those first principles may be disputed. The key issue is that movements of this kind seek to mould society and the state according to what they claim to be Islamic principles.

5. On North Africa, see the work of Roy and Esposito; also Francois Burgat, *L'islamisme au Maghreb, La voix du Sud*, (Paris: Karthala, 1988); *L'Algerie par ses islamistes* (Paris; Karthala, 1991).

6. James Piscatori (ed.), *Islamic Fundamentalisms and the Gulf Crisis* (Chicago: American Academy of Arts and Sciences, The Fundamentalism Project, 1991).

7. On Islamic communities in Western Europe, see G. Kepel, *Les Banlieues de l'Islam* (Paris, 1988), T. Gerholm and Y. Georg (eds.) *The New Islamic presence in Western Europe* (London, 1988), and Jorgen Nielsen, *Muslims in Western Europe* (Edinburgh: Edinburgh University Press, 1992). See also my review article, 'The Struggle for the Migrant Soul', *Times Literary Supplement*, 14-20 April 1989, in which I discuss the Rushdie affair and political uses made of it. On the ramifications of the Rushdie affair, L. Appignanesi and S. Maitland, *The Rushdie File* (London, 1989), and M. Ruthven, *A Satanic Affair: Salman Rushdie and the Rage of Islam* (London: Chatto & Windus, 1990).

8. For further analysis of the Iranian case, and comparisons with Pakistan, Israel and Arab states, F. Halliday and H. Alavi (eds.), *State and Ideology in the Middle East and Pakistan* (London, 1988). In my chapter on Iran in this book, I have developed an account of the causes of the Iranian revolution. For my earlier study of the Shah's regime and its internal contradictions, see *Iran: Dictatorship and Development* (Harmondsworth: Penguin, 1978).

9. For comparative studies, see Martin Marty and R. Scott Appleby, *Fundamentalisms Observed* (Chicago: American Academy of Arts and Sciences, the Fundamentalism Project 1991); David Landau, *Piety and Power: The World of Jewish Fundamentalism* (London: Secker, 1993).

10. For one of the most lucid expositions of this contingency, see Sami Zubaida, *Islam, the People and the State* (London: Routledge, 1989).

11. Islamist movements from below are covered in E. Burke III and I. Lapidus (eds.), *Islam, Politics and Social Movements* (London, 1988) and in Halliday and Alavi, *State and Ideology.*

12. For analysis, see Zubaida, *Islam, the People and the State*; Ervand Abrahmanian, *Khomeinism, Essays on the Islamic Republic* (London: I.B. Tauris, 1993); Paul Vieille and F. Khosrokhavar, *Le discours populaire de la révolution iranienne* (Paris: Contemporanéité, 1990).

13. Text of Khomeini's letter to Khamene'i in *BBC Summary of World Broadcasts*, part 4, 8 January 1988. For analysis, see J. Reissner, 'Der Imam und die Verfassung', *Orient*, 29, 2, June 1988. Khomeini's theorization of how an Islamic State can, for reasons of state interest, override religious precepts has an ironic relevance to the Rushdie affair: Iranian and other defenders of the death sentence on Rushdie claim that Khomeini's condemnation of Rushdie to death cannot be overridden because it is necessitated by religious principle. Application of Khomeini's *maslahat* principle would suggest that, if Iranian political leaders thought it was in their interests to do so, they could cancel the death sentence. That they do not so is not because of some religious compulsion but because, within the politics of the Islamic world, it is still profitable for them to maintain their stance.

14. On Iranian foreign policy since 1979 and the place within it of Islamic themes, see my 'Iranian Foreign Policy Since 1979: Internationalism and nationalism in the Islamic Revolution', in J. Cole and N. Keddie (eds.), *Shi'ism and Social Protest*, (New Haven, 1986).

15. The concept of *zuhd* or austerity, often associated with forms of mysticism, was important in Khomeini's rhetoric and fused conveniently with the anti-

consumerism of third world populist and revolutionary ideology. In some ways Khomeini's use of anti-imperialist *zuhd* was analogous to the usage of the concept by the Imam of Yemen who in the 1950s declared that Yemen would prefer to be poor and independent than rich and dependent. How far the Iranian or Yemeni people were committed to such austerity was and is another matter.

16. For the Tunisian background, see the work of Esposito and Burgat; N. Keddie, 'The Islamist Movement in Tunisia', *The Maghreb Review*, vol. 11., no. 1, 1986; C. Moore, *Tunisia since Independence* (Berkeley, 1965); N. Salem, *Habib Bourguiba, Islam and the Creation of Tunisia* (London, 1984).

17. Interview with Ghannoushi in the Tunisian weekly, *Realités*, 192, 21-27 April 1989. Further Islamist critiques of the Ben Ali regime reported in *Le Monde*, 9 June, 5 September, 10 November, 6 December 1989.

18. The trial of those arrested, held a year later, seemed to indicate that the coup attempt had not been as serious as claimed at the time; some of the defendants were released, whilst others received unexpectedly light sentences (*Le Monde*, 19 January 1994).

19. This was classically the case in the Iranian revolution: the Islamists allowed the left to ally with them in the initial revolutionary period and then isolated and destroyed them one by one.

20. On the 'modernity' of Khomeini's theories and the contemporary preconditions for the emergence of his movement, see the very perceptive study by Zubaida, *Islam, the People and the State*.

21. For a critique of contemporary Islamism from within the Muslim world, and the weakening of Islamic society and culture it entails, A. Akbar, *Discovering Islam, Making Sense of Muslim History and Society* (London, 1988).

*Chapter 9*

1. Technically the English translation of the state, the Kingdom of Saudi Arabia, is misleading. There is no Arabic word corresponding to English 'Arabia' – it is normally referred to as *al-jazira*, 'the peninsula'. The title of the country *al-mamlaka al-arabia al-saudia* literally means 'the Arab Saudi Kingdom'.

2. Hasan Abdulla al-Qurashi, *Spectres of Exile* (Echoes); Abd al-Rahman Munif, *Cities of Salt* (Vintage); Ghazi Algosaibi, *An Apartment Called Freedom* (Routledge).

3. *Voices of Change, Short Stories by Saudi Arabian Women Writers* (Lynne Reinner).

*Chapter 11*

1. The painting, a spirit fresco on canvas which was then plastered to the wall, is in the Royal Exchange building in London and is considered to be one of Leighton's less distinguished works. He himself had visited Egypt, Greece and Syria in the 1860s and 1870s, and developed an interest in the Middle East that was also evident in the Arab room at Leighton House, West London.

2. A. Redford, *Manchester Merchants and Foreign Trade*, (Manchester 1934), vol. 1, p. 199.

3. A listing of foreign merchants trading in Manchester, compiled up to 1870 on an annual basis, is to be found in *Scholes Manchester Foreign Merchants*, Manchester Central Library, MS FF 382-S35. Scholes distinguishes only between Turkish and Moroccan traders, the former comprising anyone from the Ottoman empire,

irrespective of place of origin or religion. The first house he records was that of Abdullah Yalibi, established in 1833, but by the mid-1860s there are over thirty: the listing for 1864 gives twenty-five 'Turkish', including several Armenians. His cut-off date, 1870, precedes the largest influx of Lebanese/Syrians.

4. As reported by Mr Emile Abu-Fadil: interview with author, Manchester, October 1975.

5. *The Condition of the Working Class in England* (1844). Friedrich Engels visited Manchester first in 1843 to work in his father's firm, and managed it from 1850 to 1870.

6. Roger le Tourneau, *Fès avant le Protectorat* (Casablanca 1949), p. 433.

7. Albert Hourani gives the 1830s date, while the first Moroccan house listed in Scholes is that of Isaac Pariente, 1847.

8. Louis M. Hayes, *Reminiscences of Manchester, And some of its Local Surroundings from the Year 1840,* (London: Sherratt & Hughes, 1905), pp. 205-12.

9. Hayes, *Reminiscences of Manchester*, p. 209, gives several names of these traders, as follows: Luarzazi, Elofer, Benquiran, Lehluh, Benabsolam, Dris, Benassi, Benani, Guessus, Lushi, Meecoe, Bombar, Larashe, Benmassoud. From Fasi sources cited by Le Tourneau we have the names of at least seven of these merchants, in the following spellings: Ben Khalef, Mefdhel ben A'ist, El Hajj bin Naser bin Nani, Si Mohammed Qesous bin Bou Bakr, Ahmed bin Jelloul, Si Mohammad Felloul, Si Abdel Ghani Kabbaj, in Le Tourneau, *Fès avant le Protectorat*, p. 446.

10. *Manchester City News*, 2 October 1936.

11. Abd al-Majid bin Jilloun, *Fi al-Tufula* (Maktabat al-Ma'arif, Rabat, n.d.)

12. *Manchester City News*, 2 October 1936.

13. One member, John Abulafia, became a fiction writer, see *Introduction 6:* stories by John Abulafia and others, (London: Faber, 1977).

14. Scholes lists a Paul and Peter Cababe as having started buisness in 1840, while his first 'Turkish' entry is Abdullah Yalibi, 1933.

15. Scholes first mentions Turadh in his list for 1865, with the date of establishment of his firm as 1862. For the general background on Turad, see Fadlo Hourani, 'Nubdha Ta'rikhiyya min Hayyat al-Jaliyyya al-Suriyya fi Manchester', *al-Mustami' al-Arabi*, vol. 1, no.3, p. 4. On Tarad and the centenary celebrations of his arrival in Manchester, see note 31 below.

16. R. Bayley Winder, 'The Lebanese in West Africa', in L. A. Fallers (ed), *Immigrants and Associations* (Paris, 1967) p. 103.

17. Elie Safa, *L'émigration Libanaise*, (Beirut, 1960).

18. See report by Sir Mark Sykes, note 28 below.

19. See Safa, *L'émigration Libanaise*, and Nadim Shehadi and Albert Hourani, *The Lebanese in the World* (London: I. B. Tauris, 1993).

20. Edward Atiyah, *An Arab Tells his Story* (London, 1946), p. 2.

21. Two of Edward Atiyah's sons were to have noted academic careers. Sir Michael Atiya (b. 1929) became a mathematician, and was President of the Royal Society and Master of Trinity College Cambridge; Professor Patrick Atiyah (b. 1931) became Professor of English Law at the University of Oxford.

22. Atiyah, *An Arab Tells his Story*, p. 27.

23. The author was present on that occasion. It was his first visit to the Oxford Union, and the first time he had heard a public discussion of the Arab-Israeli question.

24. On the general background to Jewish settlement, see Bill Williams, *The Making of Manchester Jewry, 1740-1875*, (Manchester: Manchester University Press, 1976); and Bill Williams, *Manchester Jewry. A pictorial history 1788-1988*, (Manchester, Archive Publications, 1988). In *The Making of Manchester Jewry*, table 12, p. 354, gives the names of the founder members of the Sephardi Spanish and Portugese Synagogue at 190 Cheetham Hill in 1872. The synagogue was built in a Moorish style and, with its reopening as the Manchester Jewish Museum in 1984, has been restored to its original form. Williams also identifies those who broke away to form the south Manchester 'Arab' synagogue at Old Landsdowne Road in 1874: Abadi, Bensaud, Besso, Bianaco, Bigio.

25. Haim Nahmad: interview with authors, Oxford, 30 October 1976.

26. The term *schlecht* was also used amongst Sephardim in Cairo to refer to the Ashkenazis, apparently because the latter used the term amongst themselves to refer to local inhabitants, and were then categorized by the Sephardim in the same way: I am grateful to Claudia Roden for this point.

27. H.M. Nahmad, *From the Arabic Press, A language reader in economic and social affairs*, (London: Lund Humphries, 1970).

28. Elias Canetti, *The Tongue Set Free*, (London: Picador, 1989), pp. 35-75.

29. Canetti, *The Tongue Set Free*, pp, 51-2.

30. Albert Hourani: interview with author, Oxford, October 1975.

31. Cecil Hourani, *An Unfinished Odyssey: Lebanon and Beyond*, (London: Weidenfeld & Nicolson, 1984), p.3. Another of Fadlo Hourani's sons, Cecil, later to become an adviser to President Bourguiba of Tunisia, was to give an account of his Manchester upbringing in chapter 1 of his memoirs.

32. *The Manchester City News*, 19 November 1892.

33. *The Manchester City News*, 30 January 1892.

34. *The Manchester City News*, 20 February 1892.

35. *The Manchester City News*, 27 August 1892.

36. *The Manchester City News*, 15 October 1892. The historian Simon Schama, author of the best-selling study of the French revolution, *Citizens*, published in 1989, was a descendant of this family.

37. *The Times*, 11 September 1892, as quoted in *The Manchester City News*, 4 November 1893.

38. *Spy*, 13 August 1892.

39. *Spy*, 5 November 1892.

40. *The Manchester City News*, 11 March 1893. Original articles against Besso, in *Spy*, 24 September 1892, 26 November 1892, 3 December 1892.

41. Bayley Winder, 'The Lebanese in West Africa', p. 110.

42. *al-Kifah*, 13 April 1962. Other accounts of the anniversary celebrations, in *al-Nahar*, 20 April 1962, *Le Jour* of the same day. *Magazine, L'Illustré du Proche-Orient*, no. 278, 19 April 1962, p. 61, reports the visit of the Lord Mayor 'dont les fonctions sont analogues à celles de notre Mohafez'.

43. Bayley Winder, 'The Lebanese in West Africa,' p. 149.

44. It may be indicative of the political sentiments of the Manchester Syrians that there is no mention of them in a report of a banquet in August 1908, held at the Midland Hotel to welcome the Young Turk revolution at which a declaration in the name of 'the Mussulmans and Armenians of Manchester' was read out. The meeting was reportedly attended by 'a hundred leading Armenians and Turks' and addressed by Bishop Utudjian, the head of the Armenian church in Europe, Djevad Bey, from the Turkish embassy in London, and Enver Bey, Turkish consul in Liverpool. Amongst those presented was a Mr. Shahnazar, who had as a newspaper editor been condemned to death for sedition, and was now a merchant in Manchester ('Turkey's Liberty, Manchester Gathering', *The Manchester City News*, 29 August 1908).

45. Sir Mark Sykes, Report to the Secretary of State on Visit to Manchester Syrians, 26 June 1918, Public Record Documents FO 371/3409 72477.

46. Copy of the memorandum in FO 371/3410 90513.

47. FO 371/ 3410 90513, 2 August 1918.

48. Fadlo Hourani, 'Nubdha Ta'rikhiyya'.

49. FO 371/3411 90513, copies of three 'illuminated addresses dated 6 September 1918, with individual replies by Lloyd George to each'.

50. FO 371/4178 90513, 'Future of Syria', 11 January 1919.

51. Haim Nahmad reported an incident that occurred in the 1920s during a visit by the Zionist leader Chaim Weizmann to Manchester: at a gathering of the Jewish community each spoke in the language of his country of origin – Russian, Yiddish, Polish, etc – but when some of the Arab Jews spoke in Arabic members of the audience objected. The first rabbi of the Sephardi synagogue in Mauldeth Road, Withington, South Manchester, which opened in 1904, was Rev. Fragi Nimni, an Arabic speaker from Tripoli. His grandson, Dr Ephraim Nimni, is the noted scholar of nationalism, author of *Marxism and Nationalism* (1992).

52. *The Monastery*, 1945, *Cassino, Portrait of a Battle*, 1953. While Majdalany focusses on the role of British forces in this battle, an important role was also played by (North African French-officered) Arab troops.

# Bibliography

Abdel-Malek, Anouar, ed., *Contemporary Arab Political Thought*, Zed Books, 1984.

Abrahamian, Ervand, *Khomeinism*, I.B. Tauris, 1993.

Abrahamian, Ervand, *Iran Between Two Revolutions*, Princeton University Press, 1982.

Ajami, Fuad, *The Dream Palace of the Arabs: A Generation's Odyssey*, Pantheon, 1998.

Ajami, Fuad, *The Arab Predicament*, Cambridge University Press, 1981.

Arkoun, Mohamed, *Rethinking Islam: Common Questions, Uncommon Answers*, Westview, 1994.

Asad, Talal and Owen, Roger, *Sociology of Developing Societies: The Middle East*, Macmillan, 1983.

Ayubi, Nazih, *Over-State the Arab State: Politics and Society in the Middle East*, I.B. Tauris, 1995.

Ayubi, Nazih, *Political Islam: Religion and Politics in the Arab World*, Routledge, 1991.

Bakhash, Shaul, *The Reign of the Ayatollahs*, I.B. Tauris, 1985.

Bromley, Simon, *Rethinking Middle East Politics: State Formation and Development*, Polity Press, 1994 .

Cammack, Paul, Pool, David and Tordoff, William, *Third World Politics: A Comparative Introduction*, Macmillan, 1988.

Cole, Juan and Keddie, Nikki, eds., *Shi'ism and Social Protest*, Yale University Press, 1986.

Dalacoura, Katerina, *Islam, Liberalism and Human Rights*, I.B. Tauris, 1999.

Deegan, Heather, *The Middle East and Problems of Democracy*, Open University Press, 1993.

Dwyer, Kevin, *Arab Voices: The Human Rights Debate in the Middle East*, Routledge, 1991.

Eickleman, Dale and Piscatori, James, *Muslim Politics*, Princeton University Press, 1996.

Gilsenan, Michael, *Recognizing Islam*, Croom Helm, 1982.

Guazzone, Laura, *The Middle East in Global Change: The Politics and Economics of Interdependence versus Fragmentation*, Macmillan, 1997.

Haim, Sylvia, ed., *Arab Nationalism: An Anthology*, University of California Press, 1974.

Halliday, Fred, *Islam and the Myth of Confrontation*, I.B. Tauris, 1996.

Halliday, Fred and Alavi, Hamza, eds., *State and Ideology in the Middle East and Pakistan*, Macmillan, 1988.

Hourani, Albert, *A History of the Arab Peoples*, Faber, 1991.

Hourani, Albert, *Arabic Thought in the Liberal Age*, Oxford University Press, 1970.

Hourani, Albert, Khoury, Philip, and Wilson, Mary, eds., *The Modern Middle East*, I.B. Tauris, 1993.

Keddie, Nikki, *Roots of Revolution: An Interpretive History of Modern Iran*, Yale University Press, 1981.

Kepel, G., *The Revenge of God: The Resurgence of Islam, Christianity and Judaism in the Modern World*, Polity Press, 1994.

Keyder, Caglar, *State and Class in Turkey, A Study in Capitalist Development*, Verso, 1987.

Kishtainy, Khalid, *Arab Political Humour*, Quartet Books, 1983.

Lewis, Bernard, *The Middle East: 2000 Years of History from the Birth of Christianity to the Present Day*, Weidenfeld & Nicolson, 1995.

Lewis, Bernard, *The Emergence of Modern Turkey*, Oxford University Press, 1968.

Lewis, Bernard, *The Arabs in History*, 4th edition, Hutchinson, 1966.

Owen, Roger, *State, Power and Politics in the Making of the Modern Middle East*, Routledge, 1992.

Pope, Nicole and Hugh, *Turkey Unveiled: Atatürk and After*, John Murray, 1997..

Roberts, John, *Visions and Mirages: the Middle East in a New Era*, Mainstream, 1995.

Rodinson, Maxine, *Cult, Ghetto and State*, Saqi Books, 1983.

Rodinson, Maxime, *The Arabs*, Croom Helm, 1981.

Rodinson, Maxime, *Islam and Capitalism*, Allen Lane, 1974.

Rodinson, Maxime, *Marxism and the Muslim World*, Zed Books, 1979.

Roy, Olivier, *The Failure of Political Islam*, I.B. Tauris, 1994.

Salam, G., ed., *Democracy Without Democrats? The Renewal of Politics in the Muslim World*, I.B. Tauris, 1994.

Sayigh, Yezid and Shlaim, Avi, eds., *The Cold War and the Middle East*, Clarendon Press, 1997.

Tibi, Bassam, *The Challenge of Fundamentalism: Political Islam and the New World Disorder*, University of California Press, 1998.

Tibi, Bassam, *Arab Nationalism: A Critical Enquiry*, 3rd edition, Macmillan, 1990.

Yapp, Malcolm, *The Near East Since the First World War*, Longman, 1991.

Zubeida, Sami, *Islam, the People and the State*, Routledge, 1993

# Index